PROFILING

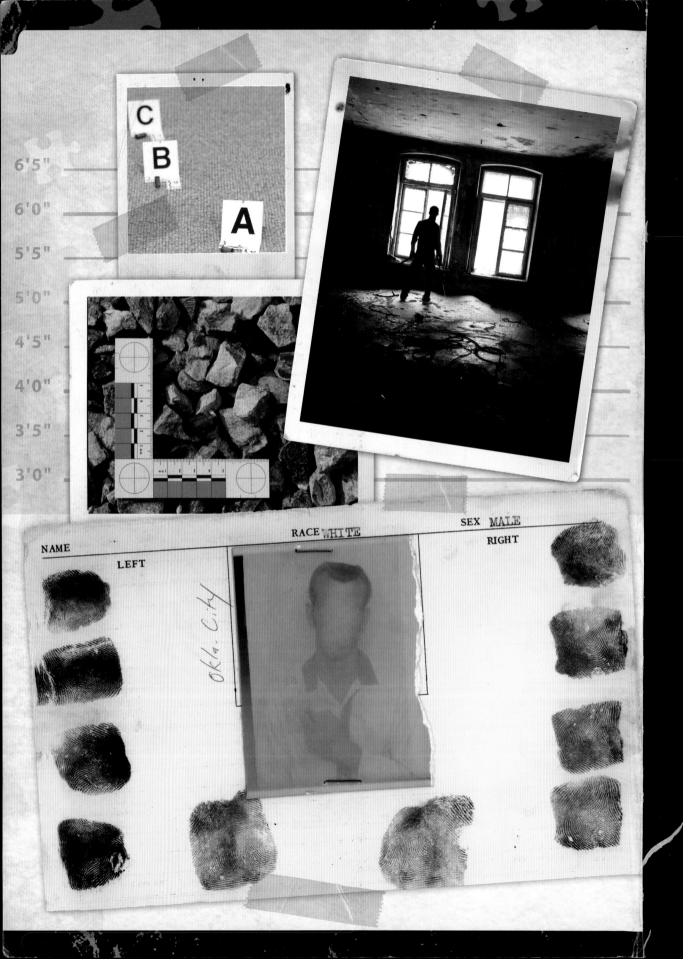

PROFILING

the psychology of catching killers

David Owen

FIREFLY BOOKS

A FIREFLY BOOK

Published by Firefly Books Ltd. 2010
Copyright © 2010 Quintet Publishing

First printing

Publisher Cataloging-in-Publication Data (U.S.)
Owen, David.
Profiling : the psychology of catching killers / David Owen.
[288] p. : photos. (some col.) ;   cm.
Includes index.
Summary: Information about psychological clues left at crime scenes, and how it helps to capture murderers. Includes infamous and terrible crimes, revelations, and the profiler's arsenal of psychological tips and tricks.
ISBN-10: 1-55407-725-7 (pbk.)
ISBN-13: 978-1-55407-725-0 (pbk.)
1. Criminal psychology. 2. Criminal profilers.   3. Criminal investigation -- Psychological aspects. I. Title.
364.3 dc22   HV6080.0946   2010

Library and Archives Canada Cataloguing in Publication
Owen, David
Profiling : the psychology of catching killers / David Owen.
Includes index.
ISBN-10: 1-55407-725-7 (pbk.)
ISBN-13: 978-1-55407-725-0 (pbk.)
1. Criminal behavior, Prediction of. 2. Criminal investigation-- Psychological aspects. 3. Murderers--Psychology. I. Title.
HV8073.5.094 2010   363.25'8   C2010-901658-0

Published in the United States by
Firefly Books (U.S.) Inc.
P.O. Box 1338, Ellicott Station
Buffalo, New York 14205

Published in Canada by
Firefly Books Ltd.
66 Leek Crescent
Richmond Hill, Ontario L4B 1H1

QTT.CPR

Project Editor: Asha Savjani
Editorial Assistant: Holly Willsher
Designer: Emma Wicks
Art Editors: Zoë White, Jane Laurie
Art Director: Michael Charles
Managing Editor: Donna Gregory
Publisher: James Tavendale

Printed in China

CONTENTS

INTRODUCTION
In the Beginning............................6

CHAPTER 1
How Profiling Works 30

CHAPTER 2
One Step at a Time 50

CHAPTER 3
At the Crime Scene......................74

CHAPTER 4
Organized or Disorganized?........100

CHAPTER 5
Commuters or Marauders? 130

CHAPTER 6
Power, Anger, and Retaliation.....156

CHAPTER 7
Finding the Signature 186

CHAPTER 8
Suffer the Little Children...........204

CHAPTER 9
Getting it in Writing..................222

CHAPTER 10
Questions and Answers..............240

CHAPTER 11
What Profiling Can Do................256

IN THE BEGINNING

The twenty-first century is an increasingly difficult time for the worst of violent criminals. At one time, thieves, murderers, and rapists could have a reasonable hope of getting away with the outrages they committed, provided they managed to escape the scenes of their crimes ahead of police searching for them. Equally, if they could break free of their own backgrounds, family relationships, or the wider communities they lived in, there might be no definite link with the evidence left with their victims to reveal their identities and lead justice to their doors. Blown safes, broken bodies, and terrified victims could in many cases show how a crime was carried out, but not by whom. Unless the witness knew the criminal by name, even an eyewitness description might not prove enough to identify the perpetrator. And if the criminal was new to crime, or seizing a random opportunity to do wrong, then even fingerprints could offer no direct route to their identity, except as a link to further crimes at the same hands.

In time, the development of powerful weapons of forensic science would change the odds facing the potential criminal. Fingerprinting and blood-group analysis, ballistics and tire-print comparisons, toxicology and trace elements, and the ultimate weapon of DNA identification have made almost any crime much more risky. In a world where even a few cells of genetic material can offer a precise match to a single individual, the chances of avoiding retribution are lessening year by year. Even improvements in the infrastructure of law and order, from intercepting cell phone signals to recording images on CCTV cameras, and number-plate recognition software in vehicle monitoring systems for highway junctions and busy city centers, help to tie a criminal to a particular location at a particular time, and in many cases to the commission of the crime itself.

WHO DID IT?

The ironic truth behind the power and sophistication of modern forensic science is that it still leaves a yawning gap around the first vital step in carrying out a criminal investigation: identifying a potential subject. In many crimes this may not prove an insuperable problem. A high proportion of murders, for example, involve a victim and a killer who are known to one another or even related. Police know to take an especially close look at whoever claims to have found a body, to see if they really were completely unaware of its presence prior to the moment of discovery. In other cases, such as those involving high-profile robberies with spectacular hauls of cash or valuables, jealousy within the criminal community itself may trigger the tip-off that leads police to their quarry. And where crimes of violence are particularly horrifying, those in the know may overcome their normal scruples of loyalty and silence to put the police on the trail of the person or persons responsible.

That still leaves those crimes committed outside these networks of friends, relatives, associates, or rivals. Where a killer chooses victims apparently at random, with no clear link to create a trail police can follow, identifying the murderer may be all but impossible on the evidence left at the crime scene alone. If the perpetrator has no previous criminal record, there will be nothing with which to compare DNA or fingerprints, or any other evidence found on or near the victim. If a crime of extortion or kidnapping reveals handwritten notes carrying demands or instructions, there will normally be nothing to compare the writing with. Though it may prove crucial in securing a conviction once the kidnapper is arrested and brought to court, the initial process of finding the suspect depends on other factors being present. The case is similar with most other types of evidence wherever the suspect cannot be isolated from the population at large. Unless something can be found to point the way for

Closed-circuit television (CCTV) and fingerprint analysis, while offering vital evidence, provide no clues to the motivation or intent of a criminal.

the forces of law and order across this initial gap, the likelihood that a crime, however serious, will remain unsolved is unfortunately high. Even a series of crimes may still not reveal enough about the person who carried them out to make it possible to catch them.

Two classic examples from the past show in sharp relief the difficulty of catching a criminal without a link between incident and suspect.

In the contemporary environment of sophisticated forensic investigations and DNA identification, crime has become a riskier business.

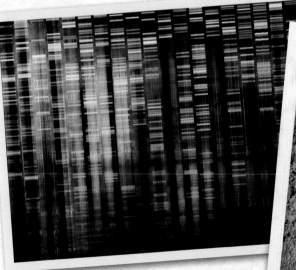

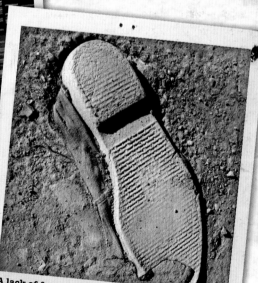

A lack of forensic evidence forces investigators to examine other contributing factors to try to solve a crime.

CASE

WHEN:	**1880s**
WHERE:	**London, U.K**
VICTIMS:	**Multiple**
CULPRIT:	**Jack the Ripper**

CASE STUDY 1: THE WHITECHAPEL KILLINGS

In the closing decades of the Victorian age, a series of horrific murders haunted the streets of Whitechapel in London's East End. This was an area where new groups of immigrants first tended to settle, before moving on to more prosperous neighborhoods, so it was poor, overcrowded, and infested with criminal activity of every kind. But by the 1880s two outside forces had made things even worse than usual. Huge numbers of Irish laborers working on building the canals and railway lines of industrial England had flocked with their families to England's major cities during the 1850s and 60s, and they came in particularly large numbers to Whitechapel. More recently, the spread of anti-Jewish pogroms in tsarist Russia had brought many more refugees from Eastern Europe, who also contributed to the overcrowded conditions.

The Ten Bells public house in Whitechapel, east London, was frequented by Jack the Ripper and his victims.

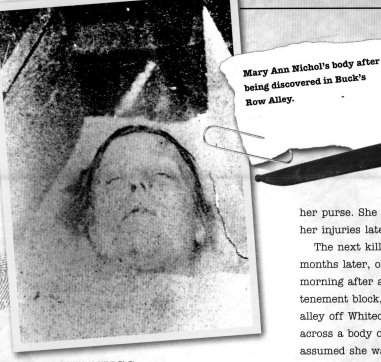

Mary Ann Nichol's body after being discovered in Buck's Row Alley.

THE KILLINGS

As unemployment increased, incomes fell and people were forced into more and more cramped living conditions. Prostitution was the only source of income for many poor women, and policing the narrow alleys and courts of the area was all but impossible. Official police figures from 1888 estimated that there were 1,200 prostitutes and 62 brothels within the borough of Whitechapel alone. All this added up to a powerful recipe for violent crime, and the storm broke on April 4, 1888, when a 45-year-old prostitute named Emma Elizabeth Smith suffered a violent sexual attack and robbery on Osborn Street in Whitechapel. It was 4 a.m. on the morning after the Easter Monday bank holiday, when she was set upon by a group of attackers who forced an object into her vagina that tore her perineum and left her badly bleeding. Despite her injuries, she managed to stagger back to her lodgings at 18 George Street, where the other occupants insisted on taking her to the London Hospital for treatment. There she was interviewed by the surgeon on duty, and told him that she had been attacked by three, possibly four, young men who had taken

her purse. She fell into a coma and died from her injuries later that day.

The next killing took place just over four months later, on August 7, 1888, again the morning after a bank holiday. A resident of a tenement block, George Yard Buildings, in an alley off Whitechapel High Street, stumbled across a body on the first-floor landing, but assumed she was a vagrant sleeping in the shelter of the stairwell. Only when a second resident noticed the body at 4:50 a.m. was it realized she was dead. She was later identified as 39-year-old prostitute Martha Tabram, last seen with a soldier several hours before. She had been stabbed 39 times with a knife or possibly a bayonet, which inflicted lethal wounds to her neck, lungs, heart, spleen, and liver. The police interviewed residents in the block and established she must have been killed between 1:50 and 3:30 a.m. that morning, but no one had heard anything out of the ordinary during that time.

The third victim was discovered at 3:40 a.m. on August 31, 1888, in an alley called Buck's Row, not far from the London Hospital where the first victim had died from her injuries. Two market porters were on their way to work when they spotted a body in a gateway. When they took a closer look, they were horrified to find it was a woman, whose throat had been cut with two slashing wounds so deep that her head had almost been separated from her body, and that she had also suffered a deep slashing wound to her abdomen and other deep cuts in the same area. The victim was identified as Mary Ann Nichols, a 42-year-old prostitute who went under the name of Polly, but no one had seen the killing, and there was no information from local people to help identify the killer. The fury of the attacks seemed to be increasing, a trend confirmed by the next killing, eight days later on Hanbury Street in nearby Spitalfields.

More and More Murders

The victim this time was Eliza Chapman, usually known as Annie, who was 47 years old and living apart from her family. She made a living from needlework and selling flowers, and only turned to prostitution when in abject need. On the night of September 7, 1888, she realized she was in desperate straits, lacking money to pay the rent on her room, so she was forced to go looking for clients. She had been seen with a man at about 5:30 a.m. on September 8, but this evidence became suspect when the police surgeon carrying out the post-mortem examination insisted that even he, with all his training, would not have been able to inflict such damage on the corpse during the 20 minutes between the last sighting of the victim and the time the body was found.

Once again she showed the two horrific slashes to the throat that had killed the previous victim, but in this case her abdomen had been cut open and it was later found that her uterus had been removed. As before, there was no information to lead to the identity of her killer, even though the murder had been carried out at first light, in clear view of the tenement buildings overlooking the site. Examination of the wounds suggested they had been inflicted by a long thin blade, similar to the type of knife that might be used by a surgeon or a slaughterman, but not by a bayonet.

An artist's rendering of the discovery of Elizabeth Stride's body. Her windpipe had been severed and she was still bleeding profusely when her body was found.

On the last day of the month two more victims were discovered, within close distance of one another. The body of Elizabeth Stride, a Swedish-born widow of 45, was found at 1 a.m. on September 30 in Dutfield's Yard off Berner Street, in Whitechapel. This must have been the killer's narrowest escape. Her body was discovered by the steward of a neighboring club, who was driving a pony and trap into the yard where she lay. It was very dark, but when he took a closer look, she was still bleeding profusely from a deep wound to the neck, which suggested the murder had taken place just moments before. The steward looked around, fearing the killer might still be nearby, but he had clearly escaped before anyone saw him, and in this case had no time to inflict any other wounds.

The second victim, 46-year-old Kate Eddowes, was another local woman who occasionally worked as a prostitute to raise rent money for her room. She had been found lying in the road extremely drunk at 8:30 p.m. the previous evening and locked up at Bishopsgate Police Station to sober up. She had then been released at 1 a.m., at the time Elizabeth Stride was being killed. Just 45 minutes later she was herself cut down in Mitre Square, just across the Whitechapel boundary in the City of London. She had been killed with a massive slashing wound to the throat, which severed the main artery on the left-hand side of the neck, and part of her uterus and her left kidney had been removed. Part of her intestines had also been cut out of her abdomen and arranged about the corpse.

Another victim was found in her room in 13 Miller's Court off Dorset Street, Spitalfields, at 10:45 a.m. on Friday, November 9. Perhaps because this was the first killing not to have been carried out in the open air, the murderer had inflicted the worst mutilations on the body of Mary Jane Kelly, a 25-year-old prostitute. She was several weeks behind with the rent, and Thomas Bowyer, her landlord's assistant, had called to collect the arrears when he found her lying on her back in the bed with all her internal organs cut out and placed on or around the body, but with her heart missing. Her breasts had been cut off, and her face mutilated beyond recognition. She was dressed only in a shift, with the rest of her clothes neatly folded and left on a chair, except for some garments burned in the fireplace, and she had been almost beheaded by a deep slash to the throat.

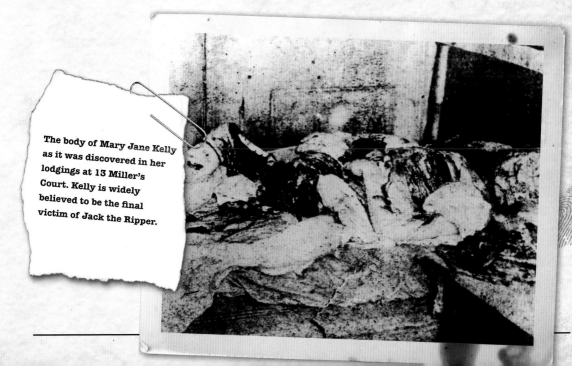

The body of Mary Jane Kelly as it was discovered in her lodgings at 13 Miller's Court. Kelly is widely believed to be the final victim of Jack the Ripper.

The Last Finds

Even this killing was not to be the last. On December 20, 1888, a 29-year-old prostitute named Rose Mylett was found by a patrolling police constable, apparently strangled in Clarke's Yard, Poplar, 2 miles east of Whitechapel. She had shared lodgings with the first victim, Emma Elizabeth Smith, but otherwise there was little direct evidence of any link between the murders. There were no wounds or mutilations and two of the doctors who examined her thought she might have unintentionally killed herself while in an extreme drunken stupor, but the inquest jury returned a verdict of willful murder by person or persons unknown.

Early the following year, a 40-year-old woman named Alice McKenzie, who lived in lodgings at 52 Gun Street in Whitechapel, was found dead in Castle Alley, not far from the earlier murders, early on the morning of July 17, 1889. Her throat had been cut, severing the left carotid artery, and there were cuts to her abdomen as in several of the earlier victims. Next, at 5:15 a.m. on September 10 an unidentified woman's torso was found under a railway bridge in Pinchin Street, Whitechapel, also close to the sites of several of the earlier killings. Suggestions were made by local people as to her possible identity, but these were discounted when the people referred to reappeared on the streets of the East End of London.

Finally, more than a year and a half later, the body of 25-year-old prostitute Frances Coles was found under another railway arch, along the same line but to the west of the Pinchin Street torso discovery, at 2:15 a.m. on February 13, 1891. The body was found by a patrolling constable who was probably on the scene only moments after the woman had died. There were

An 1888 engraving showing the discovery of the dismembered torso of an unidentified woman found on September 10 of that year.

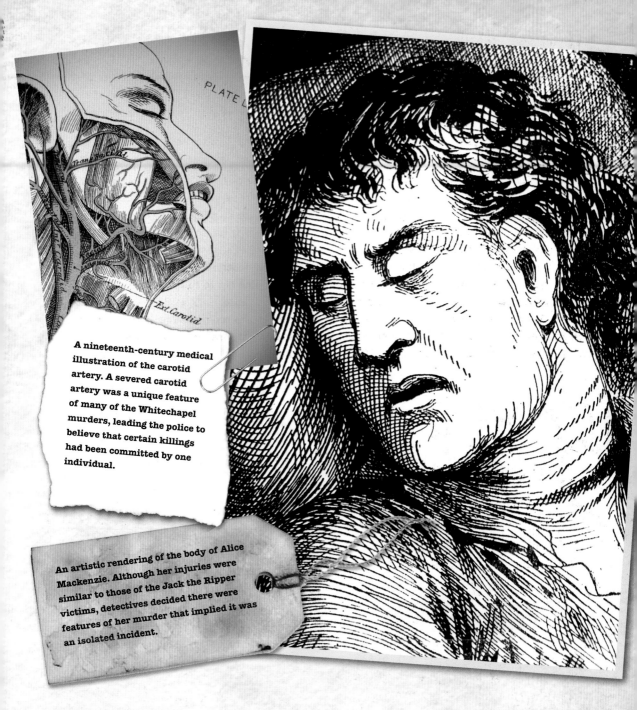

A nineteenth-century medical illustration of the carotid artery. A severed carotid artery was a unique feature of many of the Whitechapel murders, leading the police to believe that certain killings had been committed by one individual.

An artistic rendering of the body of Alice Mackenzie. Although her injuries were similar to those of the Jack the Ripper victims, detectives decided there were features of her murder that implied it was an isolated incident.

signs that she had been thrown violently on her back to the ground, before a double slash had cut her throat, but she suffered no other mutilations, possibly because of the arrival of the policeman. A man she had been known to associate with was arrested for questioning, but later released for lack of evidence. This was the last of what became known as the Whitechapel murders, which were originally thought to be the work of a single individual.

THE HUNT FOR THE KILLER

Psychological profiling did not exist at the time of the Whitechapel murders, but one of the duties of the Metropolitan Police of the time, if faced with a series of unexplained murders, was the same as that of their counterparts today. They studied each of the crimes to establish any common factors that might show whether or not these were simply random killings carried out in a small geographical area over a short time span, or whether they were the work of a serial killer.

First, just as modern profilers would do, they began with the victims and how they were killed. In one case, that of Rose Mylett, they decided that strangulation, even if carried out by a murderer rather than the victim herself, did not point to her being the victim of a serial killer. Emma Elizabeth Smith had at least survived long enough to describe her attackers, but apart from the fact that there were several of them, whereas the other cases suggested a lone attacker, the type of attack had little in common with the other murders. Likewise, Martha Tabram had been stabbed multiple times, but there were none of the slashing wounds that killed and mutilated most of the other victims. There was insufficient evidence of the method of the killer to link the mystery torso with the other cases, and detectives finally decided there were features about the murder of Alice McKenzie that set it apart from the other killings.

This left five victims—Mary Anne Nichols, Eliza Chapman, Elizabeth Stride, Kate Eddowes, and Mary Jane Kelly—whose murders shared similarities that were too close to ignore. All were prostitutes, living and soliciting in the same small area of the East End, and therefore all visible and vulnerable targets, since no one was likely to know they had disappeared until the killer had made his escape. Furthermore, they might be seen with a series of different clients during the course of a night, so witness identification of a possible attacker would be almost impossible. All had been killed in the same way and with the same type of weapon, with a trend of increasing violence and hatred in the disfigurement and mutilation applied to the corpses. The single exception to this rule had been caused by the victim's body being discovered too soon after the murder for the killer to finish his grisly work.

ESTABLISHING THE KILLER'S PROFILE

The opinions of doctors and police surgeons differed over whether the murders and mutilations suggested special anatomical knowledge on the part of the killer. Some felt he would need a reasonably sound knowledge of anatomy to be able to remove organs as quickly as he did, but others said even a competent butcher could have carried out his terrible task rapidly and efficiently.

Detectives analyzed the times and nature of the crimes, to see what they suggested about the man responsible. He had not simply attacked passing women in the street, since these attempts would have been seen and reported. He must have been able to pose as a client, and persuade each victim to go with him to the relatively secluded murder sites, before they realized the fate that awaited them. Given the women's wariness of potential violence, this would suggest that he must almost certainly

Under increasing pressure from the public, police detectives used every means at their disposal, including bloodhound dogs, to try to catch the Whitechapel killer. Unfortunately, it was all to no avail.

have been relatively well dressed and well spoken, appearing to belong to the professional classes rather than a laborer or a down-and-out. He must also have had a close knowledge of the district, to find his way between the murder sites and the places where his victims would be found. It was also likely he was in regular employment, since most of the killings took place on weekends or in the night following a public holiday. It was also decided that he must have had a secure address, probably well outside the Whitechapel area, where he could change his clothes, clean or hide the murder weapon, and wash away any bloodstains.

Police surgeon Dr. Thomas Bond, who carried out the post-mortem on the body of Mary Jane Kelly, noticed particularly that the blood-soaked bedsheet next to the victim's head had been cut in a similar way to the cuts that mutilated her face, and deduced that this might have been because the killer covered her face with it to protect his clothing while cutting up her body. This, he felt, would suggest that even at the moment of greatest frenzy, he was careful about his appearance, indicating he might well project an entirely conventional and respectable image to those who saw him in the street.

Given the details of the crimes and the public fear of further killings, the Metropolitan Police came under enormous pressure to identify the killer, arrest him, and bring him to justice. The problem was not that there was too little evidence resulting from the attacks: in a sense there was too much, since the known facts gave rise to a number of conflicting theories and suggestions as to what type of person might be responsible. The real problem was that none of the evidence, either in detail or taken as a whole, was able to lead police to the killer. The only certain fact was that after February 1891 there were no more killings that anyone even attempted to link to Jack the Ripper, or whoever had been responsible for the Whitechapel killings.

The Suspects

In the end, Jack the Ripper was, if not the first, arguably the most famous serial killer never to

A television depiction of Jack the Ripper attacking one of his victims. Countless works of fiction, film, and television have been based on the story of Jack the Ripper and the Whitechapel murders.

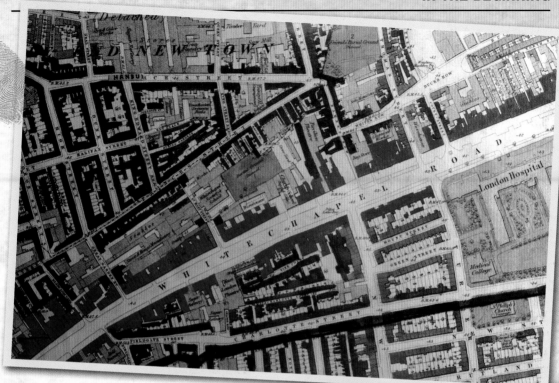

Charles Booth's *Master Map of Poverty* depicts the East London area where Jack the Ripper operated. Booth used color-coding to indicate the social class of the area: black, at the bottom of the social scale, implied vicious and semi-criminal residents.

have been caught. Up to the present day, a series of books, articles, movies, and television documentaries have tried to prove a particular individual must have been behind the murders. Suspects have included Prince Albert Victor, son of Prince Albert and Queen Victoria, the Victorian Impressionist painter Walter Sickert, the Freemasons, and more than a hundred different individuals. Since all are long dead, the truth is as impossible to determine now as it proved to be when they were alive, but police records show that only four were taken seriously. These were Aaron (or Isaac) Kosminski, Michael Ostrog, Montague John Druitt, and Dr. Francis John Tumblety.

Kosminski was a poor Polish-born Jew with a history of insanity who lived in Whitechapel and was identified by a witness as having been seen in the area of the murders. However, the

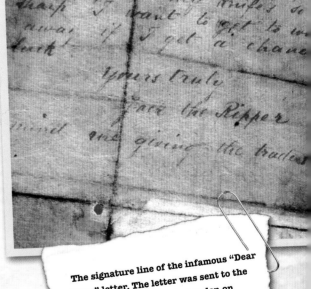

The signature line of the infamous "Dear Boss" letter. The letter was sent to the Central News Agency in London on September 27, 1888. This is the first recorded use of the pseudonym Jack the Ripper. Experts today still remain divided over whether the letter can be attributed to the actual killer.

witness later withdrew his statement, on the grounds that he did not wish to testify against a fellow Jew.

Michael Ostrog was a shadowy figure, Russian or Polish, who worked under more than 20 different identities as a thief and petty criminal, stealing valuables from both Eton College and Oxford University. He was described in a police report as "habitually cruel to women" and known to carry "surgical knives and other instruments" with him. He showed signs of madness and was unable to prove his whereabouts at the time of the murders, but the police were equally unable to prove he was present when the women were killed.

James Maybrick, a local cotton merchant, was one of the many historical figures suspected to be Jack the Ripper.

Montague John Druitt was a successful sportsman, barrister, and schoolmaster, who entered a deep depression after the death of his father and the committal of his mother to a mental home, finally killing himself by jumping into the Thames with his coat pockets weighted down with stones, soon after the last of the murders. It was believed that members of his family had become convinced he was the Ripper, but positive evidence was lacking and, apart from his mental problems, he had shown no signs of the kind of personality disorder that would suggest he had carried out the murders.

Finally, Tumblety was notorious as a self-styled medical doctor with several brushes with the law in Canada and the United States, who was alleged to have a violent hatred of women and especially prostitutes, and to have built up a collection of preserved physical specimens of body parts, especially the uterus. He escaped to England to avoid arrest on charges relating to the assassination of Abraham Lincoln, resulting from one of his many aliases. He returned to America when the hunt died down, and came back to the United Kingdom in 1888. He was seen by several members of the police team as the most likely suspect, but he fled back to America in December 1888 and never returned.

Prince Albert Victor, Duke of Clarence and Avondale, was another one of the more popular suspects thought to be Jack the Ripper. Contemporary research has disproved this theory, as Albert was not in London during the time of murders.

LEFT Montague John Druitt was one of the four police suspects at the time of the murders. His suicide coincided with the end of the murders in 1888.
RIGHT Walter Sickert, Victorian Impressionist painter and Jack the Ripper suspect.

NOT ENOUGH KNOWLEDGE

This was the closest investigators got to trapping the Ripper, and without more positive evidence there was nothing more they could do. Ironically, they had some of the information they needed to build up an accurate profile, but lacked the knowledge of the psychological signs that the killer's behavior revealed, and the light these could throw on how his mind worked, the pressures that drove him, and the background that might have helped identify him. So the crimes remain unsolved, and probably always will.

A knife thought to be Jack the Ripper's murder weapon.

CASE

WHEN:	**1940s**
WHERE:	**New York, USA**
VICTIMS:	**15 injured**
CULPRIT:	**George Metesky**

CASE STUDY 2: THE MAD BOMBER

Crossing the Atlantic and moving forward in time just over 50 years, another example arises where a series of crimes had detectives baffled and unable to lay their hands on a single suspect. The person they were looking for was no serial killer, but a small-time terrorist with a grievance, who was planting bombs in different places around New York City. No mutilated victims faced police when they turned up at the scenes of his activities, but there was every possibility that the bombs would grow in power and destructiveness, to the point where people would die in the resulting explosions.

Compared with the atrocities of the Whitechapel murders, there was an equally challenging gap between the police detectives and the unknown man they were seeking. Yet the power of criminal profiling would eventually

The police examined what little evidence they had in the case of the Mad Bomber, but it was criminal profiling that eventually cracked the case.

AGO- ACTS···— AS
BY THE BE BOMBED···
CON. EDISON CO.···
CALL ME A COMPLIMENTS

···DEPENDING ON ENERGY
FEAR GAS IN PACKAGE
GHOULS GET
I NOTIFIED IS
JUSTICE··
LOCATED LIFE
MAKES NO MENTION
MANHATTAN HOTELS
MY SUFFERINGS - ALL MY

OF THE OF THESE GHOULISH
PSYCHO PATH··· RUN FROM
SAME SEVERAL SEEING
SKILL

TARGET:··· THAT THEY
THAT STAND BY TOOK
THESE 2 BOMBS TIMING MAY

···WHILE WOULD
WILL BE WELL COUPLING···
2 YEARS YELLOW PRESS
YOUR

NYC POL.LAB.

tell them exactly what kind of man they were looking for, where he came from, what kind of family he belonged to, and even what kind of clothes he would be wearing when they finally arrested him. This astonishing prescription seemed to owe more to a Sherlock Holmes story, but it was based on expert reasoning and remorseless logic. However, as with any series of crimes, it took investigators a long time to build up enough information to narrow down the search.

A letter sent to the *New York Journal American* by the Mad Bomber. The letter was in response to an open letter the newspaper published in cooperation with the police, asking the bomber to turn himself in.

THE BOMBS

The first bomb incident happened on November 16, 1940, just over a year before America entered World War II with the Japanese attack on Pearl Harbor. A bomb consisting of a small pipe packed with explosives inside a wooden toolbox had been left on a windowsill at the headquarters of the Consolidated Edison power supply company on New York's West 64th Street. The bomb had failed to detonate, and when police dismantled it they found it also contained a note printed in capitals and carrying a brief message: "CON EDISON CROOKS, THIS IS FOR YOU."

Lacking any hint as to who had left the device, and since no fingerprint matches showed up in the records, all the police could do was watch for any more bombs to show up. The note was an encouraging sign, since it was almost certain the person placing the bomb wanted the message to be read, and had it gone off, the note would have been destroyed. They therefore hoped the bomb was a wake-up call to show the bomber's grievance against the company, as a prelude to some demand or some additional publicity. Nothing more showed up until February 1942, when the bomber left a note

for the police, explaining that as a patriotic American he would be suspending his campaign until the war was over.

He kept his word, though through the war years he left more messages and one other unexploded bomb, again close to Con Edison's offices, in early 1943. The truce lasted just over eight years, until March 29, 1950, when the latest bomb was found, this time at Grand Central Station rather than the Con Edison offices. While the gap had been welcome to police, they were concerned to notice that this device was much more carefully made than the first, and likely to cause a lot more damage if it actually went off.

The line was finally crossed when a bomb detonated in a phone box at the New York Public Library not long afterward, followed by another explosion at Grand Central Station. A succession of explosions followed, still without any casualties, but also without any evidence to show who was responsible. The pressure on the police increased dramatically on December 2, 1956, when a device hidden inside the padding of a seat at the Paramount Theater in Brooklyn exploded at 7:55 p.m., injuring eight people, three of them seriously. This was a new situation. With the cinema crowded with pre-Christmas visitors, the time and place had almost certainly been chosen to cause casualties, and it must only be a matter of time before deaths resulted.

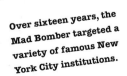

Over sixteen years, the Mad Bomber targeted a variety of famous New York City institutions.

The New York Public Library, pictured here, was the site of the first detonation. Thankfully, no one was injured.

The officer leading the search for the man who had become known as the "Mad Bomber of New York" was Inspector Howard Finney. In desperation he asked a colleague, Captain James Cronin of the Missing Persons Bureau, if he could think of any way of tracking the perpetrator down before he began killing people. Cronin could think of no solution himself, but he knew someone who might be able to help, New York criminal psychiatrist Dr. James Brussel. Cronin felt that at the very least Brussel might be able to suggest something useful about the kind of person the police should be watching out for.

THE FIRST CRIMINAL PROFILE

Finney was a policeman in the traditional mold, deeply skeptical of what he might tend to dismiss as psychological mumbo-jumbo, but with nothing to lose, he passed over his notes on the case and asked the analyst what he could

Another explosion occurred at Grand Central Station. Again, no one was hurt.

Dr. James Brussel was able to deduce that the subject lived somewhere in Westchester County near the border with Connecticut, based on the postmarks on the letters the bomber had sent to police.

suggest. His reply became legendary in profiling circles, to rival the effortless precision of Sherlock Holmes. The person they needed to find would be middle-aged, born outside the United States and heavily built. He would be a Roman Catholic, unmarried, with an obsessively good relationship with his mother and a deep hatred for his father. As a result he was likely to be sharing a household with a brother or sister, probably in the nearby state of Connecticut. As a final touch, the psychiatrist said that if the police did find the man and arrested him, they would probably find him wearing a double-breasted suit, and that it would be buttoned up.

Detectives hardly knew how to deal with such precise information apparently plucked out of the air. But all Brussel's theories were firmly grounded on a mixture of experience and specialist knowledge. Nearly all previous bomb threats in the city had been delivered by males, so the police were bound to be looking for a man rather than a woman. The targeting of Con Edison pointed to his having a real or imagined grievance against the company, either as a customer or a former employee, and the language used in the notes scattered about the city revealed further clues. Key words and phrases pointed to paranoia, or a conviction that the entire world was against him. This condition normally peaks at around the age of 35, and if this were the case when the first bomb was left in 1940, his age at the end of 1956 would be around 50. The neatness with which the notes had been printed, and the careful assembly of the later devices, also tended to confirm this estimate of his age.

More clues emerged from the words and phrases used in the notes. Formal but old-fashioned phrases, including a reference to "dastardly deeds" and even to "the Con Edison" instead of merely "Con Edison," suggested someone who was not a native-born New Yorker. However, since the grammar and spelling were correct, the unknown suspect had clearly completed high-school education, if not college.

As to his ethnic and religious background, police statistics showed the foreign racial grouping most associated with bombs as weapons tended to be Slavs, and the majority were Roman Catholics.

Dr. Brussel then turned his attention to the postmarks on those letters and messages sent through the mail. Some showed they had been posted in Westchester County between the city and the commuter communities of nearby Connecticut, where many Slav immigrants were based. Other more abstruse clues hinted to the psychiatrist that the bomber was suffering from an Oedipus complex, which would reflect a violent dislike of a father and the loss of a mother when young. This in turn suggested a single life, in a house shared with a surviving brother or sister. Finally, the fashions of the time implied he would wear a double-breasted suit, and his response to his paranoia would be to keep it buttoned up at all times as a protection from the outside world.

This was priceless material to the police, but it still did not lead them directly to their quarry. What bridged the gap was good old-fashioned police work, though the first step was suggested

Using criminal profiling and police statistics, Brussel suggested that the suspect would be Slavic and possibly Roman Catholic.

by Dr. Brussel. So far, all the letters and messages had been kept from the press, to starve the bomber of publicity, and the psychiatrist felt this had almost certainly made him more and more angry. Releasing the information to the press might tempt him into revealing himself. What it did, at first at least, was produce calls from a host of impostors, but eventually the man himself called, though without revealing his name or address. However, armed with Dr. Brussel's advice, police were able to narrow down the focus of their search.

THE BOMBER REVEALED

One of the bomber's letters had contained a reference to suffering an accident for which he had been denied compensation. Now the investigators searched the records of Con Edison and other companies taken over in the previous decades, looking for details of injuries to personnel. At last they found the details of one man, working for the United Electric and Power Company, which had been taken over by Con Edison, who had suffered an accident on the date quoted in the bomber's letter. There was even a record of his claim for compensation on the grounds that he had suffered tuberculosis as a consequence of the accident, but this claim had been denied by the company's lawyers, and Con Edison had received angry letters of protest as a result. The man's name was George Metesky, who lived at number 17, 4th Street, Waterbury, Connecticut. Only one detail in the profile remained slightly adrift. When police turned up to arrest him, he answered the door wearing a dressing gown. They asked him to get dressed and accompany them to the station. He disappeared and returned wearing a formal three-piece suit, with all the buttons fastened.

George Metesky was put on trial at New York's Criminal Court for making and planting 20 bombs in public places over the course of 17 years, so as to endanger life. He was found guilty by reason of insanity, and given a possible life sentence in a criminal asylum. In fact, he was thought to present no real danger when released in 1973. He returned to the house from which he had been arrested and lived on there until his death in 1994 at the age of 90. After his arrest he claimed to have planted a total of 32 bombs around the city, which if true meant that many of his devices were not found, or not ascribed to him.

Metesky, showing little remorse on the day of his arrest, was found criminally insane and spent the next sixteen years in a criminal asylum. Brussel's profiling of the subject was accurate down to the outfit he wore.

PAVING THE WAY FOR CRIMINAL PROFILING

The huge difference in the outcome of the cases of Jack the Ripper and the Mad Bomber of New York rested almost entirely on the skill of the criminal profiler and the improvement in the capabilities of criminal psychiatry. Had these not been available, it remains difficult to see how the Bomber could have been tracked down, unless the police had been lucky enough to catch him in the act of placing an explosive device. Given his respectable appearance and the care he took to avoid being caught, this might easily never have happened. The publicity given to the case of the Mad Bomber and the insights used to track down the person responsible made it clear that the forces of law and order would want to make increasingly frequent use of this powerful new weapon at their command.

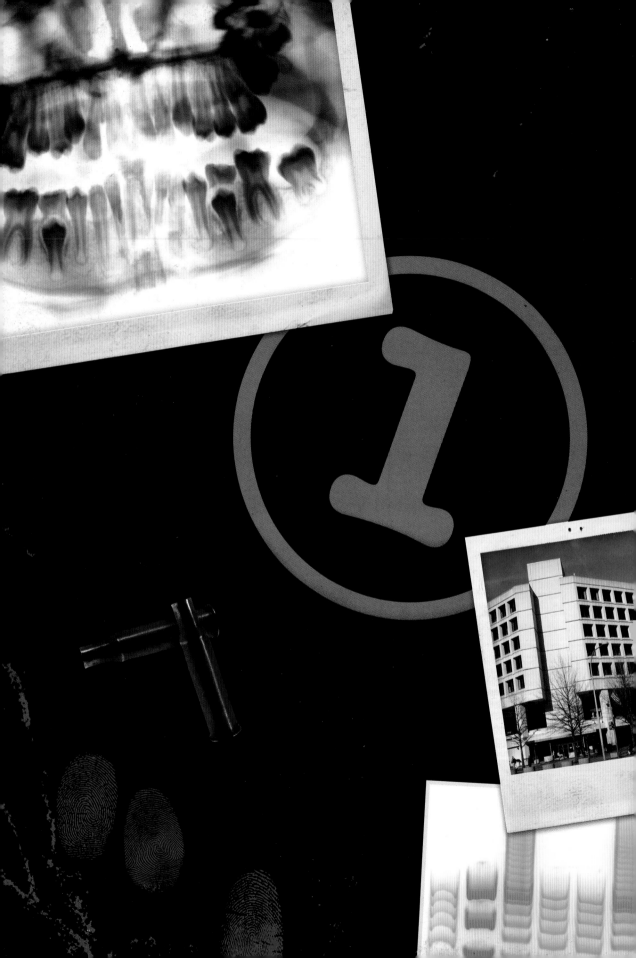

HOW PROFILING WORKS

Given the spectacular success of the campaign to track down and arrest the Mad Bomber of New York, were there any lessons to learn with regard to how profiling could be used in the hunt for other types of criminal? Even before Dr. James Brussel's clear insight into the background and motives of the Bomber, crime fighters had become aware of the possibilities of targeting criminals through focusing on their psychology, and in particular the thinking behind the crimes they chose to commit and how they committed them. Howard Teten, a detective working for the police department of the city of San Leandro in California, recruited academics from the School of Criminology at the University of California to help advise on the best way to track down suspects who were difficult to identify. Working for a local police department was merely the beginning. In 1962, five years after the arrest of George Metesky, Teten was appointed a Special Investigator for the Federal Bureau of Investigation (FBI). In 1970 he used his experience to set up a course in Applied Criminology at the FBI's own academy at Quantico in Virginia. Finally, when he met Brussel in 1972, he discussed his methods as possible inputs for teaching the other FBI agents what profiling could achieve, and the right way to carry out the technique effectively. Approaching the subject from a psychological viewpoint rather than as a psychiatrist, he was guarded about Brussel's Freudian approach, but welcomed his logical reasoning about the background factors that helped to trap the Bomber. It soon became clear to those who joined the course that rapid revelations similar to those produced in the Metesky case could appear in other investigations too.

Teten and Brussel met at the time the FBI formed the Behavioral Science Unit at Quantico, when Teten was appointed a member of a team headed by Patrick Mullany, an Academy instructor. Teten and Mullany collaborated on designing a method for profiling the unknown offenders responsible for unsolved crimes, which examined the crime scenes for evidence of behavioral quirks that could reveal specific mental disorders, useful to help narrow down the search for the individual involved.

CASE

WHEN: 1973

WHERE: Rocky Mountains

VICTIMS: Children

CULPRIT: David Meirhofer

CASE STUDY 3: ROCKY MOUNTAIN CHILD KILLER

In the year following the foundation of the Behavioral Science Unit, the FBI was called in to track down the abductor of 7-year-old Susan Jaeger, who went missing from a Rocky Mountains campsite in Montana in June 1973. The child had been subdued without waking her parents, and a series of searches had failed to find her. With the aid of Robert Ressler, another FBI investigator who was to play a key role in the development of profiling, Teten and Mullany drew up a profile from the available evidence that stated that the abductor was a young, white male with severe mental problems. Not only was he a peeping Tom, he was also a violent sex killer who would think nothing of mutilating his victims after they were dead, and who might even keep some of their body parts as grisly souvenirs. On its own, this information was helpful, but did not provide a direct link to the abductor. However, when a 23-year-old single man, David Meirhofer, was arrested on suspicion of another local murder, officers searched his house, and found body parts later identified as belonging to two different victims: the one for which he was arrested, and the missing Susan Jaeger. Profiling may not have caught him unaided, but it helped ensure his conviction for killing both his victims.

PSYCHOLOGICAL CLASSIFICATION AND ANALYSIS

Two years later, profiling was called in to help in the hunt for two serial killers who were responsible for lengthening lists of victims, but who stubbornly eluded capture: Ted Bundy and the

FBI investigator Robert Ressler aided in the profiling of the Rocky Mountain Child Killer, David Meirhofer.

The Montana Rocky Mountains where 7-year-old Susan Jaeger was abducted.

Green River Killer (see page 148). Investigating officer Robert Keppel used another criminal psychologist, Richard Walter, who had worked in the state prison system in Michigan, and had interviewed more than 2,000 killers and sex attackers. The information he gathered enabled him to group all killings and violent sex attacks into four different subtypes: power-reassurance; power-assertive; anger-retaliatory; and anger-excitation, or sadism. He also underlined the importance of looking at the behavior of suspects before and after the crime as well as at the time the crime was carried out. The two men collaborated on the creation of the Homicide Information Tracking System (HITS) database, which classified crimes by specific characteristics to allow investigators and profilers to search for records matching these characteristics.

Howard Teten left the Behavioral Science Unit in 1978, but Robert Ressler teamed up with another FBI agent, John Douglas, to continue the Bureau's profiling work. In particular, they carried out a detailed series of interviews between 1979 and 1983 with more than 20 serial killers in American prisons, and their families, to add to their knowledge of how and why criminals functioned as they did. In 1985 the FBI set up its National Center for the Analysis of Violent Crime (NCAVC), which absorbed the Behavioral Science Unit and brought profiling to bear in helping a much wider section of the law-enforcement community, and instituted the Violent Criminal Apprehension Program (VICAP). This was another database,

American serial killer Ted Bundy after his 1978 arrest for theft. Bundy was later charged with the murders of more than 30 women. Profiling was successfully used in the case.

is especially important in profiling. So many examples of successful profiling, from George Metesky to notorious killers like Jeffrey Dahmer and Ted Bundy, involve a list of crimes carried out by the same person. By examining repeated crimes it is possible to isolate factors individual to the person who carried them out, rather than similar killers who have no involvement in these particular crimes. In the case of serial killers, for example, their tortured psychology can more readily be understood when seen against the background of repeated attacks, and it is these cases that call most for rapid and effective success to limit the toll of victims as quickly as possible.

BRITISH PROFILING: CANTER'S METHODS

Just one year after the NCAVC was set up in Virginia, British police forces were quick to see how potentially useful profiling could be, when detectives in southern England were faced with a series of murders by the so-called Railway Rapist. Following the example of their American counterparts, they called in a criminal psychologist, in this case David Canter from the University of Surrey, who drew up the first U.K. offender profile. Canter brought an academic approach to the task of profiling, based on continually updated statistics on offender populations. By studying crimes committed by an unknown offender, his method makes it possible to determine a series of characteristics that the offender is likely to show, which can help narrow down the search. This was especially useful in the Railway Rapist cases, which began as a series of violent sex attacks with shared features suggesting they were the work of a single assailant.

Canter's university courses in Investigative Psychology involve five different factors governing the interaction between a criminal and his victim. The first one, interpersonal

fed with up to 100 key details of each new violent crime to allow rapid comparison and identification with crimes already existing in its files, and showing the same complex patterns. In particular, the program can present experts with information to help them decide whether apparently unrelated crimes have possibly been committed by the same person. This last facility coherence, assumes that criminals relate to their victims in much the same way as they relate to people in their normal lives. It also suggests that victims may be chosen to reflect characteristics of individuals who played a particular part in the criminal's earlier life. Canter's method also looks at the significance of time and place in the crime, since these factors are usually under the criminal's control. For example, the timing and location of an attack may reflect the criminal's work schedule, his leisure preferences, or his personal life. It also examines the particular characteristics the criminal is likely to possess, and any signs pointing to an earlier criminal career—if a criminal can force entry into a building, for example, this may mean he has been a burglar. Likewise, signs at the crime scene of deliberate attempts to remove evidence, such as the wiping of fingerprints or removal of items likely to be contaminated with bodily fluids, suggest earlier criminal experience that may show up in the records. Finally, Canter also developed a theory relating to the two different approaches adopted by criminals in traveling from their home base to the scenes of their crimes. He classified a marauder criminal as one who tends to travel short distances from his home to commit crimes, while a commuter criminal will set out to make longer journeys before looking for victims. (The marauder and commuter types of criminal are covered in more detail in Chapter 5).

Jeffrey Dahmer murdered 17 men and boys in the period 1978–1991. As a teenager he showed little interest in hobbies or social interactions, and became increasingly withdrawn.

Professor David Canter successfully applied his theories and methods in the profiling of John Duffy, the Railway Rapist.

WHEN: 1980s

WHERE: Railway stations, England

VICTIMS: Multiple

CULPRITS: David Mulcahy (above), John Duffy

CASE STUDY 4: THE RAILWAY RAPIST

Canter's first success was the case of the Railway Rapist. From June 1982, a whole series of rapes took place around suburban London. The first victim was a 23-year-old woman attacked and raped near Hampstead railway station in June 1982, though she claimed she had been attacked by two men. Between that attack and the following summer, 18 more women were raped, but in the fall of 1983, the attacks suddenly stopped. They began again in early 1984 in different parts of north and west London, always in the vicinity of railway stations, and police urgently needed to know whether or not all these crimes had been committed by a single offender, or were the work of more attackers with no real connection between them. The task became much more urgent from December 23, 1985, when the unknown rapist began killing his victims. First, he raped and murdered 19-year-

Hackney Wick Station, the site of Alison Day's rape and murder in 1985.

David Canter used criminal profiling to identify rapist John Duffy and his accomplice David Mulcahy, leading to the eventual arrest of both men. Maartje Tamboezer (left) and Alison Day were two of their victims.

old secretary Alison Day near Hackney Wick station. Now known to the public as the Railway Killer, he then raped and murdered 15-year-old schoolgirl Maartje Tamboezer on April 17, 1986, near West Horsley station, and on May 18 he abducted, raped, and killed TV presenter Anne Locke after she stepped off a train at Brookmans Park station.

Canter applied his study of violent criminals to suggest that the killer lived in Kilburn, North London, the central point between all of the attacks.

PROFILING THE ATTACKER

David Canter was commissioned to produce a profile. His study of how violent criminals tended to travel to and from crime scenes, and how this related to where they lived, led to his suggesting the person responsible for the rapes lived in Kilburn, in northwest London, since this was approximately the central point between the locations of his first three rapes. Since then, he had traveled by train to find his victims over a wider area. Canter concluded the criminal was probably married, since he must

John Duffy, pictured here in 2001, was eventually charged with three murders and eight counts of rape.

CATCHING THE KILLER

This profile was added to details about the attacker revealed by the victims who had survived. They recalled he was around 5 feet 9 inches tall, aged between 25 and 30 and was right-handed. He threatened the women with a knife, and tied their wrists together with string before attacking them. In addition, the police noted that he tried to remove evidence by wiping the bodies of his victims, and in the case of those he had killed, usually by strangulation, he tried to burn their bodies, suggesting he was familiar with how evidence was collected and used to identify rapists. Police had already drawn up a list of more than 2,000 potential suspects living in the area of the attacks, and when the profile information was checked against this record, one name stood out, that of martial arts instructor John Duffy, who had been added to the sex offenders' register after the rape of his wife in August 1985. When he was found stalking another potential victim through a local park on November 7, 1986, he was arrested on suspicion of rape and murder. Police searched his home in Kilburn, just a five-minute walk from the scene of one of the first rapes, and found a sweater that they matched with fibers found on the body of Alison Day. Other fibers and pieces of rope were linked to Maartje Tamboezer, and on the following day he was charged with the murders of both women and with that of Anne Locke, together with seven of the rapes. Police checked his background and found that Canter's profile was an extremely close match, with Duffy corresponding with 12 of the 17 predictions it

have been sufficiently at ease with women to persuade them to talk to him and allow him into a position where he could control and attack them. However, since his youngest victim was just 15 years old, it was unlikely he had children of his own, since there would be too much likelihood of his being inhibited by the resemblance between the victim and members of his own family. Canter was also struck by the gap in attacks between 1983 and 1984, which he assumed might have been because the attacker was out of circulation, possibly serving time in prison for a crime of violence. He concluded the attacker was employed in a low-level, semicasual skilled or semiskilled job that would allow him time off to stalk and attack his victims. He would have little direct contact with the public and might have just one or two male friends, though the hatred he displayed toward his female victims suggested he had little contact with women at work, and was probably a loner. More puzzling was his use of a tourniquet to strangle those victims he killed.

contained. He worked as a railway carpenter, which gave him time to commit the crimes and also accounted for his knowledge of the railway system which allowed him to travel to and from the scenes of the attacks. Furthermore, his training as a carpenter would almost certainly have taught him how to cope with serious injuries with sharp tools, including the use of tourniquets. One of the discrepancies was that he was shorter than the witnesses had suggested, although this is fairly common in violent crimes, when victims tend to overestimate the size of their attacker.

One Killer, or Two?

However, there still remained another marked discrepancy. Some of the earlier victims had referred to two men, though this could not be followed up at the time. Only when Duffy, on February 26, 1986, had been found guilty of the murders of Alison Day and Maartje Tamboezer and four of the rapes, resulting in a 30-year sentence, did he confide in a prison psychologist. He admitted he had indeed had an accomplice for some of the rapes and murders, including the killing of Anne Locke, for which he had been found not guilty by the jury at his trial. Then he refused to say who his collaborator was, but in 1997 he finally identified him as a childhood friend, David Mulcahy. Police tightened the net around Mulcahy and put him under close surveillance. He was a married man with four children, and by the time police were ready to arrest him in 1999, they were able to take a DNA sample and positively match it to genetic material found on the victims' bodies, which landed Mulcahy with guilty verdicts for all three murders and seven of the rapes. Evidence presented by Duffy against his old friend helped establish him as the prime instigator of most of the attacks, and in particular the switch to murdering the victims as a more stimulating experience than the original rapes. However, there is abundant evidence that both men carried out violent attacks on their own, in

addition to those they carried out together. Another suggestion for the transition to murder is that Duffy saw and recognized one of his former victims when he had to attend court for the rape of his wife, and realized there was a very genuine danger that his victims could still identify him long after the event—killing them at the time would eliminate this danger.

UNDERSTANDING THE VALUE OF PROFILING

The case of the Railway Killers was, for the British police and media, the equivalent of the George Metesky case in the United States, convincing them of the value of profiling as an investigative technique and, as time passed, the skill and experience of the profilers resulted in more remarkable arrests and convictions of violent and deranged serial killers. In America, even before Canter's profiling had helped catch the Railway Rapist and ultimately his accomplice, the Trailside Killer had provided another example of clever profiling helping to catch a killer.

David Mulcahy and his wife Sandra.

CASE

WHEN: 1979

WHERE: California, USA

VICTIMS: Multiple

CULPRIT: David Carpenter

CASE STUDY 5: THE TRAILSIDE KILLER

In this case, rape did not appear to be a factor, at least at first. The first victim of the killer was 44-year-old bank manager Edda Kane, who disappeared in August 1979 while hiking in Mount Tamalpais State Park close to San Francisco. Searchers eventually found her naked body in a kneeling position, with a single gunshot wound to the head. Her cash and credit cards had been taken, but she had not been sexually assaulted. The next missing person in the same park was found in March the following year. Once again the victim's body had been undressed and left in a kneeling position, but instead of a single shot, 23-year-old Barbara Schwartz had died from 10 stab wounds to the chest from a 10-inch knife. The murder weapon was found nearby, but no usable fingerprints were recovered. On October 15, 1980, 26-year-

The bodies of the Trailside Killer's victims were discovered in two public parks near San Francisco.

Point Reyes National Seashore Park, where the bodies of Shauna May, Diana O'Connell, Cynthia Moreland, and Richard Stowers were discovered.

old Anne Alderson had been jogging in the park and was seen by several witnesses. When her body was found it was clear she had been killed close to the spot where Edda Kane had been murdered, and by the same method, a single gunshot to the back of the head. However, this time the victim had clearly been raped and then allowed to get dressed again before being killed. In later November, the murder count more than doubled, with four bodies discovered in Point Reyes National Seashore Park. First to disappear was Shauna May, who had failed to turn up to hike with friends. They raised the alarm, but it took two days of searching to retrieve her body, buried in a shallow grave. She had been stripped, trussed with picture-framing wire, raped and shot three times in the head. But right next to her remains was the body of 22-year-old Diana O'Connell, shot on the same day. She too had been stripped and raped, before being strangled with wire and buried. Police concluded that the killer had lain in wait and killed the first victim, only to be surprised by the arrival of the second. But before the two bodies had been found, searchers had stumbled across the remains of a young couple, 18-year-old Cynthia Moreland and 19-year-old Richard Stowers, missing since October 11. Police did not

assume at first these were all the victims of the same killer, but when the bullets were retrieved and compared, it was certain that all those who had died from gunshot wounds had been killed by the same weapon, and the same murderer from Mount Tamalpais State Park, dubbed in the press as the Trailside Killer.

REFINING THE PROFILE

The first profile was drawn up by local psychologists, who assumed the killer was plausible enough and good-looking enough to approach his victims openly before attacking and killing them. When the search led nowhere, the police contacted the FBI. They called in John Douglas and Roy Hazelwood, who had developed their theories on separating sex murderers into organized or disorganized killers. Organized killers were those who carefully planned their crimes and tended to follow a ritual over how to derive maximum pleasure and satisfaction from the killings. Disorganized killers tended instead to act on opportunity and impulse, and were generally poorer in intelligence or earning power. Both men were unhappy with the assumptions of the existing profile, which suggested a personable, sophisticated individual

The area in which the bodies were discovered was too wide to allow police to catch the killer in the act, but profiling helped to reveal that the suspect was local, as he was familiar with the area.

In addition, the selection of the murder sites suggested someone who was very familiar with the area and therefore almost certainly a local man. In keeping with this type of personality, he was probably white, since all his victims had been white. He was probably reasonably intelligent, with a blue-collar job and a high level of aggression. This might mean he had spent time in prison, which was in line with the discovery of a pair of prison-issue spectacles close to one of the victims. Douglas also considered that the killer would be in his 30s, but in his younger years might have shown three classic indicators of later problems: bed-wetting; cruelty to animals; and a tendency to start fires. He might well have committed rapes previously, but these were almost certainly his first murders. The reason for Douglas' suggestion of a speech impediment was that he thought this might have acted as a trigger for the killer's aggression, which he relieved by overpowering and killing his victims. But as yet, despite the detail in the profile, there was no way to link it to an individual suspect, and the area of the killings was too wide to allow surveillance to trap the killer in the act of approaching a victim.

THE HUNT CLOSES

In the end it was the killer who made two fatal mistakes. On March 29, 1981, he approached a couple in the Henry Cowell Redwoods State Park near Santa Cruz, and held them up at gunpoint. He insisted on having sex with the woman, undergraduate student Ellen Hansen, but when she refused he shot her dead, and then turned his gun on her companion Steve Haertle, before fleeing the area. Though he was shot through the neck, Haertle survived and was able to give a partial description of an older man, about 50, with stained and crooked teeth, and wearing a gold-colored jacket with lettering on the back. Other witnesses saw a man running out of the

who would almost certainly be an organized, ritualistic killer. Although some victims had been found in a kneeling position, which might suggest a degree of ritual was involved, they found that other indicators carried much greater weight. For example, the fact that several victims had been shot in the back or side of the head suggested that the killer had not approached them directly, but had sneaked up from behind to catch them unawares. This pointed to someone of much lower self-confidence, shy and reclusive, unhappy about his appearance, and possibly suffering from a speech impediment or disfiguring acne.

park and driving off in a red car, possibly a Fiat. The police published an impression of the killer, revealed by ballistic evidence to be the one responsible for the earlier murders, and to their surprise they had a positive result. A woman who had been on a cruise to Japan 26 years before had complained about the attentions paid by a purser to her young daughter. He had suffered from a stutter and his name was David Carpenter, unfortunately a reasonably common name in California.

The publishing of the picture had a negative result as well. The killer realized the danger and grew a large beard to change his appearance. Then he made his other mistake, and sealed his fate. On May 2, 20-year-old Heather Roxanne Scaggs made an appointment to see David Carpenter about a used car he had agreed to help her buy from his friend. She told her boyfriend, Dan Pingle, about the arrangement and gave him Carpenter's address and phone number and the time she expected to return. Apparently Carpenter had been teaching people to use computer typesetting machines at a printing company where she was a student, and, knowing she needed a car, had insisted on being allowed to help. On several occasions he had even given her a lift home in his own car, but this time she never returned from visiting him at home. The net was closing in. The police were busy finding reasons why they hadn't located the killer earlier. Their search of prison records had failed on a legal technicality that left Carpenter out of the lists of released inmates, and other mistakes had left him off a sex offenders' list too. Finally the FBI set up surveillance of David Carpenter, and when they arrested him they found his car, a red Fiat, crammed with books and maps of local hiking trails. His former fiancée reported that he had had his gold jacket stolen,

though she was dubious about this. Finally, when put in identity parades, both he and his car were positively identified by witnesses. Carpenter was charged with six of the murders, with direct ballistics evidence linking him to them. Police recovered the murder weapon from a bank robber to whom Carpenter had given the .38 in an attempt to hide it. When they checked his personal background, they found he had had strict and domineering parents whose pressure had intensified his stuttering problems and made him shy and resentful. He had wet his bed and mistreated animals, and at 17 had been arrested for molesting two younger cousins. He finally married at the age of 25 and had three children with his wife, but the relationship finally broke up due to his insatiable sex drive, and by the time of the murders he was living with his now aged parents. Carpenter was eventually brought to trial in October 1983 and on July 6, 1984, he was convicted of the first-degree murder of Ellen Hansen and Heather Scaggs, and the attempted murder of Steve Haertle. In May 1988 he was tried and found guilty of another five murders, with both trials resulting in him being sentenced to death in the gas chamber at San Quentin.

San Quentin Prison in San Quentin, California, where David Carpenter remains on death row for the rape and murder of more than five women.

WHEN:	**1980s**
WHERE:	**New York, USA**
VICTIMS:	**Multiple**
CULPRIT:	**Arthur Shawcross**

CASE STUDY 6: ARTHUR SHAWCROSS

Profiling was clearly capable of providing considerable help in tracking down and identifying even the most elusive criminals, and as it was used in more and more landmark cases, it emerged that on some occasions even lapses in accuracy could actually be explained once more information was available. A prime example of this was the Arthur Shawcross case, which involved the murder of prostitutes in upper New York State during the late 1980s. The killings began in March 1988, and by the end of the following year a total of 16 bodies had been found in different places around the town of Rochester. The FBI had been called in to advise the police, and profiler Gregg McCrary, working with Lieutenant Ed Grant of

The Genesee River Gorge in Rochester, New York, where Arthur Shawcross took his victims.

the New York State Police, began by sifting through the evidence collected so far to look for significant patterns.

There was one main problem: by the time most of the victims' bodies were retrieved, they had deteriorated too much to yield significant material to identify their killer. Only one victim, whose naked body had been thrown into a deep ravine, was reasonably fresh, but even that provided no clues. The death toll was continuing to rise and on Thanksgiving Day 1989, a man who was walking his dog through a marshy stretch alongside the Genesee River reported finding a woman's naked body covered by a piece of carpet. Despite the decomposition that had already set in, the victim was soon identified as 30-year-old June Stott. However, there were two disturbing differences in this case: unlike all the other victims found so far, she was not a prostitute, and her body was the only one to be badly mutilated after death. She had been cut open by a long vertical incision from the top of her chest to between her legs, inflicted so long after death that the killer must have returned to the murder scene to carry it out.

Examining the locations of the murders was key in the profiling of Arthur Shawcross.

UNDERSTANDING THE KILLER

McCrary and Grant started work on December 13, 1989, with the area slushy with melting snow. For the time being, the only pattern that would help them establish a profile was the killer's usual routine, which had been to pick up a prostitute on Lyell Avenue, the only place in the area where his white victims plied their trade. From there, they had been taken to different murder sites along the scenic Genesee River gorge, a 22-mile-long stretch of parkland with three waterfalls. Most of the bodies had been found in the parts of the park nearest to Rochester itself, which suggested the killer was a local man who knew the area well. He had carried his victims a relatively short distance from the pick-up area to the murder spots, and because killers recognize that dumping a victim's body in the open is fraught with risks to them, they normally only do this in an area they know well. How would he know the area? Probably through being a keen fisherman, investigators thought. They spoke to the prostitutes working in the area who quoted their charges, showing that the killer was targeting women in his own price range, suggesting he had a fairly low educational and earning level. However, he must have a car to transport his victims from Lyell Avenue to the places where their bodies had been found. Furthermore, since his victims were happy enough to enter his vehicle even after the first killings had been publicized, he must be known to them as a regular client who presented no real threat. In cases where the victims had been found soon after death, there was no evidence of sexual activity, so there was the possibility that the killer had been unable to perform sexually, which would be a powerful trigger for rage and anger. Some of the victims showed signs of violence inflicted at around the time of death, and in some cases the probable cause of death was almost certainly strangulation. But had this always been the case, and were all the killings the work of the same criminal? When the profilers compared similarities, it seemed likely that seven of the cases related to prostitutes picked up around Lyell Avenue, killed, and then dumped in the gorge area after being suffocated. But what about the other cases—in particular that of June

McCrary and Grant used profiling to suggest that the killer was probably an active fisherman, which explained his knowledge of the area.

Helicopters were used to patrol the area where the previous killings had occurred.

totally normal, familiar, and unthreatening to the prostitutes he approached, given the widespread fear inspired by the killings. He was probably married.

FIRST SIGHTING

Stott, which failed to fit the pattern? Experience with previous serial killers told McCrary that mutilating victims after death was an extra routine that several murderers graduated to, once they became accustomed to killing and were reassured that they could commit murder and dump the bodies without being caught. So what might appear to be a marked divergence from the previous pattern of killings actually related to an increase in the killer's confidence, and could well be repeated in future murders— unless he was caught. The completed profile suggested a criminal aged from late 20s to early 30s, since this was the age of most of the victims, and the two age groups were usually closely correlated, with the killer's emotional range at least. To carry out this type of crime the suspect must have had previous experience, which suggested he would appear on the sex offenders' register. In addition, he would appear

When criminal records failed to show any matches, and more women were found to be missing, the profilers decided on a different strategy. Thus far the bodies had been discovered by passers-by, mostly walkers or fishermen. If the killer was likely to return to similar murder sites to carry out more mutilations, then keeping a close watch through police patrols and helicopter flights might result in him being caught in the act. Finally, on January 3, 1990, a helicopter patrol spotted a body lying on top of the ice close to the site of an earlier killing in Salmon Creek. It was almost hidden under a bridge where a road that was a continuation of Lyell Avenue crossed the creek, but most important of all, they had a glimpse of a man standing on the bridge, apparently urinating. Closer inspection identified the body as that of June Cicero—one of the missing prostitutes—mutilated after death by the removal of her vagina. On the nearby bridge the man who had apparently been urinating was actually found to have been masturbating. His name was Arthur Shawcross, and he was 45 years old. But was he the killer? Checks revealed he had been on parole for manslaughter, following his conviction 17 years earlier for killing and mutilating two young children in his hometown of Watertown, New York. He had behaved well while in prison and had convinced the parole board that he no longer represented a threat to the community. Two years earlier, he had been released with eight years of his sentence still to complete, on condition that he kept well away from young children. However, whenever the parole team found him somewhere to live, the news would leak out and the local community would demand he was moved away. Without at this stage charging him, the police questioned him about his presence in the area where the body was found and about his background. They then took his photograph and showed it to the prostitutes who were helping the investigation. They identified him as a regular client they knew as

Mitch, and one in particular said he had scared her when he asked her to pretend she was dead when he had sex with her.

THE FIRST MURDERS

Once his full criminal history had been extracted, it was clear that Shawcross had been on a steadily deteriorating spiral of anger and extreme violence. He had served a tour of duty in Vietnam, had been married four times, and spent time in custody for burglary, including one theft during which he had set the local Watertown branch of Sears on fire. Finally, in May 1972, a 10-year-old boy, Jack Blake, had disappeared after being seen fishing with Shawcross, though the body was not found for months. In September, 8-year-old Karen Ann Hill had been raped and murdered, and her body was found close to the spot where Shawcross had been seen fishing. After careful questioning, the police managed to extract a confession from Shawcross for the killings and also find where the badly decomposed body of Jack Blake had been dumped.

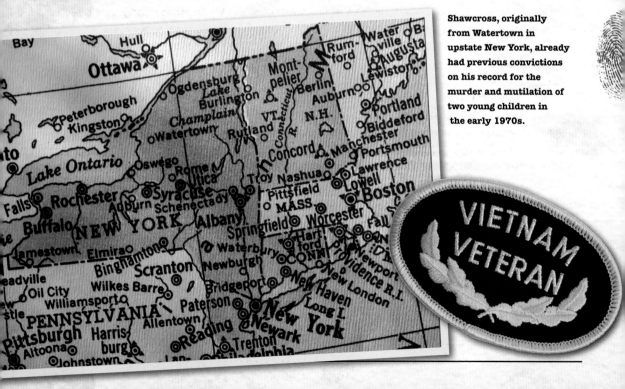

Shawcross, originally from Watertown in upstate New York, already had previous convictions on his record for the murder and mutilation of two young children in the early 1970s.

Shawcross had settled in Rochester with his fourth wife, working at a catering company packing salads. Later he would find himself working nights, when it was possible to finish his shift early, leaving him time to visit prostitutes, pick up victims, and carry out the murders. With no car of his own, he would borrow one belonging to a girlfriend, Clara Neal, and this proved crucial in persuading him to reveal what he had done, when police suggested that since he was known to have been driving her car when in the vicinity of the killings, she too might have been involved. For Shawcross, this was the sticking point. Bit by bit the truth emerged as he identified his victims from photographs. All of them were prostitutes apart from June Stott, who had been a friend of himself and his wife, often having dinner with the two of them in their home.

BACKGROUND KNOWLEDGE

When profilers looked more closely into Shawcross' background, they realized his original crimes against children reflected that he was a situational child molester, someone who did not fixate on child victims but merely chose them as vulnerable targets to be controlled and used for the criminal's pleasure. Prostitutes gave him a different kind of victim, but one who could still be dominated and controlled, given his limited social skills, and while they were available, he ceased to present a specific threat to children. He was undoubtedly cunning, and able to evade police surveillance. When they ran patrols along Lyell Avenue, he was waiting on nearby side streets where prostitutes looking for clients might occasionally stray. Despite the defense at his trial claiming he was insane at the time of each murder, the court rejected this strategy, and he was sentenced to 25 years in jail for each of the 10 murders to which he had confessed.

But what about the only real discrepancy between the profile and the reality—the question of the killer's age? This was readily explained by considering the difference between Shawcross' real age, of 45 at the time of the investigation, and his emotional age, which had been retarded by the 15 years spent in prison. With those taken out of the reckoning, his emotional age remained at 30, well within the range predicted by the profilers.

HELPING TO FIND THE CRIMINAL

In all these examples, profiling played an essential part in tracking down and identifying the perpetrator of the crimes. But there are other, more detailed ways in which information on a crime can be made to add detail to a profile to make it more effective, and the next chapter will examine some of the characteristics and descriptor factors that can be used to help define and identify an unknown criminal.

ONE STEP AT A TIME

Profiling has been described as the third great advance in the effective investigation of crime. The first advance was the technique of studying clues at the scene of the crime, largely pioneered by London's Metropolitan Police during the nineteenth century. This has since been developed to embrace many of the methods of modern forensic science. The second advance has been the collection of background data on different types of crime, to show how relatively rare or common they are, and detailed record-keeping to link potential subjects and their relative probability. Finally, criminal profiling extends this same search for background information to the psychology of different types of criminal. In the view of FBI profiling pioneer Howard Teten: "Offender profiling is a method of identifying the perpetrator of a crime based on an analysis of the nature of the offense and the manner in which it was committed. Various aspects of the criminal's personality makeup are determined from his or her choice of actions before, during, and after the crime. This information is combined with other pertinent details and physical evidence, and then compared with the characteristics of known personality types and mental abnormalities to develop a practical working description of the offender."

Officers of the London Metropolitan Police in 1864. The Met are widely credited with making the first advances in criminal investigation.

STEP ONE

In practice, profiling involves taking a series of different steps to collect and assess the evidence and then convert it into the finished profile. First, investigators have to gather as much evidence and information as possible from the crime scene, from the victim and from any potential witnesses, always being aware of the possibility that missing vital information might skew the profile and render it potentially misleading—as was the case with Arthur Shawcross, reviewed on pages 44–9. Sometimes the information can include autopsy reports, police statements, and comments from those who discovered the crime or who may have glimpsed the perpetrator on their way to or from the crime itself.

Clues From The Victim

Sometimes, too, the victim is profiled, since this information can also relate to the crime and the person responsible. For example, if the victim followed a set routine from day to day, this might suggest that an organized criminal had planned the crime carefully, studying this pattern to understand where the victim would be at the time of committing the crime. The victim's type of work might also reflect more light on the crime, since the degree of risk undergone by the victim would be much greater in some jobs than others: a prostitute has the ultimate high-risk occupation, involving casual contact with strangers on the fringes of society, and a lifestyle that means a person may not be noticed as missing for some considerable time. Perhaps the ultimate low-risk role would be a member of the police or the armed forces, since they are in constant close contact with their peers and colleagues, and any disappearance would be immediately followed up by professionals. Outside these two limits, a victim's social circle and their close family members may also generate more detail about the life of the victim and how and why this may have contributed to their fate.

STEP TWO

The second step is to use the information gathered at the first juncture to uncover more about the person responsible for the crime. Profilers can analyze the personality of the as yet unknown offender through studying what is known about their behavior just before the

Investigators collecting evidence at the scene of a crime. Police must ensure that they make every effort to gather as much evidence as possible so as to avoid gaps in the investigation.

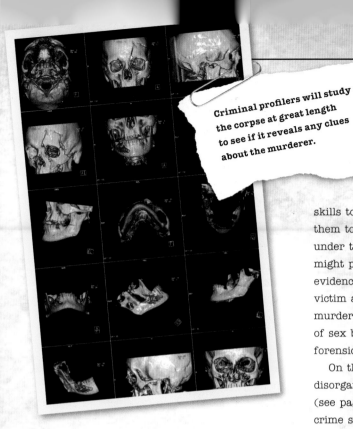

Criminal profilers will study the corpse at great length to see if it reveals any clues about the murderer.

distinction relates to different personalities and backgrounds. The characteristics of an organized killer are usually associated with a person having an outwardly normal appearance and behavior and adequate social skills to persuade a potential victim to trust them to the point where they can be brought under the criminal's control. Telltale signs that might point to an organized killer would include evidence of advance planning in choosing the victim and the murder site, the seclusion of the murder scene from potential witnesses, evidence of sex before the killing, and a lack of obvious forensic evidence at the scene.

On the other hand, indications of a disorganized killer, such as the Trailside Killer (see page 40), would imply the opposite. The crime scene would suggest they carried out the killing on the spur of the moment, having seized the opportunity when they spotted a suitable victim. There would normally be more evidence at the crime scene, because these killers usually operate in a more frenzied and less controlled manner. They might leave traces of sexual activity with the victim after the killing, since they lack the control needed to achieve their desired result beforehand. In addition, they show fewer signs of any measures to make detection more difficult.

crime was committed. Did they have a plan, routine, or fantasy they appeared to be following when they set the crime in motion? Are there any factors to explain why the murderer chose that day to find and kill his victim rather than any other day? In terms of the crime itself, profilers try to understand how the murderer selected the type of victim or victims, and what this reveals about his motivation. They will study how the victim's body was disposed of afterward, whether it was simply left at the scene of the killing, or whether it was disposed of somewhere else, or even at several different sites after being dismembered. And they will watch in particular for the presence of anyone showing an undue interest in the investigation, or even seeking to become involved in it, since this is often an indicator of a potential suspect.

Organized or Disorganized?
The Crucial Question

FBI profilers normally use the evidence in a murder case to suggest whether the killer was an organized or disorganized criminal, since this

The way a body is disposed of can tell profilers a great deal about their criminal.

STEP THREE

The third step is to reconstruct how the crime was carried out and try to ascertain what this shows of the perpetrator's method and motives. In particular, investigators look for the killer's "signature," signs of the psychological pressures that induce them to commit the crime. Another crucial factor is "staging," or the degree to which the killer modifies the crime scene after the killing, either to fulfill a particular fantasy or to throw investigators off the scent.

With their experience of similar cases, profilers can use this information to suggest the likely age range of the killer, their social class, their educational level, their outward personality and appearance, their family relationships, their possible occupation, the type of car they probably drive, and whether or not they served in the armed forces. Some of this information can be obtained from a profile relating to a single crime, but in the case of serial killers, the level of detail will almost certainly increase with successive murders, except in the case of the most careful and organized offenders of all. Finally, the profile can sometimes suggest appropriate ways of questioning a suspect, by predicting their likely psychological strengths and weaknesses, so as to persuade them to reveal more about themselves or even give a full confession.

BALANCING THE PROBABILITIES

The following chapters of this book explain how these aspects of profiling have been used to track down the criminals responsible for a range

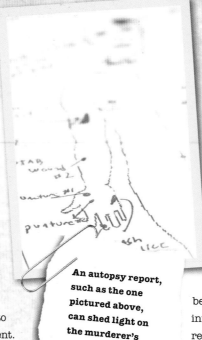

An autopsy report, such as the one pictured above, can shed light on the murderer's motivations and tendencies.

of rapes, sex attacks, and murders, in many different countries and against a variety of backgrounds. Some of the examples will show organized and disorganized killers, and how the signs they leave when they carry out their crimes have helped lead to their arrest and conviction. Others will show how criminals have staged their crime scenes, and how they leave evidence of their signatures, no matter how much they try to disguise these. Particular aspects of profiling have been developed to deal with cases involving children, and those relating to written documents, and these too are outlined in later chapters.

However, in all cases it is vital to remember that profiling is not an exact science. It deals with probabilities and possibilities, rather than providing direct physical evidence, though physical evidence may be vitally important in leading profilers to the conclusions that help identify the perpetrator responsible for a particular crime. So a profile can never be treated as a hard-and-fast prescription that must be correct in every detail before it can be applied to a potential suspect. Human beings vary in countless different ways, and there is always the possibility that a normally safe conclusion may prove unreliable when searching for a particular individual. On the other hand, increasing experience of the complexities of human behavior as each case unfolds helps make future profiles more informed and more accurate. Furthermore, a clearer understanding of the psychological priorities of violent criminals has enabled profiling to find a valuable role in individual murder cases, as well as those involving serial killers.

CASE

WHEN:	**1980s**
WHERE:	**Rhode Island, USA**
VICTIMS:	**Multiple**
CULPRIT:	**Craig Price**

CASE STUDY 7: A FAMILY MURDERED

Even before becoming involved in the maximum effort needed to bring about a successful conclusion of the Shawcross case, FBI profiler Gregg McCrary had been faced with a gruesome family murder in Warwick, Rhode Island. In the Warwick case, the target was not a serial killer, but a lone individual who made a savage and lethal attack on a mother and two young daughters. All three were found at home, dead from multiple frenzied stab wounds and beatings with a blunt instrument. There was no obvious motive, but there were clear signs of a disorganized killer at work, reinforced by the use of a knife from the kitchen as a murder weapon. Had the murderer been an organized killer, he would certainly have chosen a weapon and brought it with him to the house.

LOCAL SIMILIARITIES

The body of the mother, 39-year-old Joan Heaton, was found next to that of her elder daughter, 10-year-old Jennifer, lying in the hallway of the house and partially covered by bedsheets soaked in their blood. Apart from their horrific wounds, the knife used to kill them had actually broken off in Jennifer's neck, adding mute testimony to the frenzy of the killer. In addition to 57 separate stab wounds, Joan Heaton had also been strangled and her head had been battered with a heavy object. A search of the house revealed the body of the other daughter, 8-year-old Melissa, lying in the kitchen. She had been stabbed over and over again, and finally beaten about the head with a bloodstained footstool lying nearby.

Detectives checked the other evidence and tried to reconstruct what had happened. It appeared the killer had entered the house by forcing a kitchen window and stepping through it onto a table that had broken under his weight. He had then attacked the mother and elder daughter. The younger child had run into the kitchen to reach the phone to call for help when she too had been killed. There was no clue as to who might have done this, but the only unusual

Profilers used forensic evidence, such as the murder weapon, to deduce that the murderer in the Warwick case had also lived in the small state of Rhode Island.

RHODE ISLAND

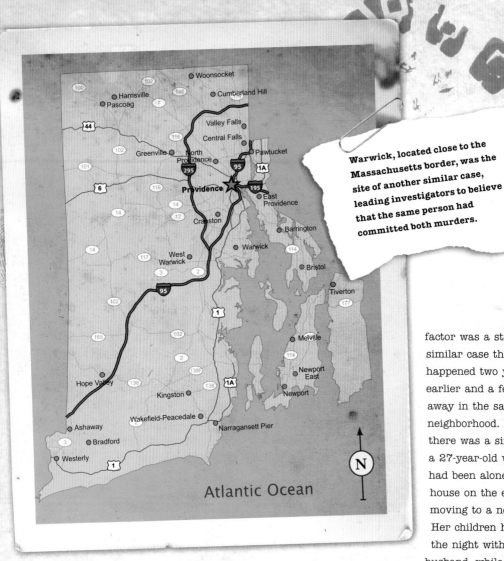

Warwick, located close to the Massachusetts border, was the site of another similar case, leading investigators to believe that the same person had committed both murders.

factor was a strikingly similar case that had happened two years earlier and a few houses away in the same neighborhood. In that case there was a single victim, a 27-year-old woman who had been alone in the house on the eve of moving to a new address. Her children had spent the night with her husband, while her brother, who shared the house with her, had been out completing a night shift as a security guard. She had spent the day packing items ready for the move, and had slept on a pile of blankets in front of the television.

The next morning, the victim's brother returned home to find his sister dead as a result of multiple stab wounds from a knife she had been using to cut string for her packing. With neither motive nor suspects, the murder had remained unsolved. However, McCrary was struck by the fact that the killer in this case, too, was disorganized and had picked up a weapon at the crime scene to kill his victim.

Two telltale signs came to mind. With the killer almost certainly local, there was a high chance he knew his victims personally, an assessment borne out by the attempt to cover their bodies with the sheets. Another, more hopeful, possibility was that after carrying out a particularly frenzied attack, using a very sharp kitchen knife, the killer may well have cut his own hand. Officers searching the house had found bloodstains, possibly from the killer, in the hall of the house but some distance from the victims' bodies, and also in a bathroom.

THE UNREPORTED KILLER

No one in the neighborhood had reported seeing any strangers in the vicinity during the day of the murders, which suggested to McCrary that the murderer was likely to be someone known to them. Most people living in the area were of Irish Catholic origin, so it would be safe to conclude the killer was white and—given the type of killing and the age range of the victims—probably in his late teens. Another pointer was the fairly difficult entry through the forced kitchen window, which suggested someone who was fit, well-built and agile.

Blood tests showed the samples in the hallway and the bathroom came from none of the victims, so were almost certainly left by the killer. Then one policeman spotted a teenager he knew, named Craig Price. Though only 15 years old, he was 6 feet tall and lived close to the houses where the murders had been committed. He was friendly, and black, but he was wearing a bandage around his hand. If he was a genuine suspect, why did he not fit the profile in all respects? Normally witnesses would notice someone from a different racial group compared with the rest of the neighborhood, yet a boy raised in the neighborhood with plenty of white friends would not be seen as a potential threat, so did not even register on witnesses' radar.

His record, though, contained much significant information. He had been arrested for theft, including breaking and entering, and scouting people's houses to determine where valuables could be found. In the light of the murders, it was clear he had no compunction about attacking those smaller and weaker than he was, since his record showed he had been arrested two months earlier for assaulting his younger sister. When finally arrested for the Heaton family killings, he claimed he had cut his hand on a broken car window. However, checks revealed no fragments of broken glass had been found where the vehicle had been parked. Shoeprints and a large handprint in the kitchen produced close matches, and the blood analysis proved his presence at the scene of the crime. He was tried and found guilty, but as a juvenile, he could be detained by the state only until the age of 21, when in theory he would walk free to commit further crimes. However, he soon committed another crime, which resulted in his being sentenced to seven more years in prison. During this term after turning 21, he attacked two prison guards and earned another 25-year sentence. A young man whom McCrary saw as well on the way to developing into a future serial killer was securely behind bars at last.

After concluding that the killer lived in the neighborhood, McCrary was able to make an educated guess about his ethnic and religious background.

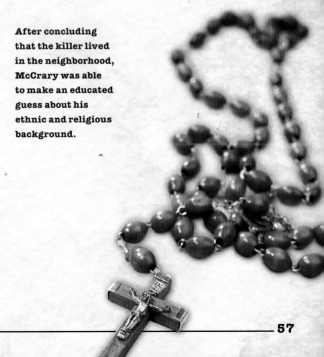

CASE

WHEN: 1989

WHERE: Dryden,
New York State

VICTIMS: Harris Family

CULPRIT: Anthony
Turner, also
known as
Michael Kinge

CASE STUDY 8: DEADLY CHANGE OF MIND

Just three months after the murders of the Heaton family, the FBI were called in to help track down the criminal responsible for another family murder. This time the victims were a husband, wife, and two teenage children in the community of Dryden, near Ithaca in New York State.

DISCOVERING THE CRIME

At around 4:30 p.m. on December 22, 1989, a postman delivering mail in Ellis Hollow Road noticed an unfamiliar hooded figure riding a bicycle with some difficulty along the snow-covered road. He saw the cyclist approaching the home of Tony and Dodie Harris and their children, 14-year-old Marc and 16-year-old Shelby, and thought little more about it. Then

When a police officer arrived at the Harrises' home he discovered two used cans of gasoline that the murderer had used in a failed attempt to set the house on fire.

A police officer called to the house by concerned neighbors found the phone wires ripped out and ran to his car to radio for backup.

around 15 minutes later, a neighbor across the street from the Harrises saw two figures standing in the drive in front of the small gift shop, Grey Goose, which Mrs. Harris ran as an additional family business next to their house. In the failing light, the neighbor thought one of the figures was Dodie Harris, but did not recognize the other person. An hour later, a witness walking past the house noticed all the lights were out, but someone else driving past the property at a 7:15 p.m. saw a figure in the house, walking past a lighted window.

At 7:30 p.m. Shelby Harris' boyfriend called the house, worried because she had failed to meet him for a date they had arranged that evening. Puzzled because there was no reply, he called again and again at 30-minute intervals, still with no response. Finally at 6:30 a.m. the following morning, the Harris security alarm woke their neighbors who called the police. An officer in a car reached the house at 7:20 a.m., where he found the alarm turned off and the front and side doors of the house locked, but the garage door was open and the outside lights to the property were still on. Inside the garage was a family saloon car with a portable air compressor placed on top of it, and a space for a second car, which seemed to be missing. He walked through the door into the kitchen where he found a man's briefcase on the floor and two bags of groceries. There was a sharp smell of burning in the house, and smoke detectors were sounding.

Walking into the living room, he found Christmas gifts with the wrapping torn away,

and a red and yellow fuel can lying on the floor. On the banisters in the hallway were a man's blue jacket and a pair of gloves. With no response to his calls, the police officer went back into the kitchen to ring the station for backup, but found the phone wires had been ripped away. He used his car radio to call-in assistance, and then began searching the upstairs rooms. He found another gasoline can and a smashed telephone before three of his colleagues arrived to help continue the search. In one room they found a body with its upper half so charred it was unrecognizable, but the lower half showed clearly it was that of a woman. A mattress appeared to have been set on fire deliberately, and in the bathroom they found a dead dog. A fire was still burning in another room, so they called the fire department and waited for the blaze to be extinguished.

THE FIRE THAT FAILED

Once the fire was out, they found the charred body of a second adult, this time male. Both bodies had bags over their heads and twisted wire coathangers binding them to the bedposts. On another bed in the same room was a smaller body, that of 14-year-old Marc Harris, and in the main bedroom the naked body of Shelby Harris was lying face down with a torn dress spread out to cover her. She was bound and gagged and had been shot three times in the head. Both her parents had been shot twice in the head, and her brother had also been shot three times. A neighbor noticed that the family's van was missing from the garage, and it appeared credit cards had been stolen from the study. Finally, crude attempts had been made to set the house on fire and destroy the evidence of the killings, using cans of gasoline. However, closing the doors to the individual rooms had starved the flames of oxygen, stopping them from taking hold. Two more features were noted by the police: all surfaces had been wiped clear of fingerprints, indicating an experienced criminal, but the gift shop next to the house had not been robbed.

The missing van was found empty near a local bank. Witnesses had noticed it there on the night of the murders, but it had then vanished and returned the following day. At the same time, one of the police at the crime scene noticed fresh tire tracks in the snow across the lawn in front of the Harris house, which might suggest the killer had returned to the scene of the crime after his original visit.

BACKGROUND CHECK

Gregg McCrary's first step was to explore the family's background, to establish whether there was any possible reason for the horrific attack. He drew a complete blank, with no apparent enemies and no skeletons in the family closet. Tony Harris was almost 40 and worked as a director of marketing for an electronics company, with a good reputation at work. His wife ran the antique and gift shop and had recently recovered from several episodes of breast cancer, which had eventually persuaded the family to move from Georgia to New York State, closer to her family, to live in a house built for them by her father. The only potential trigger for the crime appeared to be the gift shop business, which in the approach to the Christmas holiday would be enjoying a brisk turnover and might have attracted the attention of robbers.

WHAT KIND OF KILLER?

Given the facts, it made a great deal of sense to assume the killings had been carried out by a stranger to the area, with some previous experience of crime. Wiping off the fingerprints

had been effective, but the attempt to start a fire was not—and while the phone wires had been torn out to prevent any calls for help, a phone in the basement of the house was left intact. There were marked discrepancies in the way the daughter had been treated, compared with the rest of the family. Where they had simply been shot and burned, she had been tied to a chair, then released and retied, forced to change into a new dress, then made to undress and endure a sexual assault before being shot. Only when the unavailing attempts to start a fire triggered the house smoke alarms did the killer panic and leave the scene.

There were several apparent inconsistencies in the evidence. For example, cutting the phone wires only made sense while the family remained alive. Did this mean the intruder did not originally plan to kill his captives? Given the amount of time between the original witness sighting and the setting off of the alarms, was he confident enough to spend the entire interval in the house, risking discovery? Or had he left the scene, thought again about the danger of any evidence remaining to identify him, and taken the even greater risk of returning to try to set the house ablaze?

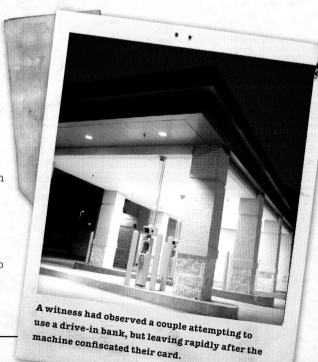

A witness had observed a couple attempting to use a drive-in bank, but leaving rapidly after the machine confiscated their card.

After initial inquiries by the police, the suspect locked himself in his apartment with a vicious Doberman and a gun, in an attempt to ward off the police.

to killing the family, it was also likely the killer had been serving time for crimes of violence but not for previous murders. If he had had experience of killing, he would probably have eliminated the family immediately, without wasting time cutting the phone wires. Furthermore, given the inept failure to set the house on fire, it was likely the criminal record would not contain earlier cases of arson.

These questions were still unresolved when the investigators enjoyed a sudden break-through. They traced the use of the family's ATM cards just after the murder to withdraw cash, and later to pay for women's clothing and jewelry at a shopping mall in the area. The user was identified as a young black male, accompanied by an older black female, and the purchases suggested the male might be buying the luxury articles as gifts for a wife or girlfriend of similar age to himself.

FROM ROBBERY TO MURDER

In profiling terms, all this added up to a crime originally planned as a simple robbery, but which had escalated to rape and murder. It was likely that the killer had been watching the family long enough to decide the gift shop and those who ran it would be worth robbing, and had changed his mind once in the house, with the victims at his mercy. This behavior is typical of a criminal who has served time in jail and who is so desperate not to return there that under the stress of potential exposure at the crime scene, he decides his only hope of escaping scot-free is to eliminate all potential witnesses. Because of this probable change of mind at the scene, from cutting the phone wires

CLOSING THE NET

This added up to a profile of a dangerously volatile criminal, switching to violence in the face of the slightest threat, including any attempt to arrest him. The probability was that he would work in a fairly low-paid, unskilled job and would live with a wife or female partner. This was promising, but still fell short of pointing the way to any individual criminal. Then came a vital new lead. A customer waiting to use the ATM at a local drive-in bank reported that a black couple in a worn-out old car had been ahead in the queue for the machine, but that they had had to drive off after the machine had retained the card they were using. The police retrieved the card, and found it had been issued to Tony Harris.

Other witnesses supplied information that enabled the suspect to be named as Anthony Turner, also known as Michael Kinge, who lived with a girlfriend, Joanna White, and their 1-year-old son in an apartment not far from the murder scene. His mother, Shirley Kinge, lived in the adjacent apartment, together with the suspect's grandmother. Michael himself was constantly in debt, and, though he had a degree from a business college, could only find casual work as a cleaner or attendant at a bowling

Although the subject had a college business degree, he was only ever able to find menial jobs such as working at a bowling alley. This fitted the investigator's profile that the murderer worked in unskilled and low-paying jobs.

alley. To make ends meet he carried out a string of robberies, and had served time for armed robbery, a charge for which he had been released, and was still on parole when he committed the killings.

Police called at Kinge's apartment and he answered the door, giving his name as Michael Turner, a combination of aliases. They asked him if he had seen anything suspicious on the night of the murder. He claimed to have seen nothing out of the ordinary, though his wife might have seen something while traveling to or from her night-shift work. He then refused to talk any more and the police left, to gather more evidence. They managed to obtain samples of his mother's handwriting and matched them to the signatures on bills relating to the stolen credit cards. They also heard Kinge had gone to ground in the apartment, armed with a sawn-off shotgun, a knife, and a fierce Doberman, and living on pizzas brought back by his girlfriend.

On February 7, 1990, police arrested Joanna White while she was at work, and questioned her, explaining their intention to arrest Kinge and underlining that the profile suggested he might use their infant son as a bargaining counter to avoid arrest. She then gave them detailed information on the plan of the apartment, and two arrest teams were sent in,

one to arrest Kinge and the other to bring in his mother. As they broke in, their suspect ran into a bedroom and emerged waving a sawn-off shotgun. At first he pointed it at himself, threatening suicide, but when negotiations broke down he turned the weapon around and began firing at the police. They returned fire, and he was shot dead on the spot. When they searched the apartment, they found the weapon he had used to kill the Harris family, along with other evidence that tied him to the killings.

VALUABLE CONTRIBUTION TO FUTURE PROFILES

In both these cases profiling was a valuable aid to tracking down the criminal responsible for a series of killings, though the actual identification of the suspect had been down to conventional detective work. In both cases, though, the profile was confirmed by what was known about the perpetrator in each case, and increasing knowledge about the motivations and priorities that triggered the crimes was added to the store of information that could help explain future crimes. But in its most powerful and most urgent role of helping to apprehend serial killers, profiling was about to find a vital new area in which to demonstrate its usefulness.

WHEN: 1980s

WHERE: Cape Province, South Africa

VICTIMS: Children

CULPRIT: Avzal Norman Simons

CASE STUDY 9: THE STATION STRANGLER

So far, the art of criminal profiling had been largely confined to the United States and the United Kingdom, but profiling would soon become an established part of the weaponry available to police in the Republic of South Africa. In fact, South Africa's overall murder rate is thought to be the third highest in the world, after Colombia and Swaziland. For example, in the first six months of 1998, there were 11,500 murders recorded in South Africa, compared with only 1,000 during the whole of 1997 in France, a country with a population 30 percent larger. But a particular feature of

violent crime in South Africa is the high incidence of serial killings, at a level second only to that of the United States, which has six times the population.

YOUNG BOYS

At about the time of the killings in Rochester, Warwick, and Ithaca, a serial killer was already terrorizing the communities of Cape Province, around the town of Mitchell's Plain, a rundown and high-crime neighborhood. Beginning in 1986, the bodies of young boys had been found in different locations in the area, adding up to a consistent and sinister pattern. The ages of the victims varied between 8 and 15, and many were found with their hands tied behind their backs. Because most were found in remote hiding places amid sand dunes, they had been dead long enough for decomposition to become advanced in the warm climate, making it difficult to retrieve evidence. In those cases found quickly enough, it was clear the victims had been sexually assaulted, and in many more it was also clear they had died from strangulation with items of their own clothing.

A police officer in Cape Town covers the body of a murder victim with a blanket. South Africa has the second highest rate of serial killings in the world, exceeded only by the United States, with a much higher population.

A security guard sits inside a wooden shelter as he guards the entrance to one of Johannesburg's controversial gated streets in the suburb of Norwood. These shelters etched apartheid into the landscape of South Africa.

With advice from profilers at the FBI, the South African police had been able to produce a detailed summary of the person they were looking for, who was already being referred to in the press as the Station Strangler. In a predominantly rural group of communities where strangers of any kind would be noticed and remarked upon, the killer must be a figure so familiar—as an individual or simply as a type—that witnesses did not tend to remember him. As US experience showed, the majority of serial killers began repeating their murders in their early 20s, which suggested that by the time 21 bodies had been discovered, at the end of 1993, the killer would probably be aged between 27 and 29. There was another element in the profile peculiar to a South African context: with the divisions of apartheid still fresh in his mind, it could be assumed that the ethnic origin of the perpetrator would be the same as that of his victims, since a man seen with a boy of a different racial grouping would be unusual enough to cause witnesses to remember.

The locations in which the killer was able to conceal the bodies of his victims, and the ease with which he moved around the area, suggested to police that he must have grown up there, and had possibly played among the sand dunes when he was a child. But he would have to be sufficiently at ease with children to reassure them he presented no threat at a time when people in the area were living in fear of the unknown killer. This would imply he worked as an authority figure in contact with children, such as a teacher, a policeman, or a social worker, and that given his attacks on his victims, he must have been abused in a similar way at the same age.

PERFECTIONIST KILLER

But what kind of killer was he? When the press broke the story that a serial killer was on the loose, and revealed the number and locations of his victims, they had an unexpected, and valuable, item of feedback. The body of the next victim to be found had a note in a pocket, almost certainly from the killer himself. It read: "Number 14. Many more to score." On the published list of victims, this body was not the fourteenth to be found, though if the note was indeed from the killer, then he would know the body must belong to his fourteenth victim, and not the one that appeared as number 14 in the published list. To Dr. Micki Pistorious of the investigation team, a criminal psychologist who would rapidly become the country's most successful profiler, this pointed unmistakably to the killer being both organized, and a perfectionist in terms of his victims. For him to take the very high risk of returning to an undiscovered body to place the note, when the police might have found the corpse and been mounting surveillance on it, showed he was highly confident. This might well manifest itself in concern about his appearance, suggesting a careful and well-groomed dresser.

COMMUNITY AWARENESS

An additional problem with regard to investigating the serial murders of children in a highly volatile area like Mitchell's Plain was that police had to be particularly careful about local vigilantes monitoring their activities. Had a suspect been spotted, local feeling was running high enough to suggest a lynch mob might take events into their own hands, and preempt the law. So on March 26, 1994, when police received a tip-off, they were slow and unobtrusive in their reactions. A week before, they had found another body, this time very badly decomposed, and as yet unidentified. They then received a visit from a Mrs. Fouzia Hercules, who had been waiting for her daughter outside a shopping center near the station at the Strand, a township 12 miles away from Mitchell's Plain, two weeks earlier. There she had seen a stranger talking to two young boys who then agreed to help him carry a pile of boxes to the station. She recognized the boys as cousins, both the grandchildren of a friend, but did not see anything particularly worrying in what she had seen.

Only when at a school meeting a week later did she learn that one of the two boys, Elroy van Rooy, was still missing, and realized what must have happened. She visited her friend, and spoke to the other boy, Ryno, who explained the stranger had offered them

Mitchell's Plain, pictured here, was considered an unstable and violent area by police, so they were careful not to make any of their suspects known to the public, in case of vigilante-style retribution.

10 rand each to help him with the boxes. On realizing the boxes were empty, he had been too scared to join his cousin and the stranger on the train, and had not seen the boy again. In fact, Elroy was the most recently discovered victim, and when Ryno and Mrs. Hercules turned up at the station they were able to help a police artist draw an impression of the Strangler and give a detailed description of his appearance, which was published along with the profile.

THE UNCOOPERATIVE PATIENT

The following month the team had a lead. A nurse working at a private clinic had become convinced that a patient being treated for depression seemed to match the artist's impression and the profile of the strangler. The police mounted a surveillance operation and noticed that the suspect regularly left the clinic at night, and the staff reported that he did not take his medication or participate in the therapy sessions for depression sufferers. Finally they followed him on the night of April 13 as he drove around Mitchell's Plain, where they intercepted him and took him back to the station for questioning. His name was Avzal Norman Simons; he was a 27-year-old primary school teacher from Mitchell's Plain who was neat, softly spoken, and well-dressed. When asked for a statement, he produced a long and rambling

autobiography, but made no confession. It did, however, include a reference to his being sexually abused by his elder brother, who had died some years before.

The police took him back to the house where he lived with his mother, stepfather, and sister, only a short distance from the police station. When they spoke to the headmaster of the school where he taught, they found that members of staff had agreed to keep watch over pupils in the school grounds during breaks to ensure none were abducted by the strangler, but the suspect was the only teacher who refused to take part. He also refused to lock his pupils in their classroom during lessons as an additional safety precaution and would not give them permission to collaborate in an inter-form project on the hunt for the killer.

Bit by bit he spoke of his own background. He was born to a Xhosa father and a mother officially classified as Cape Colored, but he had never known his real father, only his stepfather, another Xhosa. In addition to possible confusion about his racial identity, he had been moved from one distant relative to another in the Mitchell's Plain area during his childhood, he had been taught elements of both the Christian and Muslim religions, and had finally admitted he was gay. He had been regularly raped by his elder brother from the age of eight to 14, though his brother was now dead. Some items of his brother's clothing were found at the house, but no explanation was given as to what had happened to him.

THE KILLER CONFESSES

Finally Simons admitted to the killings and agreed to show police where the bodies had been left, as long as this could be done at night, to avoid vigilantes. He was eventually charged

Simons had been raised in Christian and Muslim environments, which would have looked harshly on his homosexuality.

with the murder of Elroy van Rooy alone, because this was the only killing with more evidence than his own confession.

It proved to be enough. On June 14, 1995, he was sentenced to 25 years in prison for the killing and 10 years for the kidnapping, but at an appeal three years later, his sentence was changed to life imprisonment.

OF FUTURE VALUE

In all these cases and many others like them, profiling has been able to shed vital insight into how criminals think. By revealing these thought processes, profilers have shown why the crimes they commit can often show characteristic signs and items of evidence that suggest what type of perpetrator was responsible, and help to point the way to either tracking down the offender or helping to direct the search in the right direction. But there remain cases that elude even the best profilers, usually because the criminals are careful to operate well below the horizon of public perception. Often they are caught because they themselves sicken of their crimes and set out to invite arrest, or commit a crime so inept and obvious that they can be identified and arrested without the need for any profile at all. However, the truth is that even the most bizarre and inexplicable of cases have value to profilers, because they add to the knowledge of criminal behavior and help in the analysis of future cases.

REPUBLIC OF SOUTH AFRICA

CAPE TOWN
Cape of Good Hope Mitchell's Plain

Criminal profilers were correct in assuming that the killer was local to Mitchell's Plain. Simons had lived in various homes in the area throughout most of his life.

CASE

WHEN:	1970s
WHERE:	California, USA
VICTIMS:	Multiple
CULPRIT:	Ed Kemper

CASE STUDY 10: THE CO-ED KILLER

One of the strangest of such cases was that of the Co-ed Killer. Ed Kemper came from Santa Cruz in California, a beach resort town south of San Francisco, which at one time was known as the murder capital of America, even before he carried out his first killing.

TARRED REPUTATION

The reason for its lurid reputation began with a multiple murderer named John Linley Frazier, who killed a local eye surgeon, Dr. Victor Ohta, his wife, two children, and the surgeon's secretary, in October 1970. Frazier himself was a hippie who was diagnosed as suffering from paranoid schizophrenia, but was found sane enough to be tried for his crimes, which were ascribed to an extreme reaction to the drugs he was taking at the time.

The coast of Santa Cruz, California, was infamous for its gruesome murders.

At the time of the killings, Santa Cruz was about to host an additional campus of the University of California, and local people reacted sharply to the threat they claimed would result from a huge influx of young people from mixed backgrounds. The bloodbath produced by the Charles Manson commune was still all too fresh in people's minds, and when killings began again even after Frazier's arrest, trial, and sentencing, they feared the worst, and sales of handguns for individual protection increased dramatically.

This second chain of murders began late in 1972 and continued into the following year, and was eventually found to be the work of another paranoid schizophrenic, a 25-year-old named Herbert Mullin. He had been prescribed antipsychotic drugs, but had ceased to take them, and was allowed to live as an outpatient, despite being assessed as a potential danger to others. This allowed his bizarre fantasies free rein. He had become convinced that only he could prevent California from suffering a mighty earthquake that would send it crumbling into the sea. To do that, he would have to persuade 13 people either to commit suicide or to allow him to kill them in order to become human sacrifices.

Without any apparent reasons for choosing his victims, he killed a priest, a young girl, four young men on a camping trip, and a mother and

Charles Manson, pictured here, was the mastermind behind a number of cult-killings in California during the 1960s. Hippie culture was blamed for the Santa Cruz murders.

her two children, using a gun, a knife, and a baseball bat. Before he could reach his self-imposed total, a witness spotted him shooting a man digging in his garden, police arrested him, and he was finally convicted of the 10 murders. But if people hoped the town's reputation as a haunt for murderers would now be allowed to wither on the vine, they were to be sorely disappointed.

PEDIGREE OF A MURDERER

Just three months after Mullin faced his accusers, female students began to disappear from the roads in the area as they hitchhiked to and from their studies. The killer was yet another paranoid schizophrenic, a tall, heavily built, and threatening figure named Ed Kemper. From early childhood he had seen everyone, including his immediate family, as a threat to his freedom, and had nursed the most violent fantasies.

He had even shown the classic serial killer symptom of extreme cruelty to animals, having killed two of his family's pet cats, burying one alive and beheading the other with a machete. He had been devoted to his father and violently antipathetic to his mother, and when his parents divorced in 1957 he took the split very badly. He was sent to live with his mother in Montana, but his mother's treatment alienated him further. Claiming to be worried that he might abuse his younger sister, she often locked him in the basement to sleep apart from the rest of the family.

In the summer of 1963, at the age of 14, Kemper ran away to find his father, only to learn he had remarried and wanted nothing to do with his son. Instead, his father sent him to live with his own parents, Ed's grandparents, on their small mountain ranch at North Fork in California. This proved of little improvement, since he came to hate his grandmother almost as much as his mother. Finally, on August 27, 1964, while his grandmother was finishing off her latest book for children, he took down a rifle his grandfather had given him the previous Christmas. His grandmother warned him not to shoot the birds, but he turned the weapon on her instead. He shot her in the head and, as she collapsed, he shot her twice more in the back. Knowing his grandfather would soon return after shopping for groceries, he dragged her body into one of the bedrooms. Then, hearing his grandfather drawing up outside, he waited until he climbed out of the car, and shot and killed him as well. He then dragged his grandfather's body into the garage and phoned his mother to tell her what he had done. She called the police and they arrested the boy.

It seemed as if a stop had been put to Ed Kemper's murderous career. The authorities tested him and found he had an IQ of 136 as well as paranoid schizophrenia, and sent him to a hospital for the criminally insane. In spite of his appalling record and because he was able to charm people with his intelligence and friendliness, Kemper was able to find out details

Paranoid schizophrenic Ed Kemper was charged with killing female students in the area who would hitchhike to and from campus.

of the assessment procedures used to check patients for potential release back to the community. He finally managed, with his mother's help, to convince the authorities he would present no real danger if he was released once he reached adulthood, on his 21st birthday in December 1969. He was even able to ensure, after release, that the records of the murders he committed as a juvenile were destroyed.

LIVING WITH MOTHER

However, the authorities realized the problems were caused by the poor relationship he had with his mother, and it was made a condition of his parole that he kept well away from her. Unable to find a job that would provide him with support, he had no option but to live with his mother once again, and he managed to move to her new home in Santa Cruz. There she worked as an administrative assistant at the new university campus, having left her third husband, but she failed to alert the authorities about Ed's reappearance. Now 6 feet 9 inches tall and weighing more than 350 pounds, her son was a powerful and intimidating figure, yet capable of exerting great charm when he wanted to exploit this quality.

Life in his mother's house was no better than before. He was now mature, and completed a local college course as a condition of his parole.

After moving back in with his mother, Kemper became a familiar face along the Santa Cruz coastline so that when the murders began he would not be a suspect.

He applied to join the police force, but ironically was rejected as too tall. Nevertheless, he became a familiar figure at police headquarters, where officers knew him as Big Ed, and saw him as a friendly figure. He moved into an apartment with a friend, but when he ran short of money, had to move back in with his mother again. She continued to belittle him, and his anger was building to the point where he longed to find a way of releasing it.

He bought himself a Ford Galaxy and started cruising the roads in the area, where he noticed the large numbers of attractive young women hitching for lifts to and from the college. Deciding that this was the ideal prey to feed his increasing appetites, he began to prepare meticulously for his new role. He bought himself handcuffs, a blanket, a set of knives, and plastic bags, and stored them in the trunk of his car.

Kemper fitted the classic profile of an organized killer, having purchased all the tools he required in advance of the murders, including a set of knives.

He even took regular trips along popular routes, and began picking up girls who were looking for a lift. He offered them no violence, but took them quietly and politely to wherever they wanted to go, refining his manners and conversation to put them at ease and persuade them that despite his height and build, he presented no threat at all.

THE DISAPPEARING HITCHHIKERS

This killer-in-waiting situation lasted until May 7, 1972, when two hitchhikers, Anita Luchessa and Mary Ann Pesche, failed to turn up to stay with friends at Stanford University. At first, given the haphazard arrangements of students of the time, no one worried too much. Something more inviting might have turned up, or they might simply have changed their plans. There was still no evidence a serial killer might be at work. However, that evidence surfaced on August 15 when a human head was found at a remote spot in the mountains overlooking Santa Cruz. The head was later identified as that of Mary Ann Pesche, but no other trace of either missing girl was found.

On September 14, a dance student named Aiko Koo vanished while hitchhiking, and on January 7, 1973, another local student named Cindy Schall disappeared under similar circumstances. Normally, this would cause rising panic in the area, but the killings were overshadowed by the murders carried out by Herbert Mullin at the same time. In the absence of any real evidence as to how the killings were carried out, there was nothing to separate them from the other murders in profiling terms. Until, two days after Cindy's disappearance, a passer-by found human arms and legs on a cliff top, with no trace of the body from which they had been severed. Later the upper part of a

Officials questioned **Ed Kemper, aged 24,** in connection with six unsolved co-ed murders in the Santa Cruz area.

body was washed up and, when checked with X-rays of the lungs, was found to belong to Cindy Schall. Finally, a surfer found a human hand which, when checked for fingerprints, was also identified as belonging to the missing girl. This was evidence at last that another killer was at work in the area, since Mullin had not attempted to dismember any of his victims. Then, on February 5, two more female hitch-hikers, Alice Liu and Rosalind Thorpe, vanished without a trace.

On March 4, hikers found a human skull and jawbone beside a highway near Boulder Creek in San Mateo county. Checks showed they did not belong to the same victim, but a search revealed another skull not far away that did belong with the jawbone. These turned out to be the remains of the two latest missing girls, and it was revealed that Alice Liu had been shot in the head twice. The university began running a bus service to eliminate the need for its students to hitch lifts from passing drivers, and enrollment numbers began to drop as fear spread through the area.

THE LAST STRAW

Kemper was still showing the remarkable coolness of the organized serial killer. On the

way back from seizing and killing his first two victims, with their bodies jammed in the trunk of his car, he was pulled over by the police for a missing taillight. To him it was a challenge to appear normal enough to persuade the police officer not to search his car, but to be ready to kill him if he did. And on the day following his killing of 15-year-old Aiko Koo, he appeared before a panel of psychiatrists following up on his parole behavior, who found him calm and convincing enough to stand by their assessment that he presented no risk to the community.

He was even continuing to pick up hitchhikers, aided by the university parking sticker on his car obtained for him by his mother. In between the killings, he would deliver the luckier passengers to their destination without incident, since he assessed each one as a potential victim. This might have continued for months longer, because there was so little evidence to point in his direction, had matters not reached a terrible conclusion on Good Friday, 1973. The always toxic relationship with his mother had deteriorated even further, and he had finally decided she must be made to disappear from his life.

He waited for her to go to bed and fall asleep, then hit her over the head with a claw hammer to kill her. He cut off her head and placed it on a shelf, and claimed he was able to talk to her at last with all the pent-up rage from previous years, before he used the head as a dartboard, and put her vocal cords into the waste disposal. Then he calmly left the house to go for a drink with some friends in the police force, before it occurred to him that finding his dead mother would for the first time identify him as the killer. What was needed was another victim. Then he could claim it was the unknown murderer of the hitchhikers, who had often killed them in pairs, who was responsible. He returned home, rang his mother's best friend, 59-year-old Sally Hallett, and asked her to come for dinner. When she arrived, he felled her with a violent punch, then strangled her. He beheaded her and left her corpse in the house along with his mother's, before driving from the scene.

A CALL FOR ARREST

Police were still completely unaware of what had been happening with someone they knew so well. Only on April 26, when they received a phone call from Pueblo in Colorado from someone claiming to be Big Ed Kemper and insisting he had killed two people and left their corpses in the family home, were they brought face to face with the deception he had practiced so coolly. Even then, they thought it was some

kind of practical joke at Kemper's expense, and asked him to call back later. Desperate to bring an end to what was becoming a nightmare, Kemper asked them to check with Sergeant Aluffi, an officer who had come to his mother's house to confiscate a handgun some time before, and ask him to check out the house. When he did, he found the headless bodies in closets, and they realized they had found the Co-ed Killer— or more accurately, he had found them.

Local police were called in to arrest him. He made no resistance and was put on trial for eight charges of first-degree murder on May 7, 1973—the anniversary of his first hitchhiker murder. But by acting out his fantasies of rape, necrophilia, and dismemberment in private settings, he had given profilers nothing to work on, and had eluded those who were searching for him. He was found guilty in November 1973, only weeks before the law changed, and missed the death penalty by the narrowest of margins.

Kemper en route to his cell at the Pueblo City jail after being questioned by officials about the unsolved murder of 6 co-eds. Police said Kemper admitted to killing his mother and a friend during a phone call to Santa Cruz police.

AT THE CRIME SCENE

The level of control shown by Ed Kemper (see page 68) would be totally alien to most serial killers. Within their psychology, the leaving of the bodies of their victims in plain view remains a powerful part of the pleasure they take in controlling and then killing those they choose to attack. Often they try to see this blatant display of their handiwork as a challenge to the investigators whom they consider their adversaries, and a statement that, they believe, reinforces their power and invincibility. Even the knowledge that the crime scene will be studied and searched for the tiniest scraps of evidence represents a challenge to their continuing freedom, so the ways in which they try to conceal or remove pieces of evidence can provide useful indicators of the criminal's thinking and experience, as well as underlining the type of criminal that police are dealing with in a particular case.

In many cases, a crime scene may be just that, the place where the crime took place, or where the victim's body was placed or a rape or robbery was carried out. In that sense, it can simply present evidence that tells a straightforward enough story and building up a profile from that evidence is equally straightforward. In other cases, however, the killer is confident enough and experienced enough to try to muddy the evidential waters. By planting details to suggest a different course of events, a different type of criminal or a different motive, they seek to mislead investigators and put them off their trail.

Confident killers will often tamper with or disguise evidence as a way of sending investigators down the wrong track.

THE PROFILER'S VIEW OF THE SCENE

In nearly every case, the profilers will see a crime scene after police investigators and forensic experts have searched it for direct physical evidence to explain what happened on the spot and to guide the hunt for the perpetrator. However, profilers have different priorities, and often look for different kinds of information. The detectives and forensic scientists will be looking at the crime scene as an end in itself. The profiler, especially when dealing with an actual or potential serial killer, will be looking at a wider context, to compare with other crime scenes thought to be the work of the same unknown suspect, or to indicate the kind of person the perpetrator appears to be, rather than trying to reveal his or her individual identity.

If, for example, a killer has been careful to remove or destroy all items of forensic significance that might link them to the crime itself, then the crime scene will produce little factual evidence. A profiler, however, will be looking for different signs. Even a careful and rigorous removal of every physical trace of the killer's presence on the spot and of their involvement with the victim is itself an important item of evidence. It points to the involvement of an organized rather than a chaotic killer, with important implications for other aspects of the criminal's identity.

Forensic experts and profilers will look for markedly different types of evidence at a crime scene.

HAS THE SCENE BEEN STAGED?

In an initial assessment of a crime scene by a profiler, an important question is whether or not there is a clear element of staging involved. As each item of apparent evidence emerges, from the murder weapon to the reason for choosing the victim or the crime scene, profilers always have to be on their guard. Is this evidence genuine, or part of an elaborate charade by the killer to mislead their reading of the scene, and persuade them to search in entirely the wrong direction?

If it appears from the scene that an attempt at staging has been made, the next stage is to determine how convincing that attempt was. Most people may feel that if ever they found themselves having to conceal the nature of a crime—to suggest suicide rather than murder, to make a deliberate planned killing appear a matter of a chance attack, and so on—they could do it. But in a murder scene staged by a layperson with no experience of violent crime, the discrepancies between the staging and the real thing would be entirely obvious to a professional. Mistakes and inconsistencies would stand out, even on a brief inspection, and reveal the inexperience and incompetence of the criminal all too clearly.

However, when the opposite occurs, and the staging is not immediately obvious, an entirely different set of implications is created. Sometimes a profiler may assess a scene as genuinely unstaged, until some small detail reveals what actually happened. This shows the criminal involved was not only cool and confident, but had personal criminal experience to know what kind of details and evidence an investigating team would be looking for, so as to misdirect them. When a really determined effort is made to stage a scene, the illusion can sometimes be made so convincing that guilt becomes difficult to establish even after the perpetrator is caught and brought to trial, and justice itself becomes elusive.

CASE

WHEN: 1954

WHERE: Ohio, USA

VICTIMS: Marilyn Sheppard

CULPRIT: Dr. Sam Sheppard

CASE STUDY 11: DR. SAM SHEPPARD

One of the most celebrated and controversial cases involving a staged crime scene dates back to the very beginnings of profiling. The original murder conviction was reversed on appeal and the suspect was released from prison. Only when the original defendant died, 15 years after the crime, and his estate tried to mount an action for wrongful arrest and imprisonment against the authorities who had brought the case, was a profiler brought in to examine the evidence, revealing a classic case of a staged murder scene.

UNDER SUSPICION

The victim in the case was Marilyn Sheppard, wife of osteopathic surgeon Dr. Sam Sheppard. She was reported dead by her husband in the early hours of July 4, 1954, at the lakeside home they shared in Bay Village, a suburb of Cleveland, Ohio. When police arrived at the scene, they found the severely shocked doctor being cared for by his next-door neighbor, while upstairs his wife's body showed clear signs she had been beaten to death.

In cases like this the surviving partner is first to come under suspicion, unless their story holds up under questioning. In Sheppard's case, his story was vivid and apparently consistent. He claimed that the evening before, his wife had gone to bed, leaving him watching a late-night program on television. He fell asleep and woke up some time later, and, to avoid disturbing her, he had gone to sleep on a couch in the living room. Later still, though unaware of the exact time, he had been woken by screams from upstairs. On rushing to the bedroom, he was surprised, attacked, and knocked unconscious by an unknown "white" figure. When he woke up again, he went over to his wife and tried to feel for a pulse, without success. He then went to

Dr. Sam Sheppard, pictured here with his wife Marilyn, whom he was charged with murdering, had the charge appealed and then reinstated after his death.

Sheppard claimed to have followed the supposed attacker down to the beach at the end of his property before he was promptly knocked unconscious again.

check on their son, asleep in another bedroom, but before he could do so, he heard noises from downstairs that indicated the intruder was still there. He rushed downstairs and saw a large, heavily built man with a thick head of hair who ran out of the house. Sheppard followed him onto the edge of the property, which ended in a beach facing Lake Erie. There the man attacked him and once again left him unconscious. When Sheppard woke up again, for the fourth time since his wife had gone to bed the previous evening, he went back into the house to find his wife was dead. He called his neighbors, who called the police, just after 6 a.m. Because Sheppard's description of his attacker was vague and lacking in detail, he was unable to deflect police suspicions that he had actually killed his wife, though at that stage no one could suggest a motive. He was charged with her murder, found guilty, and sentenced to life imprisonment.

UNEXPLAINED INCONSISTENCIES

So far the case seemed straightforward, for the police at least. But increasing pressure for a retrial focused on some apparent inconsistencies in the existing evidence. For example, spots of blood found on Sheppard's watch had been an important part of the prosecution case against him, which he had explained by his checking her pulse when he first found her lying on the bed. Another disputed point was a part of the otherwise blood-soaked bed, where the body lay, that was actually free of blood. The defense team insisted this could only be because that was where the killer had stood while delivering the fatal blows, and that consequently he must have been soaked in the victim's blood that would otherwise have fallen on that part of the bed. But Dr. Sheppard showed only one bloodstain on his clothes, a diluted patch on

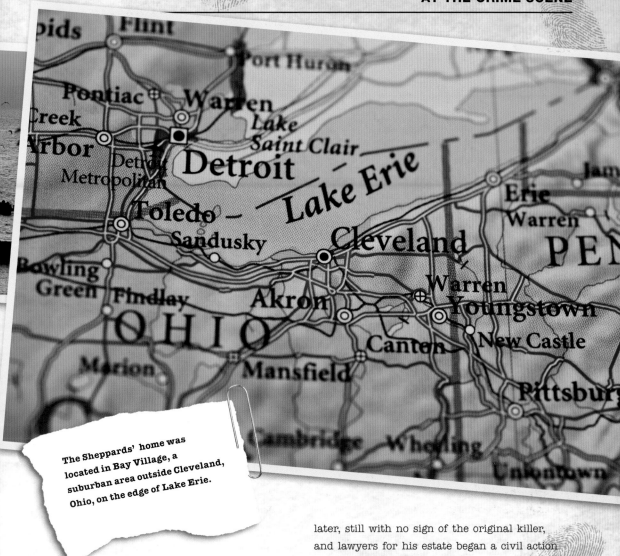

The Sheppards' home was located in Bay Village, a suburban area outside Cleveland, Ohio, on the edge of Lake Erie.

one knee of his trousers, which he said he must have been picked up when he knelt down to take his wife's pulse.

WHAT KIND OF CRIME?

The case created a media frenzy, with all kinds of theories in the press and on radio and television, and Sheppard's lawyers insisted this publicity had ensured he could not have had a fair trial. Eventually their request for a retrial was granted in November 1966. This time Sam Sheppard was acquitted of killing his wife, and released from prison after serving 11 years of his sentence. He died four years

later, still with no sign of the original killer, and lawyers for his estate began a civil action against the Ohio authorities for wrongful arrest and imprisonment. The defense then called in a criminal profiler, the FBI's Gregg McCrary, to reassess what had been found at the scene, and what this might reveal about Sheppard's innocence or guilt.

McCrary knew that one classic mistake made by inexperienced criminals was to suggest that more than one type of crime was involved, while an experienced attacker—or the truth—would suggest only one. In this crime scene, the victim's body was lying on the bed with legs parted and with some clothes removed. The drawers of the bedside desk and dressing table had all been pulled out, and Dr. Sheppard's medicine bag was found open with its contents scattered about and some items missing. These "clues" hinted at a sex attack, a conventional burglary that had escalated to extreme violence, and a case of drugs theft, without any clear link to explain them being grouped together.

FURTHER DOUBTS

Other signs failed to add up to a genuine crime scene. The sex-attack scenario failed to work, since there were no post-mortem signs of internal damage resulting from a violent rape. The robbery was unconvincing, because the articles from the pulled-out drawers were placed neatly on the floor, instead of scattered around the room as the robber searched frantically for anything of value. Furthermore, nothing of any real value seemed to be missing, which added to doubts about a robbery. Finally, the drug theft seemed false. The scene had been staged to suggest the robber opened the doctor's bag, and rummaged through it to take one or two items. A genuine drugs thief, wanting to leave the scene as quickly as possible, would take the whole bag, to go through it once in hiding.

McCrary also found telling discrepancies in the injuries suffered by Sheppard in his fight with the attacker. Marilyn Sheppard received a total of 35 injuries, including 20 that were potentially fatal. Yet in terms of the risk to the criminal carrying out the attack, she presented a relatively trivial threat. Her husband was a very different matter, and a real attacker would have subjected him to a far deadlier attack to avoid being killed or captured, probably using the murder weapon that had killed Mrs. Sheppard. Yet Sheppard said the attacker had hit him with his fist only. His only injuries were a chipped tooth, a bruised face and a neck strain that forced him to wear a collar until it recovered. The difference between these levels of violence from the attacker made no sense.

What about the blood evidence that played a vital part in securing Sheppard's acquittal and release from prison? McCrary insisted that in simply taking his wife's pulse, Sheppard

Criminal profilers questioned the supposed criminal's choice of rummaging through Dr. Sheppard's bag rather than taking the whole thing.

could not have avoided becoming much more bloodstained than he was. The upper half of his wife's body was drenched in her blood following the frenzied attack. Even the evidence about the watch was double-edged. McCrary saw that the pattern of blood droplets on its face suggested that it was spattered because Sheppard was wearing it while delivering the fatal blows.

Even the absence of bloodstains on Sheppard's clothing threw doubt on his story. Part of his case depended on the attacker being covered in Marilyn's blood while he battered her to death. Then Sheppard fought him twice, which would have transferred massive bloodstains to his own clothing. Even if the fights themselves had not happened, there was no way the attacker could have touched the medical bag, the drawers in the bedroom, and the doors through which he escaped, without leaving bloody marks on them, yet none were found by the police.

A STAGED CRIME

One final touch pointed to a staged murder. Nearly always the killer fails to contact police directly, first telling a friend, neighbor, or relative who then calls the police for them. Perhaps they feel better able to convince a layperson of their innocence than a police professional, but this is a highly significant symptom that all is not quite as it has been made to seem. Added to this, the question of motive had been suggested by the discovery of letters from Marilyn threatening a

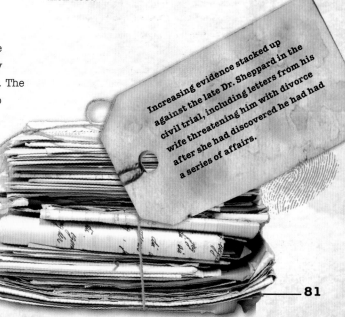

Sheppard's attorney F. Lee Bailey is pictured leaving the Cuyahoga County Criminal Court with his wife, during the original 1954 trial.

divorce following Sam's series of affairs. Though Sheppard himself was dead, and this was now a civil rather than a criminal case, the jury was unanimous in deciding the arrest and conviction were genuine and so no damages needed to be paid. Nevertheless, the case continues to attract interest, and zealots insist Sheppard was innocent in spite of all the evidence.

Clues to Staging

Several crucial factors in the Sheppard case show up in other attempts to stage a family killing as the work of an unknown intruder. The most difficult challenge for anyone trying to suggest a violent attack on themselves, to match that inflicted on the victim, is to deliver enough violence to themselves to convince investigators. Striking self-inflicted blows similar to those that actually kill someone else is almost impossible. Quite apart from the risk, suffering pain at first hand always seems worse than it really is. And since a

survivor presents a much greater risk to a criminal than a victim, they would have to experience an even more violent attack to fool a professional. In much the same way, attempts to suggest a robbery often fail because items of value to the family are unaccountably left by the robber as they escape with the rest of their loot.

Increasing evidence stacked up against the late Dr. Sheppard in the civil trial, including letters from his wife threatening him with divorce after she had discovered he had had a series of affairs.

CASE

WHEN: 1986

WHERE: Pennsylvania, USA

VICTIMS: Betty Jayne Wolsieffer

CULPRIT: Dr. Edward Glen Wolsieffer

The alleged murder of Betty Jayne Wolsieffer by an unknown intruder occurred in Wilkes-Barre in northeastern Pennsylvania.

Mansfield
6

Pennsylvan

6
81
Carbondale
15
6
Scranton
476
84
Wilkes-
Barre
11
220 Williamsport 180
80
380
81
Bellefonte
80
80 Stroudsburg
26
Lewisburg
Hazleton
476
322
State
College
61
209
522
33
11
248
22
81
309
Allentown
Easton
476 22 Bethlehem
Mt. Union
61
611
78
78
22
222
81
422
Reading
100 663
283
322
322
Lebanon
222
309
202
76
76 222 476
422 Pottstown
476
15
283
100
73
Philadelpf
81
41
Harrisburg
Chambersburg
15
83
Lancaster 322
276
30
30
York
222 30
95
202
76
Gettysburg
41
1

CASE STUDY 12: WOLSIEFFERS OF WILKES-BARRE

In the summer of 1986 another staged case, in Wilkes-Barre, Pennsylvania, gave an FBI profiler a full set of telltale clues. Dr. Edward Glen Wolsieffer was a 33-year-old dentist who lived with his wife Betty Jayne and their 5-year-old daughter Danielle, across the street from the house of his brother Neil. Early on the morning of August 30, police were called by Neil Wolsieffer to report that his brother had called him after suffering a violent attack in his home. An intruder had hit him over the head and tried to strangle him, while the victim's wife and daughter were still asleep upstairs.

FAMILIAR STAGING POINTERS

The parallels with the Sheppard case were significant to anyone searching for signs of staging. To begin with, the alarm was raised by a neighbor—in this case a family member as well—rather than the person most closely involved, and once again the call was made early on a Sunday morning.

In this case though, Glen expressed fears of suffering a fainting attack, and the possibility that the intruder might still be in the house persuaded Neil not to check upstairs. When the police arrived, they found Danielle asleep and undisturbed in her room. Her mother, however, was dead on the floor of the main bedroom. There were bloodstains on the sheets and she had been strangled. Moreover, her nightdress was pulled up over her waist, though with no evidence of sexual assault. In addition, her face had been wiped clean of blood.

Glen Wolsieffer explained he had been in bed with his wife when he woke at first light and heard an intruder in the house. He reached for a handgun from a bedside table and got up without waking his wife. As he tiptoed onto the upstairs landing, he spotted a tall and heavily built man—another unconscious but significant parallel with Sheppard's story—standing at the top of the stairs with his back to him. Seemingly unaware of his presence, the intruder descended to the ground floor of the house, with Glen Wolsieffer following him. With the downstairs floor in semidarkness, he lost sight of the other man, so he started to search room by room. He was suddenly attacked from behind, with a rope passed around his neck, forcing him to drop his gun and fight to prevent strangulation.

In a classic case of crime-scene staging, Glen Wolsieffer claimed that his wife was strangled by an unknown intruder in their family home.

Although a ladder was placed outside the house, implying that the intruder had gained entry through an upstairs window, criminal profilers were able to deduce that the scene was staged as the ladder would not have been able to support the weight of the alleged tall and heavily built attacker.

Nonetheless, he managed to wriggle free and kick his attacker in the crotch, but was knocked unconscious by a heavy blow to the head. He awoke to find the intruder gone, and called his brother for help.

Classic Signs That All is Not What It Seems

Outside, police found a ladder that suggested the intruder broke into the house through an upstairs window. But the ladder itself was far too flimsy to support anyone of moderately heavy build, and the bottom of the ladder showed no signs of having been pressed into the soft ground next to the house by anyone climbing up it. The ground was covered with dew and grass cuttings, but there was no sign of grass or moisture on the windowsill or within the house.

Furthermore, if Glen Wolsieffer's story was true, the intruder had arrived on the upstairs floor of the house and then gone downstairs, before realizing that the occupant was searching for him, armed with a handgun. He had then attacked Wolsieffer and knocked him unconscious, and gone back upstairs to attack and kill Mrs. Wolsieffer, without worrying that his first victim might have recovered consciousness and raised the alarm. Then he had left the house without stealing anything, though items of jewelry were in plain view in the bedroom.

To FBI profiler John Douglas there were several classic signs of crime-scene staging. The combination of a partial sex attack and a burglary escalating to murder was, as with the Sheppard case, another instance of a multiple crime staging, when neither really carried any credibility. The burglar stopped to kill a woman presenting no direct threat while leaving alive her husband who did offer such a threat. He took no valuables, never seriously tried to carry through the sex attack, and simply left the area.

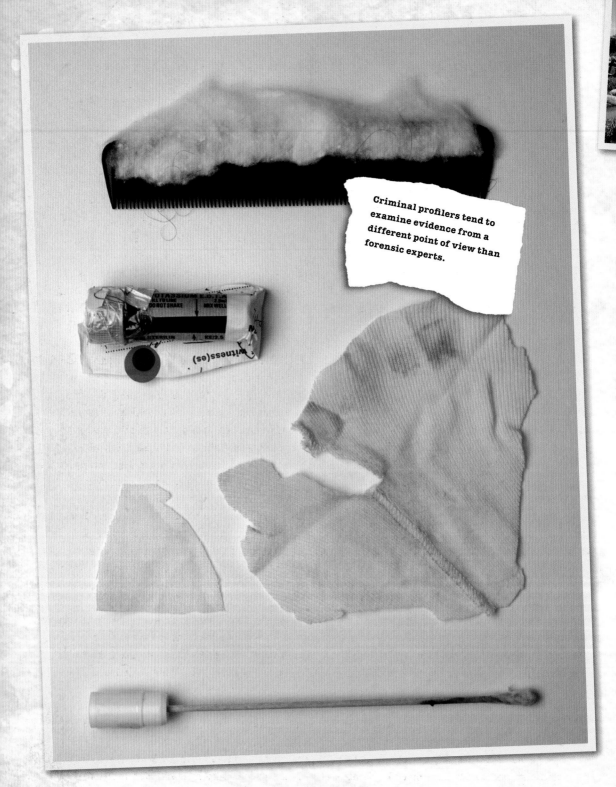

Criminal profilers tend to examine evidence from a different point of view than forensic experts.

After three years of the profilers compiling evidence, Wolsieffer was eventually tried and charged in Richmond, Virginia.

of a series of affairs, but amassing the evidence needed to convict him would take another three years. By then, Wolsieffer had moved to Virginia, and it was there he was finally brought to justice and found guilty of his wife's murder.

UNCOVERING DISCREPANCIES

Both the Sheppard and the Wolsieffer cases were reasonably straightforward from a profiler's point of view, since if those involved had known more about how real criminals operate, they could have changed the scene they were trying to stage to make it more convincing. A story that somehow explained how they failed to drive off the attacker without actually suffering grievous injuries on their own account might close one loophole. In the Sheppard case, a story of a drugs robbery gone wrong might have worked had the "intruder" fled the scene with the doctor's bag intact, while the doctor himself remained asleep. On the other hand, he would have to find a way of killing his wife consistent with the noise not waking him up. In truth, each change to the story to eliminate inconsistencies usually creates another discrepancy, and eventually the scenario fails when exposed to the experience of experts.

Another type of serious crime can often involve staging. Once again, it relates to a killing within a family, though in this case the murder of a wife by her husband is replaced by the murder of one or more children by their mother. Where an unknown attacker becomes the scapegoat in the first type of crime, with the murder of children, the usual objective of staging is to suggest a kidnap attempt which has resulted in their killing rather than their return once a ransom is paid. However, what may seem an easy crime to stage to the person involved invariably reveals as many faults as any husband–wife murder.

Furthermore, Douglas' experience of how real burglars operate told him they were highly unlikely to break into a house early on a weekend morning with two cars parked in the drive and when people in nearby houses were likely to be up and about, and able to spot intruders. They were equally unlikely to take a ladder and use it to reach the upper floor and then go downstairs without checking out the upstairs rooms first. So far as the attack was concerned, the most significant clue was that Mrs. Wolsieffer had been strangled face to face, an indicator of a highly personal crime that again failed to fit that of a burglar simply trying to remove a potential threat.

Once again, there were clear discrepancies between the injuries suffered by the victims. Mrs. Wolsieffer had been strangled, but her husband merely suffered some relatively trivial marks to the back of the neck, some scratches on the left side of his chest and a blow to the back of the head, which did at least back up his story. Perhaps feeling the signs did not add up, he began referring to a second intruder, and this added to Douglas' conviction that he was indeed the killer, who had staged the evidence at the crime scene to divert suspicion.

DELAYED JUSTICE

However, being certain of this was merely the first step. Information had to be collected and a case constructed. The apparent absence of a motive was soon explained by evidence that his wife was planning to divorce Wolsieffer because

CASE

WHERE: Secluded woodland

VICTIM: The child

CULPRIT: The mother

If the body of a victim of a fake kidnap has been carefully hidden and protected, this can suggest the involvement of a parent rather than a criminal.

CASE STUDY 13: SPOTTING A FAKED KIDNAP

Profilers look for the discrepancies between a staged version of events and the behavior of genuine abductors and kidnappers (see page 209). Sometimes an apparent case of child abduction simply wouldn't convince investigators. Former FBI agent Gregg McCrary quoted one example. Imagine a single mother claiming her two-year-old daughter had been snatched by abductors as they had been about to leave on a shopping trip. As they walk to their car, the mother is seized by sudden stomach cramps, and has to leave her daughter as she returns to the bathroom in their apartment. Though she has told her child to stay by their car until she returns, when the mother emerges again the only sign of her daughter is one of her knitted mittens lying in the parking lot. Later, she reports the abduction to the police. Only when searches have been carried out, followed by appeals in local papers, does a package arrive from the kidnappers, containing the matching child's mitten, but nothing else.

This kind of story might seem convincing enough to someone trying to cover up the accidental or deliberate loss of a child, but to investigators it would make no sense at all. Why did the mother not take the child back to the apartment with her, to guarantee her safety, rather than leave her in a public place? When the mother reported the disappearance to the police, why did she immediately report her child as abducted, when most parents cling to hope that the child has simply wandered away and will soon be found?

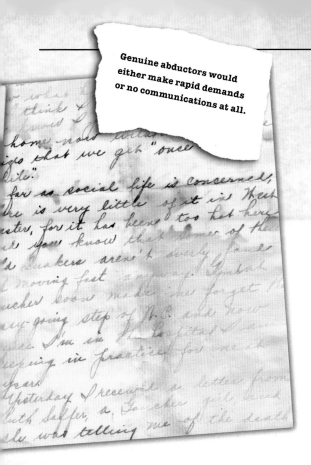

Genuine abductors would either make rapid demands or no communications at all.

involved to confess the truth. Usually the reasons involve the death of the child, either accidentally or deliberately, with the staged kidnapping being intended to cover up the resulting responsibility for the loss of life and the often overwhelming burden of guilt.

MOTHER'S TOUCH

Eventually the mother confirmed the profilers' estimate of what had happened, and admitted to having killed her own child and trying to cover up the crime with a mock kidnapping. She took the police to the site where the body had been left. Here there was no evidence of staging at all, with the little girl buried deep in secluded woodland, wrapped in thick warm garments and a blanket, and covered with a bag to deter predators. Had the body been found for any other reason, the care taken over the disposal of the child's remains would have tended to focus attention on the mother, for the combination of love and guilt shown so clearly, rather than the indifference to be expected from real kidnappers.

THE MISSING DEMAND

The apparent behavior of the so-called kidnappers would cast even more doubt on the story. Professional child abductors take an appalling risk, and they only do so because they want the child for their own purposes, perhaps to make up for a missing child of their own, or to abuse the seized child. In these cases, they would send no message at all. If they simply want money, they would normally issue demands straight away, to minimize the risk of being discovered, and this would inevitably form part of the first communication with the return of the mitten. The absence of a demand or other message would prove to profilers the attempt was staged.

Eventually in cases of this kind, the clear signs of staging and the resulting contradictions enable the investigators to persuade those

A deliberate "clue" like the example of kidnappers returning the missing mitten of an abducted child provides all-too-clear evidence of staging.

SOUTH CAROLINA
DEPT. OF CORRECTIONS

WHEN: 1994

WHERE: Monarch Mills

VICTIMS: Michael and Alexander Smith

CULPRIT: Susan Smith

CASE STUDY 14: THE PHANTOM CARJACKER

A higher-profile case, and a more elaborate attempt at staging a mock abduction, was carried out in October 1994 by the mother of two young sons, 23-year-old Susan Smith from South Carolina, whose husband was divorcing her. She was driving in the family's 1990 Mazda Protégé saloon through Monarch Mills near the town of Union on the evening of October 25, with her sons Michael and Alexander in the back seat of the car. She stopped at a red light at a crossroads, and while waiting for the light to change, the passenger door was opened and an armed black man jumped into the car. He pointed his gun at her and forced her to drive through Union and out along the road to the northeast for some four miles, past the signpost for the track leading to the John D. Long Lake. There he pushed her out of the car and drove off with her boys still in the back.

Toys and pictures of Michael and Alexander Smith are left at John D. Long Lake shore shrine, site of the drowning murder of the two boys by their mother Susan Smith.

Susan Smith, pictured here with her husband, shows distress over the supposed abduction of her two sons.

IMMEDIATE POINTERS TO STAGING

The mother ran to a nearby house and called her family and then the local police. Immediately the investigators noticed large holes in her story. First of all, it became clear she had seen no other traffic around the intersection at the time the alleged intruder had jumped into her car. But the police knew something she presumably did not: the default setting for the traffic lights at the intersection was to show a green clear signal for the road along which she was traveling. It would only turn to red when triggered by another vehicle emerging from either of the side roads, which had not been the case. Her evidence therefore begged the question: why had she stopped and given her attacker the opportunity to hijack her car? The experienced police officers also noticed something unconvincing about her grief, in that she made weeping noises but shed no real tears, and at one point actually referred to her sons

in the past tense, as if she knew they were already dead.

Another, more subtle, pointer to the staging of the scene was reported by the police artist commissioned to draw a likeness of the attacker. Though the mother had given only the vaguest of descriptions relating to his actual appearance, she had been very exacting in all matters relating to small details, a common reaction in people trying to cover up for a made-up invention and make it seem more genuine.

BACKGROUND OF THE KILLER

At this point the local police called in FBI profilers to study the evidence. If the alleged abductor did not exist and the boys had in fact been murdered by their mother, what kind of person would she have to be to commit such a crime? In their opinion she would be a troubled

PROFILING: THE PSYCHOLOGY OF CATCHING KILLERS

Police knew something that Smith did not: the lights where she claimed her car had been taken from her when she stopped at a red light would change to red only if a vehicle was coming out of a side road.

young woman, probably with limited education, who had grown up in an abusive and unhappy family with real money worries, and who consequently suffered from depression, with perhaps a history of attempted suicides. In terms of the crime itself, rejection by a lover who might otherwise have presented an escape route from her limited circumstances might have spurred her into taking the lives of her own young sons. When checked against the background for Susan Smith, it was revealed that her father, to whom she had been devoted, had taken his own life after his marriage to Susan's mother had ended in divorce. When the same fate overtook her father-in-law for the same reasons, she had been the one who found him and had to call the emergency services. It also emerged she had been carrying on a relationship with a well-heeled man living in the area, who police thought might have been willing to take her on after her divorce, but only without the added complication of the children.

Two factors were still missing. Although the profile matched Susan Smith with uncanny accuracy, the boys had still not been found and no confession was yet forthcoming. The lake close to where the alleged abductor had driven off with the boys seemed a likely site for their

disappearance, but police divers had searched the lake bottom without finding any trace of the car or the missing boys. With no other avenues remaining, they continued to question the mother about the clear discrepancies in her account, but only after nine days did she finally admit she had driven the car down to the edge of the lake, originally intending to drown herself and her boys.

Instead, she stopped the car at the lake edge, then released the handbrake, watching it roll slowly down into the water, with the boys still inside. Because it floated with doors and windows closed, it took a long time to sink below

A memorial in honor of the two boys marks the place where they were pushed to their deaths by drowning in the quiet waters of the lake.

the surface, so it traveled farther than police experts predicted. When divers resumed their search farther out from the shore, they found the missing car lying upside down on the bottom, with the two boys still strapped in their seats and dead from drowning. On July 27, 1995, Susan Smith was sentenced to 30 years to life for subjecting her two young sons to the most cruel and terrible death, slowly suffocating as the water level rose in the car in which she had left them trapped.

WHEN: 1991

WHERE: Arizona, USA

VICTIMS: Multiple

CULPRITS: Jonathan Doody, Alessandro Garcia, Michelle Hoover

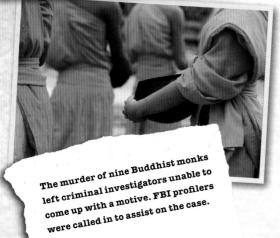

The murder of nine Buddhist monks left criminal investigators unable to come up with a motive. FBI profilers were called in to assist on the case.

CASE STUDY 15: IN THE DEPTHS OF THE TEMPLE

Sometimes staging attempts fail to deal with the aftermath of a sudden violent crime, when those responsible finally realize how vulnerable their failure to plan for what they did now leaves them. Unfortunately, there are still cases where investigators find the staged version of the crime convincing enough to let it govern their search for suspects, especially when the crime itself is well out of the ordinary.

THE CRIME SCENE AS PRESENTED

One of the most inexplicable crime scenes ever was found on the morning of August 10, 1991, in the otherwise tranquil surroundings of a Thai Buddhist temple, where nine of arguably the most peaceable people in the world had been brutally murdered. Even more unusual, the temple was not in Thailand itself, but close to a US Air Force base near Phoenix, Arizona.

So unusual was the crime at that time, and in that place, that investigators were baffled as to the identity and motive of those responsible. When FBI agents Gregg McCrary and Tom Salp arrived at the crime scene, their first reaction on seeing the saffron-robed bodies of the victims was to note that a mixture of shotgun cartridges and .22 caliber casings were scattered among them, indicating two weapons and almost

Profilers first took note of the fact that two different weapons were used at the crime scene: this suggested there were at least two killers.

Police removing bodies of two of the nine victims killed in the mass murder in Wat Promkunaram, the Thai Buddhist Temple outside Phoenix, Arizona; the victims were executed and laid out in a circle.

certainly two killers. All the victims had apparently been compelled to kneel down in a circle and put their hands behind their heads. Each one had then been shot several times in turn through the back of the head, and it seemed that all but one had accepted their inevitable death calmly and without offering resistance. Only one seemed to have tried to defend himself, suffering wounds to the arms he raised in a doomed attempt to deflect the shotgun blasts that killed him.

There was also an ashtray containing four cigarette butts in the middle of the floor of the murder room. These were of two different brands, confirming the theory that there were two killers, and suggesting they spent some time at the scene. The shotgun evidence didn't add up to the idea that this was a professional crime. The ammunition was not the 12-gauge a gunman would have used, but was a smaller 20-gauge shot for bringing down birds, and much less powerful. Consequently, it seemed to McCrary that this was the kind of opportunistic weapon a young attacker might steal from his father.

EVIDENCE

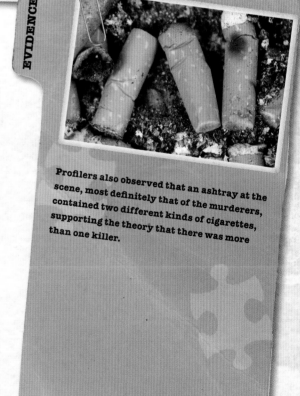

Profilers also observed that an ashtray at the scene, most definitely that of the murderers, contained two different kinds of cigarettes, supporting the theory that there was more than one killer.

The temple, located just outside Phoenix, Arizona, was an odd place for racially motivated crimes, targeted at Eastern religions, to take place.

Five men had already been arrested in Tucson, pictured here, for the murders when two teenagers were discovered with weapons matching the descriptions of those used at the scene.

SIGNS OF STAGING

On the other hand, it looked as if the criminals were trying to suggest a professional killing linked to the drugs trade. However, the way in which the staging had been carried out, by carving the word "Bloods" into one wall of the entrance lobby and setting off several fire extinguishers, was hopelessly naive. It was clear those involved had no idea of what a real drugs murder would look like. In addition, they seemed to have stolen cameras that could later be identified, a mistake professionals would never make. In addition, local inquiries showed the victims had no real enemies, and the profilers were convinced the offenders were locals.

The police began checking locally held weapons to try to trace those used to kill the monks. In fact, they had already seen and seized one of the murder weapons without realizing its significance. Police pulled up two cars driven by local teenagers on August 20 for what was recorded as "suspicious behavior." On the passenger seat of the leading car, driven by 17-year-old

Rolando Caratachea, was a .22 rifle. Initially the police took no further action until the resemblance between the gun and one of the murder weapons rang alarm bells, and the gun was added to the large number of weapons waiting for ballistic testing.

In the meantime, police had already arrested five men from Tucson for the murders, implicated by the first man who had called police to report the crime. Multiple interrogators kept them awake for nights on end, until they admitted they had gone to the temple in two cars, and carried out the murders. Police arrested all five, and revealed that two had existing criminal records. But McCrary was worried that these men didn't seem to fit. They were not local, nor were they as naive as the real killers seemed to be.

DECISIVE BALLISTICS EVIDENCE

At last, the case against the detainees began to unravel, and the ballistics lab tested the rifle seized from the teenagers, matching it with the cartridges found at the murder scene. The shotgun was found at the apartment of Jonathan Doody, driver of the other car stopped by police soon after the killings. Police arrested him and his flatmate, Alessandro Garcia, who, when questioned, admitted being at the temple,

but only as part of a larger gang. They then tried to implicate the men from Tucson, and when this failed, laid the blame on one another. It emerged they had gone to the temple to rob the monks, and Doody had decided before leaving that it would be fatal to leave any witnesses alive.

The final twist in the tale arose when 14-year-old Michelle Hoover, Garcia's girlfriend, revealed that he had pressured her to join him in killing 50-year-old Alice Cameron at a local campsite. Here, too, police had a suspect of their own, 47-year-old George Peterson, a man with mental problems who had confessed to the killing after prolonged interrogation, and who was saved from a possible death sentence by the girl's admission. Finally, the two young killers were each sentenced to more than 200 years in prison, and Michelle was given 15 years for second-degree murder.

Ballistic analysis was used to test the weapons of Rolando Caratachea and Jonathan Doody. The cartridges at the crime scene matched the guns.

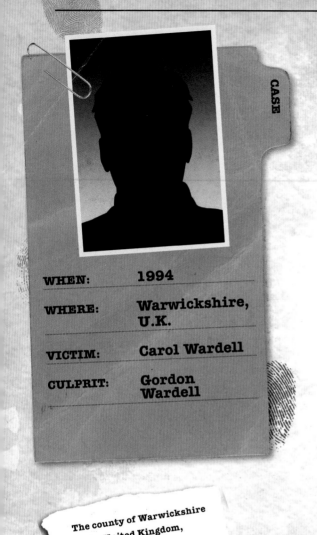

CASE

WHEN: 1994

WHERE: Warwickshire, U.K.

VICTIM: Carol Wardell

CULPRIT: Gordon Wardell

The county of Warwickshire in the United Kingdom, where the body of Carol Wardell was discovered.

CASE STUDY 16: ABDUCTOR MURDERER?

Time and again, profilers can use their experience of how real-life criminals think and behave to expose the inconsistencies of amateurs who feel clever enough to conceal the truth about their own responsibility for a crime. Even in cases where the perpetrator devises a twist in the story to reinforce their claim to be nothing more than an innocent bystander, that same ingenuity inevitably becomes a trap. Since a real criminal would have no need to behave in that way, their involvement stands exposed by the clearest of signposts to point investigators in their direction.

Even those criminals who feel they have their lives securely under their control, with ample time to plan how they mean to mislead those who will investigate their crimes, find staging amazingly difficult. Ironically, the absence of a criminal past can make them more, not less, vulnerable to exposure. It is this very lack of first-hand knowledge of a real crime scene that can reveal their efforts for what they really are—futile attempts to mislead investigators.

At 8:40 a.m. on Monday September 12, 1994, the body of Carol Wardell, 39-year-old manager of a building society branch in Nuneaton, Warwickshire, in the United Kingdom, was found by a passing motorist in a roadside rest area to the north of the town. Her upper garments had been pulled up to expose her stomach and breasts, and she had been suffocated. When police realized who she was they contacted her husband, who was found bound, gagged, and anesthetized on the floor of their home in Meriden some 10 miles away. He claimed that the previous afternoon he had returned home from the pub to find a stranger wearing a clown's mask, armed with a knife, and holding his wife hostage. He had then been hit over the head, bound

and gagged, and rendered unconscious by a chloroform pad held over his face. Early the following morning, Wardell claimed he had regained consciousness to find that the man and his accomplices had taken his wife away in a car to the building society where she worked. It was only with the discovery of his wife's body that same morning that he realized what had happened to her.

UNLIKELY STORY

When police checked at the building society branch, they found £15,000 had been taken out of the safe, and one of Mrs. Wardell's sandals had been left on the floor. Yet the story did not ring true. Once again, there was a marked discrepancy between the actual injuries suffered by Wardell, and the fact that his wife had been killed after the successful completion of the crime. Where other gangs had abducted family members to force banking officials to disable their own security to pay what was effectively a ransom to release the hostage, the chances were overwhelmingly in favor of the hostage being freed afterward. The clown mask was a warning sign, too, for it meant that Wardell could not be asked to give a description of his assailant. Finally, they found that this respectable husband had a previous conviction, at the age of 17, for sexually assaulting and stabbing the wife of his school's science teacher.

Suspicion switched to the outwardly grieving Wardell, and eventually he was charged with his wife's murder as well as the robbery. On December 20, 1995, he was found guilty and sentenced to life imprisonment. All his elaborate staging, and the additional detail of posing his wife's body to look as if she had suffered a sex attack, not to mention his own distress after the killing, failed to convince professional investigators that he was telling the truth.

NOT JUST HOW, BUT WHY

All of these case studies have involved an inexperienced criminal trying to stage the crime scene to deflect suspicion elsewhere. However, there is another entirely different type of staging for a totally different motive, which involves experienced and successful criminals. Killers who murder their victims for sexual or psychological gratification may carefully stage the crime scene as part of the ritual that confirms they are fully in control of both their victim and the overall situation. Here the objective is not so much to conceal who committed the crime as to underline it, as part of what profilers call the killer's signature. From the way they leave their victims, the positions they maneuver the body to, and the sites they choose, profilers can identify an otherwise apparently random killing as part of a continuing series. In doing so, they often reveal still more about the psychology of the killer and, in time, their weak points and limitations.

How does this differ from analyzing the methods and weapons used by a criminal to carry out a series of crimes? Perhaps the simplest way of separating the two is to emphasize that analyzing the methods used by a criminal shows how a particular crime was carried out. Analyzing the signature of the criminal used in their staging of the crime scene will, on the other hand, deal with the reason why it was committed. For example, were the victims tortured as part of the killer's invariable routine? Not only does this help determine whether or not a particular crime fits into a series, but it sheds important light on the motivation the killer had for carrying out that crime. Was it anger? Was it excitement? Was it reassuring the killer of his own power over the victim? Or confirming his own masculinity? Or from motives of pure sadism? All the factors involved in signature crime analysis are reviewed in more detail in Chapter 8.

ORGANIZED OR DISORGANIZED?

The public view of the profiler's role in fighting crime invariably focuses on serial killers, since their crimes cry out most urgently for the forces of law to identify them and bring them to justice as speedily as possible. However, serial killers remain an exception to the rules that govern most non-serial murders.

A police forensics team catalog and photograph a crime scene. The nature of the scene and how the killer left his victim will give police crucial information about whether the killer is organized or disorganized.

MOTIVE, MEANS, AND OPPORTUNITY: THE TRILOGY OF THE NON-SERIAL KILLER

In the cases of non-serial killers, police with long experience of murder investigations know that many involve close family members or at least people who know one another well. Usually this kind of murderer kills a victim because of who they are, rather than purely at random. Motive looms large: a person may be killed because of sex, money, a bitter dispute, a grudge, or a real or imagined injury attributed to the victim by the killer.

Even when killer and victim do not know one another, non-serial murders are usually triggered by a particular event: perhaps a chance confrontation between members of rival gangs, a threat to a thief carrying out a robbery, or paying off a score as part of a continuing vendetta, for example. In all these cases, detectives can apply certain rules to help identify the most likely suspects. Who would benefit most from the death of the victim, for example, either in financial terms or in the lifting of a threat? Would the death of the victim benefit a rival in love or in business? Would the killing clear the way to a much-valued inheritance, or a claim to property? Do existing disputes within an organization or a family point to an individual whose anger has boiled over, prompting them to turn to violence?

Any of these considerations can help to identify a motive. The two other factors in the trilogy that guides investigators to a prime suspect are means and opportunity. How was the victim actually killed—

what was the method used to end their life, and what light does that shed on the killer? Were they poisoned, and if so, what kind of poison was used, and how was it acquired? How did the killer know what kind of poison to use, what its effects would be, how much was needed and where to find it? If the victim was shot, then what kind of weapon was used, and how did the killer lay hands on it? If the victim was beaten over the head, what does the forensic evidence reveal to help narrow down the pool of potential subjects? What height was the killer? Were they left-handed or right-handed? How strong would he, or she, have to be to deliver the fatal blow, and what kind of weapon did they use? Where did it come from and how was it disposed of afterward?

Considering the opportunity needed by the killer to carry out the crime is another powerful factor in identifying the subject. How did the killer manage to find the victim on his or her own? How did he or she manage to ensure there were no witnesses? How did they plan to keep details of the crime hidden, and what alibi did they set up to divert suspicion? How did they

Profilers examine the motives, weapons, and opportunities the killer has in an attempt to discover their identity.

EVIDENCE
19/10/63

A murder weapon can reveal a lot about a killer. For example, it can offer insight into the killer's profession, their height and weight, and whether they are left- or right-handed.

happen to be on a particular day and at a particular time, so that predicting the crime is impossible, and using it as a link to a potential subject is almost as hopeless.

In terms of the human cost involved, the ideal solution would be for a profiler to identify someone about to begin a serial-killing spree before they target their first victim, but this remains impossible in reality. Only after a killer has struck and the victim's body has been found can profilers start to look for the telltale signs that reveal how the killer thinks: how they choose and approach their victims, decide on the location, time, and day of the crime, select the threats, weapons, and restraints to apply to the victim, and choose the method of attack. Even after the victim has fallen prey to the killer, knowing how the body has been disposed of, what kind of signs have been left on and around the victim, and what kind of trophies or souvenirs the killer has taken away afterward help profilers to determine where a new suspect fits on the spectrum of potential serial killers.

Once this has been determined, every additional sign or piece of evidence can help to point profilers toward the likely background of the person they are looking for: their educational attainments, their job, their income level, their family circumstances, the kind of home in which they live, and how they developed their murderous inclinations. Not only will this help narrow down the search, it may even tie a particular attempted killing, where the victim survives, to a given serial killer. This at last will allow a description and a potential artist's impression or composite image to give police an identifiable figure for whom to search.

reassure the victim that they presented no threat, until the moment of attacking and killing them? If the victim was careful enough or nervous enough to have security protection, even from friends, family members, or associates, how could the killer evade or outwit this to ensure the victim was alone and defenseless at the crucial moment?

HUNTING FOR SERIAL KILLERS

However, serial killers do not abide by these rules, which makes them a much more deadly and difficult problem for law and order to deal with—deadly because they are never satisfied with a single victim, but derive such excitement and satisfaction from the act of killing that they continue to find and kill victims in a macabre series of attacks; and difficult to identify and difficult to catch, because they follow none of the established rules connecting killer and victim. They almost certainly choose victims with no direct and identifiable link to themselves—even where the victims are of a particular age group, a particular profession, or a particular physical type, these consistent selection factors will only emerge when a series of their crimes can be studied as a whole. In some cases, victims may be chosen and killed because of where they

Investigators examine all the minutiae of a case to help decipher information about the killer.

REVEALING THE ORGANIZED KILLER

So where does this multistage process of identification start? The first step concerns the most basic factor of all: how does the killer approach his self-imposed task? Do they plan coolly and carefully to reduce the risk of being caught as far as possible? Do they evolve a routine that has proved successful before, and that seems watertight in terms of leaving loopholes open should anything go wrong? Do they target a particular victim early in the preparation of the crime, studying his or her routine, travel patterns, home, and place of work, and decide on a location for the attack where the victim will be at their most isolated and vulnerable and witnesses unlikely to be present? Do they find a murder site where discovery will be unlikely and a subsequent getaway simple and straightforward?

Do they plan how to reassure and, if necessary, subdue the victim while moving them from the point where the approach is made to the murder site? Does the killer ensure they have the rope, the handcuffs, the blindfolds, and other items needed to keep the victim under their control for as long as necessary? Do they take the greatest care to remove evidence, even if the chances of a clear getaway are good? And do they take highly personal mementos of the victim, rather than items that are simply valuable, as a way of recalling the event and reliving the pleasure derived from it?

If the answer to all, or even most, of these questions is "yes," then the killer can be classified as organized, which suggests a number of probable characteristics that profilers can use in identification. Organized behavior tends to be associated with a relatively good education, intelligence that is probably better than average, and a high level of social and sexual competence, to put potential victims at ease and persuade them to trust a stranger. If the killer comes from a family with several brothers or sisters, they will usually be one of the eldest, and their father will usually have a steady job, but fail to provide clear and consistent discipline for his children.

The killer himself will usually have a skilled job and a partner, and drive a medium-value, well-maintained car. They may also enjoy alcohol and social events but, in spite of their coolness in approaching their crimes, they will almost certainly suffer a high level of resulting stress. This usually appears as a need to follow details of the crime and the hunt for the killer on the radio or television, or in the newspapers. In extreme cases, where they begin to feel the hunt for the killer is approaching too close for comfort, they may even move, change jobs, and set up home in another town to distance themselves from the threat of capture.

DISORGANIZED KILLER— THE OPPOSITE EXTREME

Of course, not all serial killers are alike, and many may differ considerably from this type of highly organized individual. At the opposite end of the spectrum, a killer can be driven by the same needs to murder multiple victims but on an entirely different basis in almost every respect. This is the psychology of the disorganized or chaotic serial killer, who acts completely differently. This killer will be governed much more by impulse than carefully drawn-up plans, and will take no real trouble to minimize the chance of being caught. They may find their victims, and the weapons they need to subdue them and kill them, purely by chance. They may kill on the spot, or close to their own home or place of work, without pausing to consider the consequences.

Where an organized killer has above-average intelligence, a disorganized killer will have limited intelligence. Where an organized killer tends to be one of the older children of their generation within the family, the disorganized killer will be one of the youngest. Where the father of an organized killer will usually be in a stable job, a disorganized killer will have a father in casual work or in no work at all, and discipline will be much harsher and more arbitrary than in the household of an organized killer. Disorganized killers will be less competent, socially or sexually, and will usually only be able to take control of a victim by a sudden, violent attack, rather than through reassurance and persuasion. Consequently they do not plan ahead in sufficient detail to use restraints on their victims, but may have to fall back on rendering them unconscious to take them to the murder site, or simply kill them on the spot where they first make their attack. Their indifference to careful planning means they will tend to leave more important evidence at the crime scene. Increased stress after carrying out the crime will almost certainly translate into higher levels of drug or alcohol use, and they will usually not follow news of the investigation of their crime.

Forensic investigators look for fingerprints on any objects that the killer may have come in contact with.

BEHAVIOR CHANGES

Between these two extremes, serial killers show different proportions of both kinds of characteristics. In some cases a normally organized criminal can be triggered into behavior more characteristic of a disorganized killer, once his intended control is disturbed because of some factor he cannot influence. Perhaps an intended victim puts up unexpectedly strong resistance, or a passer-by approaches the crime scene at the wrong moment, or the intended victim escapes. At these moments of vastly increased danger and stress, normal patterns of behavior can be so disturbed that they suggest a different individual altogether. In cases like these, profilers have to watch out for the triggers that change the killer's usual behavior and not fall into the trap of assuming the crime was carried out by a different individual altogether.

CASE

Having met in prison, James Clayton Lawson Junior and James Russell Odom joined forces in Lawson's home state of South Carolina to live out their violent sexual fantasies.

WHEN:	1970s
WHERE:	California, USA
VICTIMS:	One
CULPRIT:	James Clayton Lawson Jr, James Russell Odom

CASE STUDY 17: LAWSON AND ODOM

How does a disorganized killer operate in practice? Perhaps the most dramatically disorganized killer was James Clayton Lawson Junior, a violent sex attacker who became friendly with another like-minded criminal, James Russell Odom, when they were fellow inmates of a California high-security mental hospital in the mid-1970s. Although they spent most of their time discussing violent and bloody fantasies for attacking defenseless young women, both men were finally given parole and released. Odom then traveled all the way to South Carolina where his friend was living with his parents and working as a pipe fitter. Within a matter of days, they decided to realize their fantasies and hunt for a victim.

DISORGANIZED MISTAKES

In the hands of more organized killers, this could have been the beginning of a whole series of crimes. In fact, their first victim was also their last. To begin with, they used Lawson's parents' car to hunt for a victim. A young woman working at a local convenience store struck them as ideal, so they returned late the following evening. First they bought a knife from the girl, then they used it to threaten her into going with them in the car, leaving the store open and unattended. They drove to a quiet spot nearby, where they forced her to strip, after which Odom raped her. When he climbed out of the car so Lawson could have his turn, his friend simply took out the knife and killed her by cutting her throat, before removing her breasts and carrying out other mutilations. They took her clothes with them, but left her

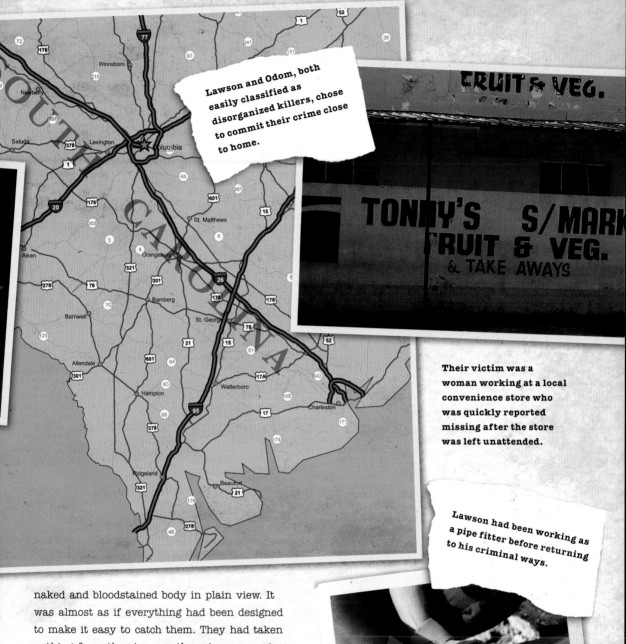

Lawson and Odom, both easily classified as disorganized killers, chose to commit their crime close to home.

Their victim was a woman working at a local convenience store who was quickly reported missing after the store was left unattended.

Lawson had been working as a pipe fitter before returning to his criminal ways.

naked and bloodstained body in plain view. It was almost as if everything had been designed to make it easy to catch them. They had taken nothing from the store, so the crime was not a robbery. Once the girl's body had been found, and a witness reported seeing the Lawsons' car outside the store, it was clear who would be the prime suspects, given the men's records. When police arrived to question them, they owned up to the killing, and were returned to spend the rest of their lives in close confinement.

CASE

WHEN: 1989, 1992

WHERE: London, U.K.

VICTIMS: Multiple

CULPRIT: Robert Napper

CASE STUDY 18: THE GREEN CHAIN KILLER

Not all disorganized killers make things so straightforward for those tracking them down. In the suburbs of South London on August 10, 1989, the so-called Green Chain Rapist carried out the first of a series of attacks on young women, choosing victims when the chance arose. He attacked his first victim inside her own home, noticing her failure to lock the back door. Where an organized attacker would have checked that his victim had no one with her at the time, the criminal in this case simply walked into her house, stepped past her young children playing in a downstairs room, and surprised her as she was drying her hair upstairs. He had

prepared to the extent of arming himself with a Stanley knife, but on this first occasion he limited his violence to gagging the woman, raping her, then leaving the scene. As a disorganized criminal he made no attempts to remove traces of semen, and took nothing from the house as stolen goods or as a souvenir.

ESCALATING VIOLENCE

The assailant failed to strike again until March 10, 1992, a relatively long interval for a serial sex attacker. In this case, the scene of the attack was different too, in that he grabbed his 17-year-old victim from behind, in the open air, and threatened her with a knife. He also punched her in the face before the rape, and his failure to penetrate his victim intensified his anger to the point where he gave her several vicious kicks to the head before escaping the scene. Nevertheless, he left traces of semen on his victim. The police checked the DNA for any matches found at other crime scenes. They immediately had a perfect match with the sample from the house of the 1989 victim. With this powerful new forensic weapon at their disposal, investigators did not need a detailed profile to reveal a series attacker at work.

New attacks began to occur at much shorter intervals. On March 18, just over a week later, a second 17-year-old was also threatened by a knife-wielding assailant, who this time wore a ski mask to conceal his identity. He confirmed his disorganized approach to his crimes by taking off the mask, and the escalating level of violence by using the knife to cut one of her breasts. Once again his rape attempt was unsuccessful, but semen traces told police this was a third attack by the same criminal. A fourth attack was carried out on May 24, 1992, when a mother pushing her 2-year-old in a stroller was grabbed from behind, hit about the head and upper body, and partly strangled with a length of rope. Once again the attacker tried to rape her before suddenly running off, and once again there was a DNA match.

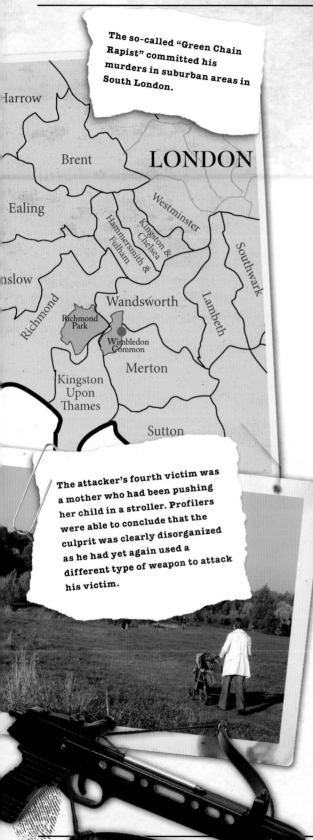

The so-called "Green Chain Rapist" committed his murders in suburban areas in South London.

The attacker's fourth victim was a mother who had been pushing her child in a stroller. Profilers were able to conclude that the culprit was clearly disorganized as he had yet again used a different type of weapon to attack his victim.

By now the evidence was adding up to tell profiler Paul Britton what kind of person was carrying out the attacks. Because the first assault failed to fit the pattern that united the later incidents, he concluded that the act of entering someone else's house to commit a crime was not as big a challenge to the criminal as the sexual violence carried out on his victims. This would suggest experience as a burglar, and it was the combination of an open door and a sexual opportunity that first took him out of an area of crime that felt familiar, and into a new and more difficult one. Having seized the opportunity offered by this one chance, he had taken much longer than usual to summon up the determination to carry out another rape, in the much more dangerous surroundings of a public place. Having carried out this new type of attack, he repeated it twice more, together with other attacks in the area where DNA evidence was not found and which could therefore not definitely be linked.

Two more links emerged from the pattern of attacks. The first attack was in Plumstead in southeast London, the third in Eltham, and the fourth on King John's Walk in Mottingham, less than a mile away. All three attack sites were on a network of footpaths signposted as part of the Green Chain Walk system, and the press began tagging the unknown criminal as the Green Chain Rapist. The second, more sinister, link was that the level of violence was escalating quite steeply between one attack and the next, as the criminal's confidence and aggression grew.

LOCAL KNOWLEDGE

The attacker's profile assumed that since the victims were all young, the rapist chose them because of what he assumed would be their vulnerability to a sudden assault. The location of the attacks suggested a knowledge of the area and the footpath system, which implied that the attacker tended to use local buses rather than traveling in his own car. These clues indicated someone probably aged between 20 and 25, sexually inexperienced, with a fairly low-level education and a job with flexible enough hours to allow him to be out and about at the time of the attacks. It was also likely that he was already known to the police for lower-level sexual crimes, such as indecent exposure, or as a peeping Tom.

DEATH COMES CALLING

No positive leads had emerged from the profile by November 3, 1993, when the Green Chain Rapist became the Green Chain Killer. Apart from the switch from rape to murder, the attacker returned to his first routine, watching a likely victim and striking when she was safely in her home and away from the eyes of passers-by. He even returned to the area of his first rape, not far from his home in Plumstead. He had seen his intended victim making love to her boyfriend through the windows of her flat, and when he saw the man leave for work, he hammered on the door of the flat.

When Samantha Bissett opened the door the rapist stabbed her so violently that he almost cut through her spinal cord. He stabbed her again and again in an uncontrollable frenzy, inflicting another 70 wounds, before looking for her 4-year-old daughter Jazmine. He raped and smothered the child, then went back to her mother. After carefully propping her up in the position in which he had watched her make love, he then slit open her ribcage and cut out part of her uterus, which he took with him as a trophy.

EVENTUAL CAPTURE

The police were now under heavy pressure to find the killer, but it took time to reveal his identity. They had published a composite picture from interviewing the girls who had survived his attacks in 1992, and received a positive response from someone in Plumstead who said the composite image was very similar to a neighbor of his, Robert Napper. The police interviewed Napper, but ruled him out of the inquiry because he was 2 inches taller than their self-imposed height of 6 feet. In fact, witnesses had differed over the stature of the man who attacked them, and Napper himself tended to walk with a stoop. Other neighbors reported his odd behavior. Although he volunteered to provide a blood sample, which would have proved his guilt beyond doubt, he failed to turn up to either of the appointments arranged for a sample to be taken, and police failed to follow it up.

In October that year, police arrested Napper for allegedly stalking a civilian working at Plumstead police station and ordering a printer to copy and print 50 sheets of official Metropolitan Police notepaper.

Robert Napper, pictured here after his arrest for the murder of Samantha and Jazmine Bissett.

When they searched his home, they found a .22 caliber pistol and 244 rounds of ammunition, together with a crossbow, a set of six crossbow bolts, and two knives. He was sentenced to six weeks in jail, but the police had missed his London A to Z map guide, which had the attack sites marked in it. In April 1993, police found a tin box buried on a local common, containing a Mauser handgun. They checked fingerprints on the box, and found they were Napper's, but took no further action. Three months later, he was questioned after being seen peering through the window of a woman's house elsewhere in Plumstead, when his behavior had him marked down as a potential rapist.

In spite of these hints, the first real action taken against Napper depended on old-fashioned police work, when his fingerprints were matched with bloodstained prints found at the Bissetts' flat. This time he was made to provide a DNA sample, and finally unmasked as the Green Chain Killer. Though police had become convinced he was probably responsible for a long list of other unsolved rapes and sex attacks in the area, there was no DNA evidence to tie Napper to these crimes, and he continued to deny them. However, he was found guilty in October 1994 of the killing of Samantha and Jazmine Bissett, and of the two earlier rapes and one attempted rape in 1992. His family records revealed a horrific childhood, marred by violence between his parents, and their eventual divorce, diagnoses of Asperger's syndrome and paranoid schizophrenia, rape by a family friend at the age of 12, and increasingly bizarre behavior, which resulted in his being sent to Broadmoor high-security psychiatric hospital.

Napper was eventually sent to Broadmoor high-security psychiatric hospital after childhood diagnoses of paranoid schizophrenia and Asperger's syndrome were discovered.

VICTIMS

Although considered the chief suspect in other cases, the courts only had enough evidence to charge Napper with two counts of rape and the murder of Samantha and Jazmine Bissett, pictured here.

CASE STUDY 19: RACHEL NICKELL

Yet the truth was that Samantha and Jazmine Bissett were not the first of Napper's victims to die. In July 1992, a 23-year-old model named Rachel Nickell had been walking with her 2-year-old son Alex and their pet dog Molly on Wimbledon Common when she was attacked, raped, and stabbed to death. She had 49 wounds, one of which almost decapitated her, and her son had witnessed the horrific killing from start to finish. Yet there was no serious attempt at this stage to draw parallels with the murder of Rachel Nickell and the other attacks and killings in southeast London. True, there was a geographical separation—Wimbledon was well to the southwest of the city—but the open common was all too reminiscent of the countryside around the Green Chain path network. The victim was young and blonde, and the attack was almost identical to those delivered by Napper, except that at this stage he had not actually killed anyone before.

SETTING THE HONEY TRAP

The result was that the police looked elsewhere for the killer, and they were convinced they had found him in the shape of Colin Stagg. Reported to have been walking his dog on Wimbledon Common at about the time

Years after the murder of Rachel Nickell, new, sophisticated forensic technology was able to match paint chips discovered in her son Alex's hair to Robert Napper's toolbox.

Nickell, pictured here with her son Alex, matched the physical profile of Napper's other victims. At the age of two, her son witnessed her murder.

of the killing, Stagg was thought to match the profile of the person responsible for this particular crime, since he belonged to a problem family and had dropped out of school before a succession of low-level jobs. In particular, he had been charged with indecent exposure for sunbathing naked on the Common, had been reported as speaking with some excitement about the killing soon afterward and had fixed a sign joking about being a pagan on the front door of his flat.

Although the killing of Rachel Nickell matched the pattern of Napper's other attacks, the police decided to pursue another suspect.

Lacking any strong evidence, the investigators set up an elaborate trap. An undercover policewoman began corresponding with Stagg, in the hope that he would reveal details of the killing to her as his trust developed. He revealed nothing, and continued to deny any involvement in the killing, but the investigators remained convinced of his guilt, due to his apparent knowledge of details of the killing that only the man responsible would know. More decisively, they believed that his letters to the policewoman showed he was suffering from "sexual deviant-based psychological disturbances." In August 1993, he was charged with the killing,

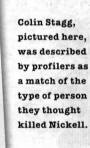

Colin Stagg, pictured here, was described by profilers as a match of the type of person they thought killed Nickell.

Police search Colin Stagg's garden. Even after being freed, Stagg was viewed with suspicion by the public, resulting in extremely detrimental effects on his life and livelihood.

In the case of Rachel Nickell, it was forensic evidence and not profiling that eventually caught the killer.

but a year later, the judge rejected the case as involving deliberate entrapment, and Stagg was freed. Nonetheless, he remained a suspect in the eyes of the public for another 14 years, was denied any chance of employment, and was subject to harassment.

FINAL RESOLUTION

The real killer was finally unveiled after a new search for evidence filled one of the yawning gaps in the original investigation. A search of the crime scene had failed to find significant traces of DNA that could have been used to reveal the killer beyond all doubt, though as more sensitive techniques were developed, a match was made possible in 2004. A footprint found at the murder scene had originally been rejected as being too small to belong to the killer, though this was reviewed when it was found to have shrunk in the wet soil, and was matched to a print of Napper's found at the scene of the Bissett murders. When the DNA was also proved to match Napper's, police returned to question him in Broadmoor. In spite

Mourners took flowers to the spot where Rachel Nickell was murdered.

of the evidence, persuading him to confess took three years. The Rachel Nickell case was concluded in 2008, when he finally admitted her murder. Colin Stagg was eventually awarded more than $1,000,000 compensation.

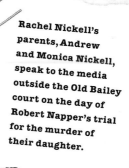

Rachel Nickell's parents, Andrew and Monica Nickell, speak to the media outside the Old Bailey court on the day of Robert Napper's trial for the murder of their daughter.

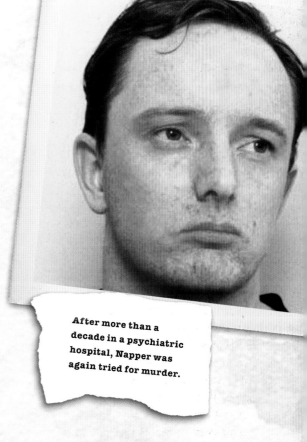

After more than a decade in a psychiatric hospital, Napper was again tried for murder.

READING THE PROFILE WELL

The Napper cases remain a sobering example of how not to handle a criminal profile. No one appeared to spot the close relationships between the portrait of the killer in the Green Chain murders and the Wimbledon Common killing, and once a suspect was identified in the Nickell murder, too much time was spent making the profile fit the single suspect, rather than looking at other, potentially better matches.

This case also provides an example of how apparently watertight assessments used to construct a profile can be blurred in practice, since, along with his predominantly disorganized tendencies, Napper actually showed some traits of an organized killer. Here, as in other areas of profiling, the problem lies in how the complete profile is constructed from the often sparse evidence initially available. The art of the profiler is heavily dependent on experience and on the knowledge of how far to narrow down the pool of potential suspects without leading the search away from the real perpetrator.

Composite released following the murder of Rachel Nickell in 1992, which bore a strong resemblance to Colin Stagg who was charged and later cleared of the murder. It also looked like Robert Napper, 42, who pleaded guilty at the Old Bailey court to the manslaughter of Rachel Nickell.

CURLING POND

WAR MEMORIAL

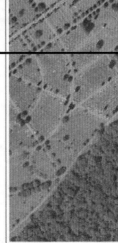

AERIAL PHOTOGRAPH OF WIMBLEDO

The photo map shows the crime scene, the car park where Nickell's car was discovered, and the two sites where Robert Napper had been seen by eyewitnesses.

Rachel Nickell, pictured here, was murdered by Robert Napper, yet it took the police years to connect him with her death.

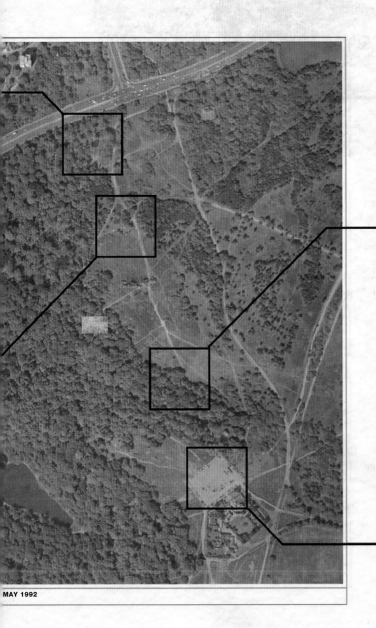

MAY 1992

SCENE

WINDMILL CAR PARK

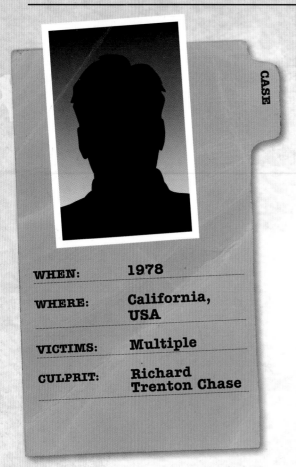

CASE

WHEN:	1978
WHERE:	California, USA
VICTIMS:	Multiple
CULPRIT:	Richard Trenton Chase

CASE STUDY 20: THE SACRAMENTO VAMPIRE

Fortunately, not all criminals present such a potentially baffling combination in their makeup. One of the earlier successes of profiling in the United States showed how an understanding of a killer's choice of victim and method of killing can not only reveal how the criminal thinks, but can suggest his lifestyle and physical appearance as well. The case began with the shooting of 22-year-old Teresa Wollin in her home in Sacramento, California, on January 23, 1978. Not only had the killer torn open her body to eviscerate her, but he had stopped long enough to drink her blood, a ghoulish ritual that earned him the title of the Sacramento Vampire.

DISORGANIZED—OR MAD?

FBI agents Robert Ressler and Russ Vorpagel were called in to advise the police on what kind

After killing his first victim, Teresa Wollin, the so-called "Sacramento Vampire" drank her blood.

The killer operated within a very confined area of Sacramento, California, making it easier for police to hunt for suspects.

of criminal they were looking for. They each produced a profile, and the close match between them confirmed the logical way both agents had approached their task. They concluded that the way in which the victim had been killed and torn apart pointed to a highly disorganized killer, almost certainly suffering from a paranoid psychosis. Not only did he not seem to have planned the crime beforehand, but his attitude to potential evidence showed a cavalier disregard for his own fate. He walked around the victim's apartment, leaving fingerprints and footprints everywhere. Because of the large amounts of blood at the scene, his clothing must have been heavily bloodstained, yet there were no signs that he had tried to clean himself up before he left the scene.

Experience showed that killings of this type tended to be carried out by people of the same ethnic origin as their victims. They would also tend to be young, aged from the middle to late 20s, and be undernourished because they lived alone and their psychosis would mean they did not look after themselves properly. The suspect would almost certainly not have a proper job, and would live off disability and unemployment allowances. They would be unlikely to drive a car and would live somewhere close to the scene of the murder, in a house or apartment left in an equally chaotic state, possibly containing ample evidence of the crimes. The most sobering conclusion the agents produced was the last: given the killer's personality type and mental disorder, they could expect a series of additional killings at fairly rapid intervals.

Just four days later, the killer struck again, this time shooting three victims in a house a

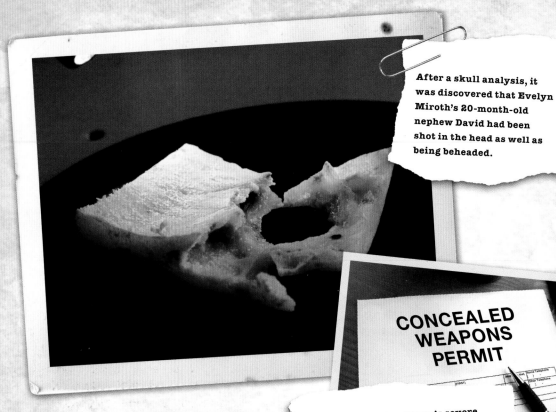

After a skull analysis, it was discovered that Evelyn Miroth's 20-month-old nephew David had been shot in the head as well as being beheaded.

CONCEALED WEAPONS PERMIT

Richard Trenton Chase's severe emotional instability labeled him as a disorganized killer. Only months before he applied for a gun license, the record of which lead the police to his home.

mile away from the first killing. He shot and raped 38-year-old Evelyn Miroth, as well as shooting her 51-year-old boyfriend Dan Meredith and her 6-year-old son, Jason. When worried neighbors called police, they found that Evelyn's 20-month-old nephew David, whom the couple had been babysitting, was missing, together with Dan Meredith's station wagon, which had been parked at the front of the house. Soon afterward the vehicle was found abandoned nearby. This so contradicted the basic precautions taken by most violent criminals that it pointed to severe mental impairment, and to the chance that the killer had retreated to the safety of his home, which must be close to both murder scenes.

A TORTURED MIND

More and more local people reported a man behaving strangely in the neighborhood, and one even remembered him from the school they had both attended years before. His name was Richard Trenton Chase, and he was now aged 27. Records showed he had applied for a gun permit, and police went to the address shown on the form, where he had previously lived with his mother prior to her moving out following his increasingly bizarre and threatening behavior. The apartment was 100 yards from the place where the car was abandoned.

Chase confirmed the profiles with absolute accuracy. As well as the match to his age, he was malnourished, lived on his own, and was out of work. When detectives searched his flat they found body parts and a bloodstained food

Upon entering Chase's home, police discovered dismembered human body parts, again pointing to a lack of organization on the part of the killer.

blender, but no sign of the missing baby, whose remains were finally found by a church janitor on March 24, 1978, left in a box. He had been beheaded and a hole in the skull showed he had been shot. Several organs were missing and Chase later admitted to having eaten them. His record showed he had been confined on psychiatric grounds several times, most recently until a matter of days before the first killing.

When the FBI questioned him, he explained the killings as being caused by outside forces, and he was therefore not responsible. He insisted his own blood was turning to sand, and it was only by drinking the blood of his victims that he could prevent it from drying up. It was also clear from documents found in his apartment that he had scheduled a series of 44 more killings on his calendar to enable him to attain his objective, killings only prevented by the speedy and accurate assessments of the profilers of his psychology and personality. He was finally brought to trial, found guilty of the killings, and sentenced to death. The verdict was never carried out, however, since on December 26, 1980, Chase was found dead in his cell, having saved his doses of medication and taken them all at once.

THE CHALLENGE OF THE ORGANIZED KILLER

Because disorganized killers tend not to plan their crimes, or take precautions to avoid leaving evidence at the scene, they tend to offer profilers a fairly fast and straightforward route to their identification and arrest. Organized killers, on the other hand, usually present a much more formidable challenge. Because everything they do is intended to conceal their identity, or their link with their victims, or even their psychological behavior, profilers have to hammer their way through these defenses to reveal the individual beneath. Furthermore, because organized killers have different ideas and routines, and ways of finding and overcoming their victims, it becomes more difficult to draw general conclusions from a few successful campaigns.

CASE

WHEN: 1980s

WHERE: Alaska, USA

VICTIMS: Multiple

CULPRIT: Robert Hansen

CASE STUDY 21: HUNTER-KILLER

Using the trackless wilderness of Alaska as his defense against the forces of law and order, Robert Hansen should have been one of the most difficult of the supremely organized killers to be found and apprehended. At first his activities were only revealed by the discovery of the bodies of prostitutes and topless dancers at different locations in the rivers and mountains around the town of Anchorage. The first victim dated back to 1980, but had been unrecognizable since her body had been left out in the open long enough for bears to have eaten much of the remains. Because they were found near Eklutna Road, she had been tagged as Eklutna Annie. The body of a second female was discovered that same year, this time in a gravel pit where she had not been found by animals. She was identified as a missing Anchorage prostitute named Joanne Messina.

The third corpse was the most significant. A 23-year-old topless dancer named Sherry Morrow was found buried in a sandbar in the Knik River in September 1982 by two off-duty policemen on a hunting trip. Because of the protection given to the corpse, it was easy for investigators to see she had been shot dead, almost certainly by rounds from a Ruger hunting rifle, a high-powered weapon common in the area. But the clothes she had been wearing showed no corresponding holes, suggesting she had almost certainly been

The state of Alaska witnessed one of the most organized killing sprees in US history.

Anchorage, Alaska. All the murders were committed in and around the coastal town.

a short, redheaded man who had offered her $200 to give him oral sex in his car. While she was complying, he snapped the handcuff around her wrist and compelled her at gunpoint to go back to his house with him.

The truck driver took her to the Big Timber Motel so she could make a phone call, while he rang the police and reported the incident. When the police arrived, she told an extraordinary tale. Back at the client's house, in the upmarket suburb of Muldoon, she had been stripped and raped, and violently assaulted. He had bitten her nipples and inserted a hammer into her vagina before handcuffing her to a fixture in the house while he slept for several hours. When he awoke, he told her that if he could fly her to his cabin in the mountains for more sex, he would bring her back to town the following morning and let her go. Then he drove her to the local airport at Merrill Field, and put her aboard a Piper Cub light aircraft, while he transferred supplies from the car to the plane's luggage compartment. Suspecting he intended to kill her once away from the city, the girl seized her opportunity—for once he had not handcuffed her to prevent her escape. She jumped out of the aircraft and ran out into the road. The man ran after her, but gave up when he saw her flagging down the truck.

naked when she was killed. Finally, a fourth victim, another topless dancer named Paula Golding, was also found buried in a shallow grave along the Knik. In this case a link was proven with the earlier killing since several Ruger cartridge cases were found near the body.

AN EARLY LEAD

Unusually, police had already identified a suspect, though they lacked the evidence to support an arrest. Before finding the bodies of the two topless dancers, a highly distressed 17-year-old prostitute had run out in front of a passing truck driver on June 13, 1982, claiming her life had been threatened by a client. She had a locked handcuff hanging from one wrist, and claimed she had been approached by

The police suspect had used handcuffs to restrain his victims.

Police took her back to the airfield, where she recognized the aircraft that belonged to her attacker, a blue and white Cub with the registration N3089Z. Checks showed the owner was a Robert C. Hansen, who lived with his wife and two children on Old Harbor Road. However, when they turned up to speak to the suspect, he angrily denied any involvement. He explained his wife and children were on holiday in Europe but he had spent the whole evening in the company of two friends, both of whom backed up his alibi when interviewed.

CONSTRUCTING A PROFILE

The police accepted the word of an outwardly respectable citizen against the claim of a prostitute, and there the matter rested, until they found the four bodies. Because whoever had killed them would have needed a light aircraft to take them to the murder sites, Hansen came back into the spotlight, but police would need much more convincing reasons to apply for a search warrant in order to see what potential evidence might be hidden at the house.

On this occasion, they asked the FBI to construct a profile of the killer, not to help find him, but to brief them on what they should look for at his house to clinch their case. FBI agent John Douglas studied the victim profiles and concluded that these were all people working and living on the fringes of society. It was common for women working in Anchorage's often violent Fourth Avenue red-light district to

vanish when they moved to find work elsewhere, so that missing persons reports were not usually assumed to reveal someone had been murdered. That showed an element of planning, since a local man could find plenty of potential victims he could select and approach personally, and who would not necessarily be missed.

Though running a successful and profitable bakery business, Hansen himself was distinctly unimpressive physically. He was short and slim with a pronounced stutter and pockmarked skin resulting from teenage acne scars. Consequently, Douglas concluded that he would have had little success with girls while growing up, and would have compensated for that in later life by abusing prostitutes, and possibly killing them. Records showed he was frequently accused of rape, but his word was invariably accepted rather than that of the prostitutes who complained. At the age of 21 he had been given a three-year jail sentence while living in Iowa for burning down the garage where the high-school bus was stored. He had been paroled early, but his psychiatric assessment had referred to his "infantile personality" that made him obsessive in paying back any hostility aimed at him. In the end the opposition of locals persuaded him to move north to Alaska to start a new life.

Much of that new life was an apparently successful sham. He claimed his hunting trophies had been stolen from his home, and he used the insurance payment to help set up his bakery business, imitating his father, an overly

A target rifle similar to that used by the killer, common in Alaska for large mammal hunting.

strict Danish immigrant who had run a bakery in Iowa. Even his light aircraft was flown without the benefit of his having a pilot's license, but he had got away with it for years.

The Importance of Hunting

In Douglas' estimation, hunting was a key factor in Hansen's life. Here at last was something he clearly took great pride in, so what better way to repay society for the injuries he thought it had inflicted on him by turning to hunting the kind of women he had previously treated violently, but who had then had the temerity to accuse him? Almost certainly he had picked up each of his victims along Fourth Avenue, before flying them out to the wilderness, landing on a suitable sandbar. Then he had stripped off their clothes and sent them off into the woods before hunting them down with his hunting rifle, killing them and then burying them to conceal their remains from the very rare passers-by.

If this was indeed the case, Douglas suggested that Hansen would treat his rifle as essential to his own lifestyle. He would also take souvenirs from his victims as a reminder of what he would see as triumphs over other people. Furthermore, Douglas was so sure of his ground that he was convinced that Hansen's friends had been lying when confirming his alibi. He suggested police should reinterview them while reminding them of the penalties they would face if it was later proved that Hansen had not been home at the time of the abduction of the woman. As he predicted, they were scared enough to retract their statements, and on October 27, 1983, a judge issued search warrants for Hansen's house and aircraft. On that day, investigators arrested him and took him to the police station while search teams went to work on his house.

There, in a hidden roof space, they found what they were looking for. A Remington rifle, a pistol, and a shotgun, together with a pilot's map of the area with locations marked on it, a driver's license, and several ID cards belonging to the missing women all helped to build the

Hunting was a skill Robert Hansen took pride in and eventually turned on women who lived on the fringes of society.

case against the suspect, but the most vital piece of evidence was a Ruger .223 rifle, which ballistic tests revealed was the one used to kill the victims. Hansen was tried for their murders, and he admitted his guilt. He also took detectives in a military helicopter to some of the grave sites, where eventually the remains of seven more missing women were identified. He was given a total of 499 years in prison without possibility of parole, and in the end all his careful planning and distancing himself from his victims availed him nothing. Even this supremely organized criminal could not eliminate the telltale signs in his background, his weaknesses, his accomplishments, and his methods, which led investigators to him just as they had to Odom and Lawson in South Carolina. All that his care achieved was to add to his total of victims and extend the story from a matter of days to one of years. In the end, though, the final result was the same—the remainder of his life in prison.

WHEN:	**2002**
WHERE:	**Baton Rouge, USA**
VICTIMS:	**Multiple**
CULPRIT:	**Derrick Todd Lee**

CASE STUDY 22: THE BATON ROUGE KILLER

Not all organized killers prove as relatively straightforward to profile and track down as Robert Hansen. Sometimes, by omitting to give one vital piece of information to the profilers, investigating police can hopelessly skew their portrait of the criminal, to the point where the hunt can be impeded. One such example was the so-called Baton Rouge Killer. His first victim, 44-year-old Pam Kinamore, left her business in Denham Springs, Louisiana, for her journey home on the evening of Friday, July 12, 2002. Her husband arrived later to find her car outside the house, but no sign of his wife. He reported her missing to police, but no further sign was found for four days, when her naked body was discovered in the water under Whisky Bay Bridge near Baton Rouge. She had been stabbed and sexually assaulted. A witness later claimed she had seen a body being driven in a pick-up truck by a white driver heading for the bridge, on the evening of the victim's abduction. Because there was no sign of a break-in at the family home on Briarwood Place, police assumed she had either left the door unlocked after

Gina Wilson Green, whose 2001 murder was linked to the Baton Rouge Killer though DNA tests.

arriving home or let her killer in without suspecting any danger.

OTHER KILLINGS

The truck seemed a vital clue, and was thought to be the vehicle used in the rape of a woman two days after the first victim disappeared. Police issued an impression of the attacker, and checked earlier unsolved murder cases for similar evidence. It emerged that a 41-year-old woman, Gina Wilson Green, who lived alone on Baton Rouge's Stanford Avenue, had been found sexually assaulted and strangled on September 23 of the previous year. On May 31, 2002, 22-year-old Charlotte Murray Pace was found in her house having been stabbed to death after signs of a fierce struggle. She too

Two months before the discovery of Pam Kinamore's body, Charlotte Murray Pace had been found dead of stab wounds in her home. Again, her murder was attributed to the same killer through DNA samples.

had been sexually assaulted, and when DNA samples were compared, it became clear the same killer was responsible for all three killings.

On November 21 the car belonging to 23-year-old Treneisha Dene Colomb was found abandoned in Grand Coteau. Unlike the other victims, she was not only black, but a serving Marine. Her body was found three days later and 30 miles away. She had also fought fiercely

All the murders were committed in and around Baton Rouge, Louisiana.

Derrick Todd Lee was tracked down in Atlanta as he was trying to make an escape to Los Angeles, California. He was eventually charged with the murders.

As the community of Baton Rouge grew more and more fearful, the police searched for any information they could find on the killer.

for her life, but had been battered to death and sexually assaulted. DNA tests confirmed she was a victim of the same serial killer.

WHITE OR BLACK?

The first profile that was produced suggested the killer was a male between 25 and 35 years old, physically strong and probably employed in a job calling for strength, but poorly paid and having little contact with the public. The FBI profilers also assumed he stalked his victims before attacking them, but lacked the confidence to interact with sophisticated women. He would be prone to extreme anger and anxiety and be obsessed by details of the police investigation. Meanwhile, they were still searching for a white suspect, and were also conducting mass DNA testing of the local population.

The fifth victim, 26-year-old Carrie Lynn Yoder, disappeared from her home on March 3, 2003. Her body was found 10 days later, and DNA evidence confirmed she too had been killed by the same man. Panic was beginning to spread, and police decided to widen the search. They wanted to know of attacks delivered by suspects of any race, and with any vehicle. Reports came in of three unsuccessful attacks where the victims had survived, but they spoke of a clean-cut, light-skinned black man who had initially not been threatening at all.

FOUND AND LOST

Finally, at the end of May 2003, police had the breakthrough they had been seeking. A DNA swab from a local man who looked like the latest composite sketch of the suspect showed a positive match with the samples taken from Carrie Lynn Yoder, and therefore a match for the earlier killings as well. He was 34-year-old Derrick Todd Lee, but he was nowhere to be found. On Monday, May 26, police issued an arrest warrant, but on visiting his home they found that on the day he had given the sample, his wife had taken their two children out of school, telling staff they were moving to Los Angeles. He was quickly tracked down to an Atlanta hotel and arrested there on the Tuesday. His criminal record revealed a succession of robberies, attacks, stalking offenses, and violence toward his girlfriend and wife.

In most respects the profile proved to be accurate in its description of his characteristics. The only major flaw was that he was initially thought to be white, since the majority of his victims were white. In Lee's case, his skin coloring was relatively light, and so the brief glimpse the first witness had of a man driving a pick-up truck could have caused them to misidentify him as a white man. As a result, when later witnesses referred to a black man seen loitering near one victim's home, police simply failed to pass this information on to profilers, since it disagreed with their picture of the killer.

Undoubtedly, this made profilers feel they must be looking for a white criminal in the apparent absence of any other leads, which may have impeded the hunt for the killer. A newspaper report referred to another witness who had earlier given Lee's name to police because he had stalked and threatened her over a two-year period, but they had done nothing because they remained convinced at that stage they were looking for a white killer.

Nevertheless, on September 24, 2003, Lee was charged with the murder of Treneisha Dene Colomb. He was also charged with killing

Carrie Lynn Yoder, the killer's fifth victim, was discovered in March 2003. Again, DNA evidence proved she had been murdered by the same man.

Lee appears here in Fulton County Superior Court for an extradition hearing. Lee waived his rights, allowing for his return to Louisiana.

Lee remains on death row for a series of murders, many of which profilers may have been able to prevent, had local police passed on all the appropriate information.

Charlotte Murray Pace by stabbing her with a screwdriver and a knife, after raping her and badly beating her. He was found guilty of this crime on October 12, 2004, and two months later was sentenced to death by lethal injection. Because of this the Colomb family decided not to press for another trial, and Lee remains on Death Row in Louisiana State Penitentiary, suspected of killing at least another seven women.

COMMUTERS OR MARAUDERS?

Classifying a killer as organized or disorganized is an important step toward understanding, describing, and finally catching them. However, there are other categories facing a profiler at the start of a new investigation. In addition to understanding how the killer thinks and approaches their crime, it is also vital to understand where they live and how they travel to meet their victims and carry out their attacks. Broadly speaking, profilers have discovered that in terms of how they move between their base and their victims, criminals can be divided into commuters and marauders, and this assessment in turn reveals other background conclusions that can help lead to their identification.

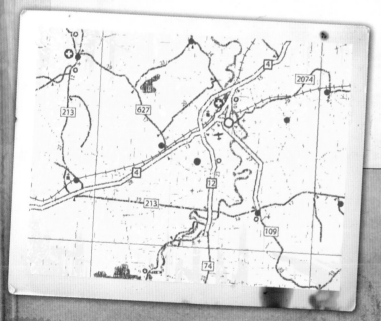

Deciding whether a criminal is a commuter or a marauder is vital to criminal profiling and can offer investigators a host of other facts about their suspect.

THE GEOGRAPHY OF A CRIMINAL MARAUDER

Much of the theory explaining these two behavior patterns was developed by British criminal psychologist David Canter, whose university researchers first examined local police records to study the geographical relationship between the scenes of successive burglaries committed in a particular area. Plotting the locations of the crime scenes relating to a single criminal revealed that they invariably operated within a remarkably restricted area. Secondly, if a line was drawn between the crime locations at the farthest limits of the area in opposite directions, and a circle was drawn around the midpoint of that line, with its radius equal to half the length of the line, it would enclose all the crime scene locations. Furthermore, the criminal's own home would normally be close to the center of the area.

Canter concluded the reason for this close physical spacing between crime scenes was that burglars would choose first to risk a robbery in an area they knew well. Not only would they know where the easiest pickings could be found, but they would also know where the most serious threats existed, and where and how to find the best escape routes. However, there was another factor they would usually bear in mind. Stealing too close to home posed a different kind of danger. Passers-by might recognize them as individuals, and seeing them close to the scene of a newly discovered crime would lead police to their door all too quickly. Or maybe the police would turn up in any case, making normal door-to-door inquiries of the local area, and finding someone with a known record would concentrate their attentions on that person to the exclusion of all else.

With these two factors in mind, the criminal would logically begin by setting out from home to the limit of his comfort zone. Then, when he needed to repeat his crime, he would set out for a similar distance but in a different direction, to avoid any danger of people in the vicinity of the first robbery still being on the lookout for potential suspects. Repeating this process a third time would mean following a different route from the thief's home base until far enough away to make it relatively safe to carry out a robbery. Successive crime scenes would mean following a series of routes in every possible direction from the home base, but never too close to it. Eventually, all the potential areas where robberies are still feasible have been targeted, and if the criminal is to continue their thieving career, they will have to return to the vicinity of the original theft. In addition, once enough crimes have been plotted in a small area, the center of the area would give a useful estimate of where the criminal lived, surrounded by a "safe zone" before reaching the closest crime scenes.

In practice, other factors could distort the simple circular pattern operating under ideal circumstances. The presence of a hazard such as a police station would obviously divert a thief's criminal activities away from that immediate vicinity to other

David Canter and his team were able to make correlations between the geographical location of crime scenes and the criminal themselves.

Criminals often leave a "safe zone" around the home, where they commit no crimes so as to try to avoid attracting attention from law enforcement.

The shape of a criminal's target area can be altered by the presence of a police station which they will be intent on avoiding.

areas within their comfort zone. Swathes of open country would also distort the pattern, for a different reason, offering fewer potential targets for the thief. Major obstacles such as rivers or railway lines would hamper getting to or from the scene of the crime and restrict potential escape routes and so skew the area into a different shape. All the same, plotting the crime scenes would still define an area in which the base of the criminal responsible would lie somewhere near the center.

EXTENDING THE AREA

So much for the shape of the area, but what about its size? Here some of the criminal's background becomes important. A thief who grew up in an inner-city background (even a different city from the one where he now operates) will be more comfortable working in crowded urban conditions than one who grew up in the country. Consequently the area covered by his crimes will be smaller, since he can be more confident of finding enough targets within that area than someone who needs wider and more open spaces to feel secure enough to steal.

The size of the area also depends on the kinds of crime involved. If a burglar specializes in rare or more valuable objects, they will have to cover a larger area to find opportunities. The same conditions will govern their thinking—traveling far enough from home to avoid leading police to their door, and avoiding areas of recent crimes to reduce the possibility of being recognized—but the distance between home and the scenes of the robberies will have to

increase, and the relative rarity of potential targets may distort the shape of the burglar's comfort zone farther from the basic circle of more routine thefts. In the case of violent criminals, such as rapists and serial killers, the distances are likely to be stretched by the needs of reaching areas where suitable victims can be found and where their crimes can be hidden, and this too can distort the shape on the map of the criminal's operating area.

FINDING THE MARAUDER

In profiling terms, the criminal who travels out and back between his home base and the scene of each crime is seen as a marauder. Once a sufficient number of victims can be tied to an individual rapist or killer through similarities in the crime scenes and other indicators, the crimes can be plotted on a local map to reveal the classic relationship of a marauder criminal, and give an indication of where the search for the home base should be concentrated.

CASE

WHEN: 1984

WHERE: Louisiana, USA

VICTIMS: Multiple

CULPRIT: Nathaniel Code

CASE STUDY 23: THE SHREVEPORT MARAUDER

Nathaniel Code, of Shreveport, Louisiana, was a classic marauder killer who concentrated his murders in a small area around his own home. He began his criminal career as a stealthy robber who would break into people's houses at night and take their possessions without alerting or confronting them, and had become happy to operate in a small semi-urban area, even when he later turned his objective from robbery to murder.

THE SWITCH TO MURDER

The switch occurred on August 31, 1984, in Cedar Grove, a suburb of Shreveport. The black, single mother who lived at 315 East 74th Street was worried about intruders, having been burgled twice before. She persuaded her father to nail the back door to her home shut, and to fit screens over all the windows to bar entry as far as possible. She then slept on a couch in her living room so as to be aware of anyone else in the house. The finding of the body of 25-year-old Deborah Ford showed that her security precautions had failed to keep her killer out. Police determined he had managed to squeeze through a small bathroom window, which hinted at an experienced burglar. The fact that the victim slept in the living room probably meant they surprised one another, and that the robber possibly fell into enough of a panic to eliminate a potential witness.

When investigators looked at the scene more closely, though, there were two clear and

Nathaniel Code operated in the small vicinity around his home in Shreveport, Louisiana.

apparently contradictory signs. On one level the killer seemed to be in complete control over his victim. She was wearing a nightdress inside out, showing that perhaps she had been forced to undress by her attacker and then dressed again before she was murdered. In addition, her wrists were tied behind her back with electrical cable, and she had been gagged. Yet the way in which she had been killed contradicted any idea that the criminal was under control. She had been stabbed in the chest nine times, and if this alone had not been enough to kill her, her attacker had cut her throat, not once but a total of six times, some of the slashes penetrating deeply enough to reach her spine.

Working on the basis that the attacker was an experienced thief and would therefore almost certainly have a criminal record, the police examiners took fingerprints at the crime scene around the frame of the window through which the attacker had entered the property. They asked the FBI for a profile, and they began with the assumption that the killer was probably around 30 years old, lived locally, and would almost certainly be on police files for either rape or burglary. Furthermore, they felt he would stay close to the inquiry to determine how likely the police would be to track him down.

Having been aware of local robberies, Deborah Ford became fearful of becoming a victim of one as well, so chose to sleep on her living room sofa. She became the victim of Code's first murder.

MISSING PRINTS

Unfortunately, police found no match for the killer's fingerprints. However, when, almost a year later and just two streets away in the same neighborhood at 213 East 72nd Street, four people were found murdered on July 19, 1985, those fingerprints would prove invaluable. The victims were 36-year-old Vivian Cheney, who had been tied at both wrists and ankles before being taken to the bathroom, partially strangled, and then drowned by forcing her head under water. Her 15-year-old daughter Carlitha had been tied like her mother and then almost decapitated by a lethal slash to her throat. Vivian's boyfriend, Billy Joe Harris, had also been tied up and then

Profilers were unable to decipher whether Ford's killer could be classified as organized or disorganized. On one hand, he had tied his victim up with electrical tape, suggesting control. On the other hand, she had been found with multiple and unnecessary wounds, implying disorganization.

shot through a pillow to muffle the sound before his throat was cut. Finally, Vivian's brother Jerry Culbert had been left sleeping until woken by the shot that killed him. Police studied the available evidence and decided the killer had used the young girl as a hostage to control the other victims, so they would allow him to tie them up. Harris had then been shot, Carlitha's throat had been cut and then her mother taken to the bathroom and drowned, before the killer slashed Harris' throat and then shot Culbert. Throughout this complex and bloody sequence he had remained in control of events apart from the totally uncontrolled violence with which he had killed those helpless under that control. But some of the signs left at the scene would ultimately lead to his capture and a place on Death Row facing execution by lethal injection.

KNOTS AS EVIDENCE

Differences to the first crime included the use of duct tape to gag the young girl—rather than the gag improvised at the killing of Deborah Ford—which was something he had brought with him, since there was none in the house. The men had been killed by shooting, though this had not prevented one of them having his throat cut, and he had forced the mother to watch him killing her daughter before he killed her too. But the victims had been tied in exactly the same way as Deborah Ford, in a complex series of knots simulating handcuffs and linking the wrist and ankle bindings together to bind them more securely. Finally, fingerprints found at the scene revealed this was not merely a similar crime to the earlier murder, but one definitely carried out by the same killer.

The third killings in the sequence were discovered just over two years later in the same suburb of Cedar Grove, this time at 641 West 66th Street. Here the identity of the victims would lead directly to the killer. The householder was 78-year-old William Code, who had been tied up in the same way as all the earlier victims, beaten over the head before being stabbed five times in the chest and seven times in the back, and slashed in the upper arm where a main artery had been cut. In the house with him were the grandsons of a friend, 8-year-old Eric Williams and 12-year-old Joe Robinson, who had been staying overnight after helping him with some gardening. Both were tied up, beaten over the head, and strangled to death.

In the aftermath of the killings, police had a visitor in keeping with the FBI's original profile. One Nathaniel Code turned up to explain he was the nephew of the householder and had called earlier to help with some household chores. In fact the killer had been brought up by his uncle in that very house, but needed a reason for his fingerprints to appear on different items of household equipment, including the telephone and the humidifier from which he had stripped cable to tie up his victims.

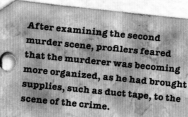

After examining the second murder scene, profilers feared that the murderer was becoming more organized, as he had brought supplies, such as duct tape, to the scene of the crime.

FAMILY REVELATIONS

In the end, this close family link was his undoing. Other members of the family revealed a disturbing past, including boyhood violence toward his late aunt, and the fact that his uncle would not let him in the house. When local people around the other crime scenes were interviewed, many of them knew him by sight and identified him as being in the area at the time of the killings. One witness placed him among the bystanders watching police dealing with the body of his first victim three years earlier, just as the profilers had predicted. But the final proof was provided by the killer himself: though he had taken care to explain why his prints might be found at the scene of this triple murder, he had no reason why his prints had been found at the earlier killings.

Unfortunately, it also emerged that he should have been included on the list of potential suspects as a result of a rape conviction. However, this information was missed because at this stage there was no connection between local police records and the nationwide fingerprint database that would have revealed the earlier crime. Instead, his prints found at the first murder scene were still being checked manually against records going back over a decade, but the rape conviction was eight months before the chosen start date for the search. The delay possibly cost the lives of the seven victims at the second and third killings, but one consolation was that Code was found guilty of four of the murders on December 28, 1990. Since then he and his lawyers have spent 20 years on appeals, all of which have been denied. Early in 2010 it seemed that a date would soon be set for his execution.

Nathaniel Code was an extreme example of a marauder killer in another sense too. His killings were spread over a single suburb of a single town. It also transpired that the reason for the final killings, leading directly to his arrest, was the only one involving a personal connection. Apart from the antipathy that had developed between him and his uncle, a direct trigger had been evidence from relatives that the killer approached his uncle on the day of his death to ask for money. His uncle had refused, effectively signing his own death warrant.

Nathaniel Code awaits execution by lethal injection in Louisiana.

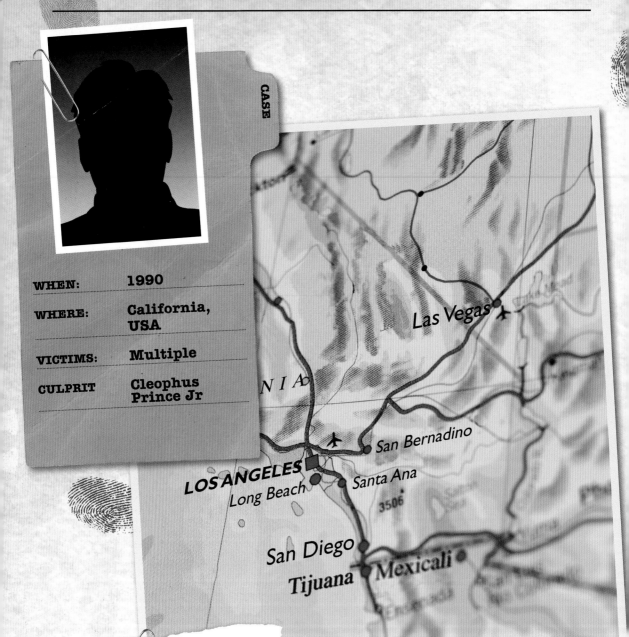

CASE

WHEN:	1990
WHERE:	California, USA
VICTIMS:	Multiple
CULPRIT	Cleophus Prince Jr

Las Vegas

San Bernadino

LOS ANGELES
Long Beach   Santa Ana

N I A

3506

San Diego
Tijuana   Mexicali

In classic marauder style, the killer limited his territory to a small area of urban San Diego, California.

The killer attacked victims in a number of apartment complexes in the Claremont area.

CASE STUDY 24: THE CLAREMONT MURDERS

Three years later, in California, another serial killer fit the marauder profile almost as closely. In this case he found his victims in a small section of the Claremont area of San Diego, and once again he had progressed from being a relatively successful cat burglar, breaking and entering houses and apartments—wearing socks over his hands to avoid leaving fingerprints—to steal rings, jewelry, and other small items of value.

FROM THIEF TO KILLER

The fatal transformation from thief to killer appeared to take place on January 12, 1990, when the body of 21-year-old Tiffany Schultz was found on the floor of the bedroom in her second-floor apartment in Canyon Ridge complex. She had been stabbed 47 times, with many of the wounds penetrating right through her body. Neighbors recalled hearing loud noises from the apartment earlier, and the manager of the complex had been approached by a young black man for the loan of a wire coat hanger to help him break into his locked car. She had noticed him walk off, not to the parking lot, but into the complex, which caused her some concern. Could this have been the killer?

A month later, another woman was killed, this time in an apartment at the Buena Vista Gardens complex, which faced the Canyon Ridge apartments across a minor road. Once again loud noises had been heard by people in adjacent apartments at around midday, when another witness saw a black man on the staircase of the complex. The body of university student Janene Weinhold was found on the floor of her bedroom when her flatmate returned from work at around 8 p.m. She too had been stabbed and left wearing only her bra, but had also been sexually assaulted, which enabled police to retrieve semen samples for DNA testing. In the kitchen sink was a bloodstained knife with the tip badly bent, identified as the murder weapon from the victim's wounds. The door of the apartment carried bloodstains in a peculiar honeycomb pattern, and it was clear the victim had been killed at around the time the noises had been heard in the other apartments, and the unknown man seen on the staircase.

The second murder was committed just across the street from the first.

MORE SIGHTINGS

On March 25 another resident of the same apartment complex was followed home from the bus stop by a black man, but managed to reach her apartment in time to lock the door before he could catch up with her. In April, two high-school seniors came to spend their spring break in the Buena Vista apartment belonging to the brother of one of them, 18-year-old Holly Tarr. When the girls were swimming in the pool belonging to the complex, they noticed a black man working out with weights beside the pool and paying them a lot of attention. Holly went back to the apartment to take a shower, while her friend Tammy followed her 10 minutes later. She heard a sound of distress from inside, but found the door was locked. She called for help, and a maintenance man managed to unlock the door and break the safety chain that held it in place. As she entered the apartment, she saw the man from the pool emerge from a bedroom with a cloth covering his face and a knife in his hand. He pushed her aside and made his escape, and she found Holly on the bedroom floor, bleeding from a deep chest wound. She died before help could arrive.

The murder scene produced some valuable pieces of evidence: the print of a man's shoe, and a bloodstained knife and T-shirt were found dumped outside. The knife was identified as having been taken from the apartment, and the blood on the shirt matched that of the victim. More significantly, the police checked the signing-in sheet for the weights at the pool. There were four names on it:

Holly and Tammy, Holly's brother, and one C. Prince, who was almost certainly the killer. He was quickly traced as Cleophus Prince Jr, who admitted to have been working out until midday, when he had left the complex to go back to his own apartment, which he shared with two friends, because he had to get ready for work. With no direct evidence to detain him, police were unable to take his fingerprints for comparison.

THE KILLER SHIFTS OPERATIONS

Nevertheless, the narrow escape persuaded him to move out of the shared apartment to avoid any follow-up. Significantly, there were no more killings in either apartment complex, but there were soon suggestions he had simply moved his attacks a little farther away. On May 2, a woman was followed into her house by a black intruder, but she managed to get away. On May 20, 38-year-old Elissa Keller spoke on the phone to her 18-year-old daughter from her apartment in the Top Of The Hill complex in Claremont. The following day she failed to show up for work or answer the phone, so her daughter went in person to confirm all was well. She found her mother's body and called the police.

The victim had been stabbed, strangled, and beaten about the face, but defense wounds showed she had tried to fight for her life. Scuff marks showed the killer had probably been able to enter the apartment through a window left ajar, and once again there was a shoeprint found on the floor. Bloody prints on the bathroom counter showed the same strange honeycomb pattern seen at earlier crime scenes.

The next killing, on September 13, was in an

The murder of Holly Tarr, the third victim, was also committed in the Buena Vista apartment complex where Janene Weinhold had been killed.

Prince consistently used knives he found within the homes of his victims as murder weapons.

All the victims, bar Holly Tarr where Prince had been caught in the act, had been stabbed brutally and repeatedly.

apartment in Universal City, again in the Claremont area. This time it was a double murder, involving 42-year-old Pamela Clarkson and her 18-year-old daughter Amber. Pamela and her husband had each left the apartment in the morning, the husband for work and Pamela going to the gym, leaving Amber still in bed. Her mother returned at 11 a.m., but when she later failed to show up at work, one of her colleagues called at the apartment to see what was the matter. She found Pamela's naked body lying in the hallway and called the police. Pamela had been stabbed 11 times in the left, upper part of her chest, and blood trails showed her body had been dragged from where she had been killed to where she was found. In one of the bedrooms, they found Amber's body. She had been killed first, and while she had not been stripped, her breasts were exposed and she too had been stabbed 11 times in the left upper chest. Pamela's wedding ring was missing and some money had been stolen from her purse.

BURGLARY AND MURDER

By this time public anxiety at the series of murders was escalating, and several suspects had been arrested, questioned, and released.

Having begun his criminal career as a burglar, Cleophus Prince Jr became a murderer, profilers hypothesized, after an incident with a women which led him to want to punish females in general.

Prince stalked women from his local gym back to their apartments.

tendencies from his young helper, his visits did not go unnoticed, and several witnesses reported to the police they had seen an old-model saloon car with a noisy exhaust in the vicinity of the burglaries at the time they had been carried out. Someone else reported the car had also been seen in the parking lot of the gym, so police asked staff to call them whenever the car next appeared.

The call was made on February 4, 1991, and police turned up to find Prince sitting in the car. When his reason for being there failed to check out, they searched the vehicle and found a selection of knives. Though he claimed to be a member of the gym, this had lapsed some time before, though witnesses testified the car was there on numerous occasions. This time they took fingerprints and blood and DNA samples. With no definite evidence, they had to release him while they waited for the tests to be completed. Finally they had a positive DNA match with the samples from Janene Weinhold, and they knew they had found their killer. They went to the address he had given, which was next door to one of the murder scenes, but were told he had gone to visit his mother in Birmingham, Alabama.

In the meantime they searched his apartment and found a ring that matched the description of the one taken from Holly Tarr's body. This ring was relatively unusual, since only 63 of this design had been made, and none had been sold anywhere in California. They also checked his background and found that he had shared a flat in the Buena Vista complex at the time of the first killings, and had then moved in with a

What police did not know at that stage was that Prince was carrying on his burglary career with a 16-year-old accomplice. Both thieves would use credit cards to trip locks and enter apartments, wearing socks over their hands to avoid prints, and looking for a knife once inside in case they were challenged. He was a member of the Family Fitness Center gym, where Pamela Clarkson had spent the last hours of her life, and would regularly follow female members home to see where they lived, then wait for the apartment to be empty before breaking in to steal. Though he concealed his murderous

Although originally unable to implicate Prince in the murder of Holly Tarr, police were finally able to take fingerprints and DNA samples after witnesses observed his suspicious behavior around the local Family Fitness Center Gym.

woman living near Universal City at the time of the later murders in that area. They searched his apartment and found shoes that matched the prints found at the murder scenes, and also a unique ring belonging to Elissa Keller.

MATCHING THE VICTIMS

Police at Birmingham called to say Prince had been arrested on March 1 for taking money from a cash register at a nightclub, and the San Diego police asked for him to be extradited. While the process was continuing, FBI profilers were called in to show how the killings that did not provide positive DNA evidence could also be shown to have been carried out by Prince. They looked at the first three killings, which presented a very high risk of discovery, and decided these showed clearly that the perpetrator must be a marauder killer working in an area with which he was familiar, and in which he could feel safe. Because he was able to enter apartments with ease, they assumed he was already on police records for breaking and entering, and that there would be other evidence of his approaching and accosting women in the vicinity before the series of murders began.

When considering what had triggered the switch from stealing to killing, the profilers believed that a stressful incident had led to the killer needing to punish women for what had happened to him. This suggests he would also have a record of violence or threatening behavior to a wife or girlfriend, but that he would probably present them with trophies stolen from people he had killed as a way of secretly being in control. In terms of the victims, all except one were aged between 18 and 21, and the 42-year-old was described as looking younger, and had almost certainly arrived at the crime scene when the killer had just murdered her daughter.

All the victims were white, physically fit, and good-looking, all had some or all of their clothing removed, some had jewelry stolen, and all were left face-up on the floors of their apartments. Other linking factors included three living in the same apartment complex and three being members of the same gym. All had been killed by a series of savage stab wounds to the chest, using a knife found at the crime scene, and the only exception, who died from a single stab wound, had resulted from him having to flee when discovered. When all the details of the crimes were fed into the VICAP database to see if they had been matched in killings elsewhere, no corresponding crimes were found.

These matching factors, together with the DNA matches, enabled prosecutors to make a convincing case, and on July 13, 1993, the jury at his trial found Cleophus Prince Jr guilty of all the murders. He was sentenced to death, and a series of appeals were finally rejected when the sentence was confirmed in May 2007 by the California Supreme Court. For the time being he remains, like Derrick Todd Lee in Louisiana, in a cell on Death Row.

Prince was found guilty of all of the murders and now sits on Death Row, awaiting execution.

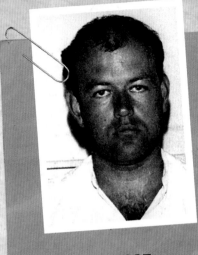

WHEN:	**1983**
WHERE:	**Leicestershire, U.K.**
VICTIMS:	**Multiple**
CULPRIT:	**Colin Pitchfork**

CASE STUDY 25: THE FIRST DNA MURDER CONVICTION

In the U.K., another marauder killer case stood out for two reasons: the criminal preferred the background of open country to help hide his crimes, and might have evaded the law altogether were it not for the first successful application of DNA profiling to tie him beyond all doubt to the crimes he committed. As a result, he was stopped after two killings, where under other circumstances he might have continued to kill several more victims until enough information was collected to bring him to justice.

THE TWO KILLINGS

Perhaps the most striking factor in the two killings he carried out was the similarities between them. The first murder was discovered in November 1983, when the body of 15-year-old schoolgirl Lynda Mann was found beside a public footpath, running through wooded countryside near the Leicestershire village of Narborough. She had been raped and strangled, but little in the way of direct evidence was left at the site except for the killer's semen.

The second killing took place in July 1986, only a few hundred yards away in the same stretch of Leicestershire countryside. The victim was Dawn Ashworth, also a 15-year-old schoolgirl. Not only had she too been raped and strangled, but her body had been left beside a footpath. This time, some additional evidence turned up, even if it led police in the wrong direction. A 17-year-old kitchen porter named Richard Buckland was reported as being in the

Both killings in this case took place in rural Leicestershire, only a short distance apart, implying that a marauder killer was clearly on the loose.

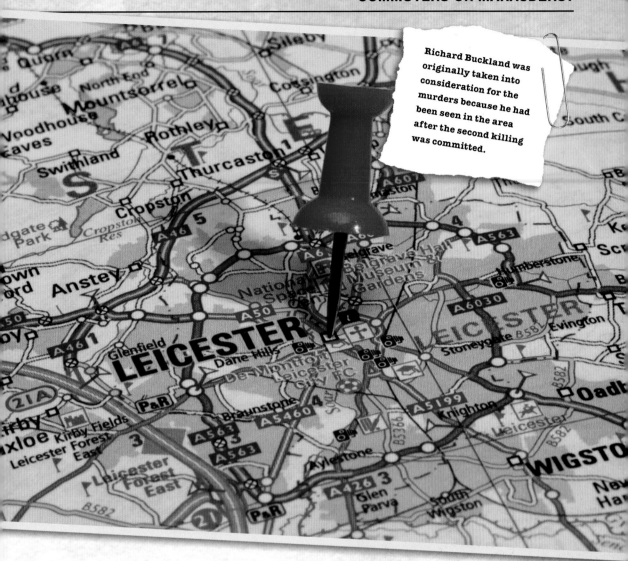

Richard Buckland was originally taken into consideration for the murders because he had been seen in the area after the second killing was committed.

area at the time of Dawn's murder, identified by his motorcycle left beside a stretch of footpath, and the sighting of someone in the area with a similar crash helmet. When challenged, Buckland admitted both killings.

CONFESSION PROVED FALSE

On the face of it, this was an encouragingly straightforward clearing up of both murders. The problem was that Buckland had definitely not been responsible, as the first use of DNA genetic marking in a murder investigation was

to prove. Comparing a sample of Buckland's DNA with the traces left by the killer at the murder scenes confirmed what police and profilers already suspected, that both young girls had been killed by the same criminal. It also proved that the criminal could not have been Buckland.

SCREENING CAMPAIGN

So who could have done it? Criminal psychologist Paul Britton drew up a profile that showed the killer was probably older than

Buckland and confident enough to approach the girls in the first place without immediately scaring them off. This suggested someone with a reasonable education who might already be in a long-term relationship with a wife or partner. Both bodies had been partially hidden from passers-by, which suggested someone who knew the locality well, an impression reinforced by the proximity of the two murder scenes to one another. The imperatives of control and domination must have been developing over time, which also suggested he might already appear on police records for low-level sexual offenses such as indecent exposure.

To find the suspect who matched the profile, police decided to use the local background of the criminal as an aid to catching him. If he really was a marauder killer, he must live relatively close to the crime scenes, and they already had his DNA. So a campaign was mounted to take samples from all males between the ages of 14 and 34 (the upper limit suggested by the profile) who lived in the village of Narborough or the neighboring hamlets of Enderby and Littlethorpe. More than 4,000 samples were obtained, but none matched those of the killer. It seemed the screening had all been in vain.

Profiling helped determine the age range and location of a DNA screen that was taken on in hopes of finding a match.

In fact, it proved to be a triumphant success, but only when the truth emerged a year later. Ian Kelly, a bakery worker, revealed in a pub conversation that he had been browbeaten by a workmate into giving a DNA sample on his behalf. The workmate in question, 27-year-old Colin Pitchfork, was worried about police harassment because his record would show a conviction for indecent exposure. Kelly had obliged, but his admission was overheard by one of the bakery managers who had been in the

Buckland's red motorcycle helmet had been seen on someone leaving the area of the crime. Yet the newly implemented DNA techniques proved that he could not be the killer.

pub at the time, and who reported the information to the police. They checked their records and found that the signature given with the DNA sample for Colin Pitchfork didn't match that given when Pitchfork had taken part in door-to-door inquiries. He was arrested and a blood sample was taken and sent to the laboratory where his DNA was matched with that from the murder scenes. So damning was the evidence that Pitchfork pleaded guilty to the double murders on January 22, 1988, and was sentenced to life imprisonment.

THE CHALLENGE OF THE COMMUTER KILLER

Of the two types of violent criminals, it may well be that marauders tend to be easier to catch, simply because they operate over a compact area and often follow a similar pattern. In the case of commuters, their arrangements are both more widespread and more complicated. The real difference is that commuter criminals have access either to good public transport or to their own vehicles, so that they can range much more widely in their search for potential victims. This shows itself in two ways: either an attacker can use public or private transport to travel a longer distance to commit an individual crime, then return home to strike out again in a different direction, in a similar way to a marauder, or he can travel to a different location and use that as a secondary base to commit a series of crimes in that area.

In practice, the choices open to a commuter criminal depend on the area in which they operate and the types of victims they choose. The targets of the so-called Yorkshire Ripper, Peter Sutcliffe, were predominantly prostitutes, which restricted his searches to the red-light districts of the cities within his reach, Leeds, Manchester, and Bradford in the United Kingdom. This commuter-killer behavior was

Peter Sutcliffe, commonly known as the Yorkshire Ripper, was a classic commuter killer with victims in all major cities within his reach.

difficult to analyze, since the pattern revealed by the locations of his crimes was distorted by the open moorland of the Pennines, and the investigation was beset by a series of problems that delayed his final arrest. Nonetheless, when his travel patterns were profiled, it seemed his most likely base was to be found close to Bradford—his house was located north of the city center.

WHEN:	**1969**
WHERE:	**USA**
VICTIMS:	**Multiple**
CULPRIT:	**Ted Bundy**

The body of Theodore "Ted" Bundy is seen here being taken to the Alachua County Medical Examiner's office following his execution in 1989.

CASE STUDY 26: INTERSTATE COMMUTER TED BUNDY

Commuter killers operating in the relatively dense conditions of a crowded island like Britain tend to offer less of a challenge to investigators than those looking for victims and eluding their pursuers across mainland Europe or the huge breadth of North America.

Perhaps the most notorious commuter killer of all time was Ted Bundy, who was, from childhood, accustomed to being uprooted and shifted across the country. When his mother remarried after splitting up with his father, they moved from Vermont in New England right across the United States to Washington state, effectively from the far northeastern corner of the United States to its northwestern extremity. This became his first area of operations, from his home in Tacoma, traveling from one casual job to another up and down the West Coast, and beginning a criminal career by breaking into homes to find extra income.

Bundy killed in his childhood home of Tacoma, Washington, as well as in nine other states, which made him extremely difficult to classify and catch.

HIDING BEHIND STATE LINES

What made Bundy unusual, even among commuter killers, was that he was able to use the geography of interstate boundaries to help him escape pursuit when one area became too much of a threat to him. His first known victim was murdered in 1969 in California. He continued killing, with victims afterward ascribed to him in Oregon and back to his childhood background in Washington, before he headed eastward into Colorado and Utah. All of these areas were ideal for his purposes, since after he had found and killed his victims he left their bodies in wilderness areas. By the time they were found, little remained in the way of solid evidence. This imposed a long delay before the forces of law and order even realized that apparently random killings were actually the work of a single serial criminal, highly organized in the way he planned and carried out his terrible crimes.

KILLING TO A PATTERN

FBI profilers were struck by two features of the killer. He clearly had the intellect to plan his crimes so as to reduce the chances of being caught to as near zero as possible. Apart from traveling between states to conceal his traces, he was confident enough to reassure potential victims of his good intentions and absence of threat until he had them within his power. The other remarkable point was the victimology. No matter where he found them, over distances of thousands of miles as his travels took him through 10 different states, ending up in Florida in the far southeast, his victims conformed extremely closely to one physical type. They were all young girls from middle-class backgrounds, they tended to be petite and slim and attractive, with long dark hair often parted in the middle. His confidence enabled him to be selective enough to pick the potential victims who matched his specification most closely.

In the end, it was two other personal defects that let him down. His overweening confidence, fed by the police's apparent inability to catch him, led to him taking increasing risks, including driving while drunk, conduct certain to cause a confrontation before long. Also, the growing anger and stress that spurred him to kill his young victims was taking over his personality, replacing the careful and controlled planner with someone much more impulsive.

The law finally caught up with Bundy in Salt Lake City in November 1974, when he told 18-year-old Carol DaRonch he was a plain-clothes policeman and offered her a lift. Once inside, he tried to handcuff her and beat her with a crowbar, but she managed to free herself and called the police. Bundy disappeared before they showed up, but he failed to move on far enough to be safe. In August 1975, in the same area, while driving without lights after dark, police pulled him over and found the handcuffs and a crowbar in the vehicle. Carol DaRonch identified him, he was found guilty of attempted abduction and sentenced to 15 years in jail.

Bundy evaded justice by escaping twice: first from jail and then, following his recapture, he disappeared a second time while en route to face additional murder charges in Colorado. This time he left his pursuers behind by moving to Florida, an area well outside the stretches of the country where he felt familiar. When he attacked four students in Tallahassee, killing two and severely injuring the others, his rigid control of events was unraveling. This time he moved, not to a different state, but less than 200 miles west to Pensacola. There he snatched his final victim, 12-year-old Kimberley Diane Leach, outside her school in broad daylight, cut her throat, and left her body in an empty pigsty nearby. The commuter killer had nowhere left to go. In desperation he stole a car and set out for Texas. It was evidence of his deteriorating control that police found him a week later sitting at the wheel completely drunk.

The old arrogance and confidence that formed part of the FBI profile drawn up when he was an unknown killer made one final appearance, when on trial for his life. His knowledge of the law, and confidence in his abilities, persuaded him he could conduct his own defense. He was wrong. In the face of a wealth of evidence, from bite marks on the bodies of some of his victims to service-station receipts proving his presence in a particular area on the days of the murders, his eloquence was powerless. He was sentenced to death for between 40 and 50 murders, and executed on January 24, 1989.

A forensic odontologist testified that the bite marks found on one of the victims did, in fact, match the teeth of Ted Bundy.

Ted Bundy, seen here in court, was eventually sentenced to death for the murder of over 40 women.

Bundy acts out in a Florida courtroom after the judge has left the room.

VICTIM

Twelve-year-old Kimberley Leach is widely considered to be the final victim of Ted Bundy.

A fraternity at Florida State University celebrates the execution of Ten Bundy. The mass murderer had attacked five women and killed two Chi Omega co-eds on the campus in 1978.

WATCH TED FRY

SEE TED DIE!

CASE

WHEN:	**1990**
WHERE:	**Europe and USA**
VICTIMS:	**Multiple**
CULPRIT:	**Jack Unterweger**

CASE STUDY 27: INTERCONTINENTAL COMMUTER KILLER

Only one commuter killer seems to have operated on a wider scale than Ted Bundy, and his career began the year following Bundy's execution. Finding his first victims in Europe, he crossed international boundaries rather than interstate lines to avoid detection and finally carried out killings in a different hemisphere. He was an Austrian citizen named Jack Unterweger, and his first victim was Blanka Bockova, who went out drinking with friends in Prague on the evening of September 14, 1990. When her companions decided it was time to go home soon before midnight, they saw her talking to a well-groomed man aged about 40, and they left her to find her own way home.

Her body was found the next morning on the banks of the River Vltava. She was naked and had been posed to suggest a sex attack, but there were no physical traces of her killer. She had been stabbed, strangled with her own stockings, and beaten, and her wounds showed she had resisted as far as she could. Her clothes were found in the river, and she was partly covered in grass, leaves and soil. Her gold ring had not been taken.

MORE VICTIMS

The first murder was followed by a series of similar killings over a wide range of central Europe. A prostitute named Brunhilde Masser went missing from Graz in southeastern Austria on October 26, 1990, followed by the disappearance of another, Heidemarie Hammerer from Bregenz, on the country's extreme western tip on the edge of Lake Constance, on December 5. This last victim was discovered on December 31 by hikers. She

The first victim of the international killer was discovered in Prague in 1990.

A POSSIBLE SUSPECT

All the signs pointed to a serial killer based in Austria. One of the sharpest critics of the police's inability to catch the criminal was a celebrated journalist who had covered the case by interviewing prostitutes and detectives about the progress of the efforts to identify the killer. Then a retired police detective named August Schenner pointed out that the writer had actually himself served time in prison for strangling 18-year-old Margaret Schaefer in 1974 with her own bra and leaving her body in the woods. His name was Johann Unterweger, known to his readers as "Jack," and he had been given a life sentence in 1976.

Unterweger had been freed because of the apparent change of character he had undergone in prison. Illiterate when arrested after an abusive childhood, he had turned to writing—everything from plays and short stories to poetry and an autobiography—which had made him famous and persuaded people that he no longer presented a threat. The prison psychologist disagreed, convinced he suffered from a toxic combination of aggression and perversion, which would mean he would always

too had been strangled with her stockings, and her jewelry left on her body. It appeared she had been stripped and then redressed, though no signs of a specifically sexual attack were found. Her body was also partly covered with leaves, but there was nothing definite to link it to the Prague killing three months earlier.

Five days into the new year, Brunhilde Masser's body was found in the bed of a stream flowing through woodland to the north of Graz. Her jewelry had not been taken, she had probably been strangled, and her body had been stripped and partly covered with leaves. The pattern, if there was one, linking the killings was far from clear. Then another Graz prostitute, Elfriede Schrempf, disappeared on March 7 the following year, and her body was not found for another seven months, once again in a forested area near the city. Public unease was growing when four more prostitutes disappeared from Vienna in less than a month. Two of the bodies were discovered later, once again left in woodland and strangled with pieces of their own clothing, while their jewelry had not been taken.

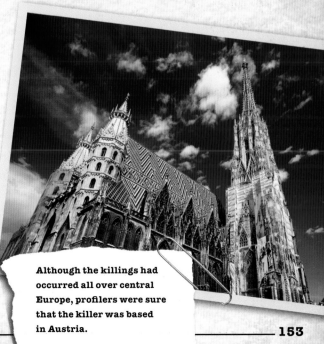

Although the killings had occurred all over central Europe, profilers were sure that the killer was based in Austria.

The Austrian investigators used forensic evidence to link Unterweger directly to one of the murders.

credit records to assemble details of his movements and timings, and found he had been in the vicinity of each of the killings at the time they were carried out. A witness testified that Unterweger was the man whom Heidemarie Hammerer had been seen with on the night that she had disappeared. The correspondence between the times and dates of the murders and Unterweger's presence in the vicinity was too close to be coincidental, and it was noticeable that when he was in California for five weeks, no further killings occurred.

Detective Ernst Geiger of the Austrian police then had the inspiration that would help nail the killer. He called his counterparts in Los Angeles to see if any unexplained killings of prostitutes had occurred while Unterweger had been in the city. Not only had there been three, but they had involved women who had vanished when close to hotels where Unterweger had been staying. Then the LA police had begun their own investigation, to find that while the Austrian had been in town, he had approached them as a European crime reporter and asked to be able to ride with police patrols covering the red-light districts. Though he wrote about what he had seen, police were now convinced he had been cool enough to persuade them to show him exactly where he could find his victims.

By now, Unterweger was back in Austria, where detectives had forensic evidence linking him with fibers found on one of the victims. They secured a search warrant and went to his apartment, only to find that he and his

be dangerous. Growing pressure from an adoring reading public and sympathetic media coverage eventually meant his opinion was overruled, and Jack Unterweger was released from prison on May 23, 1990, just under four months before the new killings began.

THE SUSPECT VANISHES

Detectives placed Unterweger under subtle surveillance, but before they could find anything suspicious, he made the ultimate marauder's move, shifting his area of operations far beyond their reach. With a commission to write about crime overseas for Austrian journals, he flew to Los Angeles just three days after Austrian police began checking on him. Without their principal suspect, all they could do was check

During his five-week stay in California, Unterweger killed three women by strangling them with material take from their bras.

girlfriend had left on vacation. Unfortunately, the newspapers revealed that his arrest was expected, and he had heard the news while vacationing in Switzerland. Rather than return to Austria, the couple fled to Paris and back across the Atlantic to Miami, where US marshals arrested him. They had been collecting evidence from his stay in California to extradite him, but the Austrian police pointed out that under Austrian law he could be charged there with all the killings wherever they had been carried out, so he was returned to his homeland to face justice. Though he continued to protest his innocence with a series of alibis, his conviction owed much to the profile drawn up by Gregg McCrary at the invitation of the Austrian authorities, since they had no profiling experience of their own at the time.

LINKING VICTIMS AND KILLER

McCrary studied the details of the murders in the order in which they were carried out, beginning with the killing of Margaret Schaefer, which had originally sent him to jail. It was clear that the strangling of the three LA victims had been carried out by removing and tearing apart their bras and then tying them in an unusual and complex knot. All three were identical, and the same as used on the first victim in Europe. Even when stockings had been used, the knot was similar enough to rule out any other killer being involved. This kind of linkage evidence was crucial, as often is the case with commuter killers, to establish guilt where forensic evidence may be patchy. In particular the FBI had been able to feed details of these killings into the VICAP database to

search for any matches elsewhere—significantly, none had been found.

The verdict given at his trial was guilty of all nine murders, except the two where decomposition made analysis uncertain. This time the life sentence meant no chance of early release, and McCrary warned that his profile suggested the shock to such a narcissistic personality might trigger a suicide attempt. Later that very day, Jack Unterweger hanged in his cell, having tied the same knot used on his victims in the drawstring of his prison overalls.

Unterweger killed himself on the day of his sentencing, an act that FBI profiler Gregg McCrary had warned he was capable of.

POWER, ANGER, AND RETALIATION

Serial rapists rank second only to serial killers as a target for criminal profilers, since both crimes involve extreme violence and are driven by the most uncontrollable psychological impulses. In fact, at the highest levels of violence the boundaries can vanish, and serial rapists switch to killing their victims as a matter of course. This imposes huge pressure to ensure such dangerous criminals are identified, tracked down, arrested, and brought to justice. Fortunately, they usually provide clear signals of their motivation and objectives. This enables profilers to understand the kind of people they are, why they commit their crimes and the background details that can help reveal who they are.

Profilers analyzing the crimes of serial rapists often rely on a classification system first drawn up by criminal psychologist Richard Walter, who carried out a series of detailed interviews similar to those undertaken by FBI agents John Douglas and Robert Ressler (see Chapter 2). In Walter's case, while working as a psychologist in Michigan's prison regime, he spoke to more than 2,000 murderers, serial killers, and sex offenders on how and why they committed their crimes. In the course of this marathon study, he began to see a pattern emerging, which enabled him to classify both killers and rapists in four clear subtypes, each one reflecting different reasons for their behavior. Applying these categories to rapists, and in ascending order of violence, the four classes are power-reassurance, power-assertive, anger-retaliatory, and anger-excitation, or sadism.

While forensic evidence, being collected here, remains vital to any rape or murder investigation, psychological classifications can reveal important details about the criminal.

POWER-REASSURANCE FANTASIES

The power-reassurance rapist is searching for a confirmation of his own masculinity, so he views the violence involved in the rape as a regrettable necessity to enable him to reach his objective. In other respects he will try to represent his relationship with the victim as a normal consensual "courtship." This controls his routine to a large extent, which helps profilers identify him from the evidence given by his victim. For example, he tends to find victims in his local area, he will normally attack between midnight and around 5 a.m, he will tend not to use threats and will rely on the minimum of violence to provide him with what he wants. The sexual assault itself will not tend to last long: simply carrying out the act will normally provide him with the reassurance he looks for.

If he has personal transport he may widen the area over which he looks for victims, but even here he will tend to seek familiarity as part of the reassurance process. He also looks for the familiar in selecting his victims. For him to portray his attacks as part of a consensual relationship, he usually targets women of around his own age, and from his own ethnic group, unless he cannot find suitable victims. Also, because the location is essential to his fantasy, he will normally break into the victim's home rather than attack her in the open. He may stalk his victim beforehand to find out all he can about her routine, the times she will be on her own, the layout of her house or apartment and potential routes in and out.

In general, power-reassurance rapists carry out attacks more frequently than other types of rapists. They behave as they do because inadequacies in appearance, personality, or social skills make it impossible—or at least extremely unlikely—that they can form close relationships with other people in the ordinary way. Their only chance to make up for their low self-esteem is through controlling another person and making them do what they want them to, providing the reassurance they are otherwise powerless to achieve. An essential part of this fantasy of a willing partner is the limitation of violence to the minimum needed. Rather than tearing off his victim's clothes, the power-reassurance attacker is more likely to ask his victim to undress herself. He often apologizes for any pain he may have inflicted, and may well take intimate souvenirs of his victim, such as jewelry or underwear, and sometimes even try to contact her again for an ordinary date.

Reassurance for Whom?

In his background, the power-reassurance rapist is probably a loner, possibly living with his parents well into adulthood. He probably

A power-reassurance rapist may stalk his victims beforehand, so that he can plan his attack.

Because women are hesitant to report power-reassurance rapes, DNA samples are rarely taken, making the serial rapist difficult to catch.

has a quiet, passive personality, a low level of education, and a poorly paid, unskilled manual job. He probably takes little care over his appearance, and may already be on police records for low-level sexual offenses such as voyeurism or indecent exposure. He may have a local reputation as a stalker, or someone who peeps into lighted windows after dark, or even enters unlocked homes and leaves again without stealing anything. But all the indications are that this extreme passivity may not persist beyond an unusually determined victim refusing to give him what he wants. This resistance may push him over his self-imposed boundary, to search for a weapon to escalate the threat level needed to ensure his victim's compliance.

FBI profiler Roy Hazelwood dealt with one power-reassurance rape where the attacker carried out the assault in just five minutes, but then lay with the victim for an hour, explaining how he managed to enter the house, and how she should go about getting counseling to help her deal with the trauma of what he had done. When he left, she checked the kitchen and found her handbag had been emptied and the contents spilled over the work surface. She called the police, but the next morning there was an envelope full of cash in her mailbox, with a letter promising she would never hear from her attacker again, and wishing her all the best for the future.

One of the strangest outcomes of the power-reassurance rapist's behavior is that very often his attacks are not reported to police, since they differ so much from what victims have been led to believe rape involves—a combination of extreme terror and violence. Since they find this behavior difficult to understand, they often feel that they will not be believed by professionals who are accustomed to handling more violent rapes. Many power-reassurance rapists have proved difficult to catch because they tend to move to other areas on a regular basis to keep ahead of any police attempts to track them down. Their fantasy means they don't hide their faces, so they realize that staying too long in one area may risk a victim pointing them out to others. Also, DNA samples are not taken in many cases, making it difficult to match crimes and see which ones have been carried out by the same perpetrator.

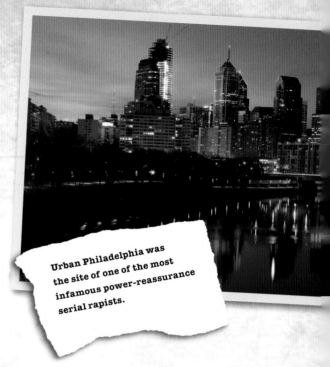

Urban Philadelphia was the site of one of the most infamous power-reassurance serial rapists.

WHEN:	1997
WHERE:	Philadelphia, USA
VICTIMS:	Multiple
CULPRIT:	Troy Graves

CASE STUDY 28: THE CENTER CITY RAPIST

Power-reassurance rapists are relatively difficult to track down, due to the care they take to select their victims and because they move on at regular intervals, therefore case studies are rare. One of the most notorious of this type of attacker is the Center City rapist, who began attacking women in the summer of 1997 in central Philadelphia.

SERIES OF ATTACKS

His first known attack was on June 20 on South 21st Street, where he entered the property through a narrow air-conditioner opening, an explanation that police rejected when the victim, a 28-year-old artist, told them about it.

On July 11 the rapist attacked his second victim, a 28-year-old office worker, in her apartment on Pine Street, close to the site of the previous rape. This time the level of violence escalated to the point where he strangled the victim to unconsciousness before raping her. The investigation was complicated by the refusal of the police to consider the attack might have been carried out by the same criminal as the earlier case. On August 6, the rapist managed to enter another Pine Street apartment, this time through a gap in antiburglar bars just 7 inches wide, to attack a 21-year-old student. Finally he broke into another Pine Street property a week later, where the occupant had fallen asleep in front of the television, only to be raped by the intruder.

Following an apparent gap of nine months, when no other rapes were reported, the attacker struck again on May 7, 1998, when he broke into the 23rd Street apartment of 23-year-old Shannon Schrieber from a second-floor balcony. This time the victim fought back, and the

The attacker would break into women's homes in the Center City area and rape them.

forced the female occupant to perform a sex act. A similar crime was committed on July 26 on Prospect Road, and on August 5 he attacked a woman on University Drive after breaking into her property. Finally, on August 23, he forced a woman to perform a sex act, but she managed to scare him away as he delivered a savage attack on her roommate.

This was the point at which DNA evidence finally caught up with the rapist. When belated comparisons were carried out between samples obtained from all the rape scenes, they proved the Philadelphia rapist and killer also carried out the Fort Collins attacks. Police checked their records, and found one person had moved from Philadelphia to Fort Collins in the gap between the two series of attacks. In the fall of 1999 he had joined the US Air Force, and after basic training was posted to a missile unit in Wyoming. He had married in 2001 and the couple moved to a new home in Fort Collins, close to the sites of the rapes that began soon after their arrival.

He was 29-year-old Troy Graves, and his background matched most of the classic profile for this type of rapist. At the age of 13, his parents had divorced and he had continued to live with his mother and elder brother. After dropping out of high school three years later, he had held a series of low-paid jobs, first in West Philadelphia and then in Center City. His mother referred to him as "painfully shy," "very quiet," and tending to be "a loner." He was arrested on April 23, 2002, for the Fort Collins rapes. On May 17 he pleaded guilty to a robbery in Fort Collins, and on May 30 he entered a plea of guilty for the Philadelphia crimes to avoid a possible death sentence. Since he was originally arrested in Colorado, he was sentenced to life imprisonment at Sterling prison in that state, and the adverse publicity given to early police reactions has ensured that power-reassurance rapes are taken much more seriously, with DNA samples taken as a matter of routine.

violence that is always close to the surface of this type of rapist resulted in him strangling her to death. He carried out one more attack in the city, on August 28, 1999, when he attacked an 18-year-old student on Naudain Street. He had unscrewed a barred security gate to enter the property.

THE SUSPECT IDENTIFIED

Though there was speculation that the unknown suspect might have been implicated in other serial rapes in different parts of the country, without regular DNA comparisons this was impossible to prove. But another series of attacks, in Fort Collins, Colorado, seemed to show distinct similarities with those in Philadelphia. On May 10, 2001, a woman was attacked on Raintree Drive, and another on the same road on June 13. On June 24, the attacker broke into a property on Battlecreek Drive and

POWER-ASSERTIVE RAPISTS

The power-assertive rapist has a much more demanding agenda altogether. He has no need of reassurance over his own masculinity, because he is much more confident, and assumes he can demand whatever he wants from his victim. He sets out to dominate women, and has a much more extroverted attitude. He is probably athletic, with a powerful ego. If he drives, it will probably be a macho-image sports car, and he will be a snappy dresser. He will probably already have a wife or a long-term partner, but these will merely be the latest in a string of relationships in which he has been the dominant half of the couple.

He will usually have worked in traditionally male roles, such as construction, the police, or the armed forces. He will hunt for victims in bars or nightclubs, especially on singles nights, when his approach is less likely to put potential victims on their guard. He is probably strong enough to impose massive physical force on his victims, and may well rape more than once during a single attack. He will be indifferent to the pain he inflicts, but will be less likely to look for souvenirs from the victim. In general, power-assertive rapists carry out attacks less often than power-reassurance attackers, but his usual frequency of once every four weeks or so may increase after an argument or dispute with his partner.

ANGER-RETALIATION RAPISTS

Next in the spectrum of violence is the anger-retaliation rapist. He is dominated by a general anger against all women in payback for some trauma in his own life. This might be abandonment by a mother, or being sent to live with relatives or strangers when young. Some of these attackers believe they are repaying abuse or neglect they suffered in early life, although in other cases the injury they suffered may exist only in their own imagination, or may be exaggerated to feed their own self-esteem. In terms of appearance, physique, and job, there will be similarities to the power-assertive rapist, but this criminal is more likely to attack on impulse, perhaps after being reprimanded, criticized or otherwise crossed by a woman, either at home or at work. For this reason, his attacks are unpredictable, and he is likely to overwhelm his victim by making her terrified and less likely to resist.

He will almost certainly force his victim into the most demeaning sex positions and routines he can think of to feed his anger. In addition, while he may choose victims close to his own age and of the same ethnic group as himself, there may be deliberate attempts to find a target close in age or appearance to the woman responsible for what he sees as the original wrong he suffered. If this person were his mother, for example, he would then choose someone older than himself to attack. As his anger and violence grows, he may find he is physically unable to complete the rapes. At this point he may switch from actual sexual attacks to symbolic ones, turning from rapist to killer and using stabbing and mutilation to assuage his fury.

The killer in Case Study 29 (opposite) entered the first victim's property by standing on a stolen rocking chair and climbing through a window.

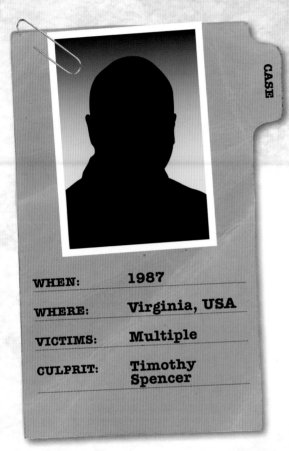

CASE

WHEN: 1987

WHERE: Virginia, USA

VICTIMS: Multiple

CULPRIT: Timothy Spencer

CASE STUDY 29: TIMOTHY SPENCER AND DAVID VASQUEZ

Timothy Spencer was an anger-retaliatory rapist who had switched to killing his victims in the vicinity of his home on the south side of Richmond, Virginia. His first victim was discovered early on the morning of September 19, 1987. Her car had been parked several hundred yards away from her house and left with its engine running. Police investigated and traced the car to 35-year-old Debbie Dudley Davis, but when they checked her property they found her body lying face downward across a bed. Not only had she been violently raped with severe internal bruising, but she had been battered across the face and strangled by means of a sock twisted around her neck and tightened with a length of vacuum cleaner pipe. The force exerted had been enough to cut deeply into the larynx and the neck muscles. Her killer had entered her property by standing on a rocking chair he had stolen the day before, to reach a window 8 feet above ground level.

MORE VIOLENT ATTACKS

His second victim, neurosurgeon Dr. Susan Elizabeth Hellems, was found two weeks later when her husband returned home on Saturday morning at about 1:30 a.m. Like the first victim,

Debbie Dudley, the first victim, had been strangled to death in her home.

she had been subjected to a violent rape with internal bruising, but had also had her nose broken and one leg damaged, which suggested her killer had stamped on her during the attack. Here, too, he had managed to scale a high wall and cross a porch roof to enter the house through his victim's bedroom window.

Both of these killings had been carried out when the victims had been alone. But the third victim, 15-year-old Diane Cho, was raped and killed while her parents slept in their own bedroom on the night of Saturday, November 21. On the Sunday morning they assumed she was still in bed asleep when they left for work, and only found her body when they returned home in the afternoon. The killer had removed the screen protecting her bedroom window to enter her room, where he had beaten her about the head, strangled her, and raped her. Finally, on December 1, the body of 44-year-old Susan Tucker was found, again lying face down on a bed. The killer had entered through a basement window, stripped her, bound her hands behind her back, then raped and strangled her.

TYPECASTING THE VICTIMS

Profilers who studied the crime scenes found the characteristic signs of an anger-retaliatory

rapist and killer. In particular, all four adult victims fitted his blueprint for the woman who had originally triggered his fury, in that they were all solidly built and aged between 32 and 44. The one exception, Diane Cho, was similarly built, which made her look older than her real age. In this case, the killer had not attacked on impulse, but clearly taken time and effort to work out how to gain entry to their homes. He had also used his considerable physical strength and agility to batter them into submission and then used ropes and ligatures to keep them under his control.

Ironically, 25-year-old Spencer had been living under parole supervision for an earlier series of burglaries, which explains why he was able to break into houses where entry would have been difficult or impossible for people without that experience. DNA evidence from all his victims firmly proved he was the rapist and killer and he was sentenced to death.

FINDING THE WRONG MAN

Spencer's conviction led to the rectification of a miscarriage of justice involving another suspect who had been convicted of an earlier killing, which bore all the marks of Spencer's later crimes. A woman living in the same area as

The killer gained access to his third victim, a teenager asleep in her bedroom, by removing a screen across her window and climbing in.

Spencer operated around his home in Richmond, Virginia.

After his sentence, Spencer fell under suspicion for the rape and murder of another woman in the area, which had been attributed to David Vasquez. Vasquez was eventually released from prison and pardoned.

Spencer's victims had been found dead in her apartment on January 24, 1984. She had been raped and strangled, and it was clear her attacker had entered through a basement window.

Suspicion fell on a local man with learning difficulties, David Vasquez, who had been reported as being in the vicinity at the time by two different witnesses. When questioned by police, he had been unable to provide an alibi for the time of the attack and had eventually confessed to the rape and murder. He was sentenced to 35 years in jail in 1985. FBI profilers maintained that the crime for which Vasquez had been imprisoned had almost certainly been committed by Spencer, and could definitely not have been carried out by someone who was mentally handicapped. However, Spencer was not charged with this killing since he had already been sentenced to death for the other murders, a sentence that was carried out on April 27, 1994. Three months earlier, David Vasquez had been given a full pardon and released from prison.

CASE STUDY 30: THE MONSTER OF FLORENCE: PIETRO PACCIANI

CASE

WHEN:	**1968**
WHERE:	**Florence, Italy**
VICTIMS:	**Multiple**
CULPRITS:	**Mario Vanni, Giancarlo Lotti, possibly more**

In August 1968 a serial killer struck in the countryside around Florence, in Italy. The first victims were a man and his mistress who had parked their car in a secluded spot to make love. They had been interrupted by their killer, who had shot them both to death. Initially suspicion fell on the woman's husband, who admitted to the crime but then retracted his confession. Police did not believe him, and he was eventually found guilty of the two murders and sentenced to 14 years in jail on the grounds of mental impairment. A gap of six years was broken by another killing, which was similar in method and target, but even more violent. On September 14, 1974, another couple were shot in secluded surroundings, but this time the woman had been stabbed in a frenzied attack that inflicted no less than 96 knife wounds. She had been left lying naked in the open with her legs spread apart and a pine branch left inside her vagina. More significantly, the bullets were positively matched with those involved in the first killing, which meant the husband of the first female victim could not have done it. But who had?

Florence was the scene of killings that were undoubtedly the work of an angry, yet disorganized, serial killer.

Barbara Locci and Antonio Lo Bianco were murdered in their car near Chianti, Italy.

VICTIM

Antonio Lo Bianco, pictured here, was one of the so-called "Monster of Florence's" first victims.

POSSIBLE DISTURBANCE

A third killing occurred on June 6, 1981, once again involving a couple. This time both had been shot inside the car, and mutilated after death. The man had been slashed twice across the throat and once in the chest, and his partner's body was found at the bottom of a bank some 20 yards away with her clothes slashed and her vagina removed. Four months later another couple were found in almost identical circumstances: the man was shot and stabbed and the woman had been shot before her vagina was removed. In this case, the post-mortem examination showed both victims had been alive when the stabbing began, and the mutilation of the female victim seemed to have been done in a much more rushed manner, suggesting the killer had been disturbed.

The Killer Reacts

Things went even more badly wrong at the scene of the next killing, where the male victim, one Paolo Mainardi, was still alive after the woman had been killed. He was able to start the car and reverse away from the killer, who ran after him to try to complete his task. The car became jammed in a ditch and the killer was able to shoot the young man several more times before escaping without carrying out the usual mutilations. Paolo survived until the next morning before dying from his injuries, but police enlisted the aid of the media to spread the knowledge that he had survived long enough to speak to detectives.

This undoubtedly shook the killer, as anonymous phone calls were made to the hospital where Paolo Mainardi's body had been left, but no positive leads resulted. Instead, another couple was found dead on September 9, 1983, this time two young German male tourists sharing a camper van. It is possible the killer mistook one of them for a female, since he had long blond hair, and certainly no mutilations were carried out, suggesting his anger was exclusively reserved for women. On July 29, 1984, another couple was murdered in the Florentine countryside. Both were shot, but this time the woman's vagina was removed together with her left breast, and she had been stabbed 100 times. The final killing in the series was discovered on September 8, 1985, when a French couple was found dead in their tent, having been shot at very close range. The woman had her vagina and left breast removed. As with all the previous murders, the same gun and the same box of ammunition had been used.

TRIAL—AND DEATH

Over the course of the following eight years police interviewed more than 100,000 people in relation to the killings. Their prime suspect was 68-year-old Pietro Pacciani, a semiliterate farmer interested in hunting and taxidermy. He had been found guilty in 1951 for killing a traveling salesman he had caught sleeping with his fiancée, certainly a possible trigger for a series of anger-retaliation killings of women sexually involved with men. Not only did he stab his victim 19 times, but evidence showed he had stamped on her corpse to relieve his anger. After serving 13 years for the crime, he was freed and settled down and married, only to be jailed for four years in 1987 for beating his wife and molesting their two young daughters.

Pacciani was put on trial for the killings in 1994, but there was little real evidence apart from his close resemblance to the profile of an anger-retaliation killer. He was found guilty and given life imprisonment, but in February 1996 was freed on appeal. The story did not end there though. He was implicated in an occult group with several individuals who were also thought to have taken part in the murders. On December 12, 1996, the Italian Supreme Court ordered

Criminal investigators believe that multiple suspects could have been at work in the anger-retaliation killings.

Pacciani to be retried for the murders in the light of new evidence, but before he could face the accusations he was found dead on February 23, 1998, in suspicious circumstances. His associates, Mario Vanni and Giancarlo Lotti, have since been charged with involvement in five of the killings, and found guilty.

In August 2001, Italian police suddenly reopened the case, saying that they now believed a larger group of up to a dozen members of a wealthy religious sect, whose beliefs demanded ritual killings and dismembering of courting couples, was involved. Later that year the homes of two psychologists were raided, not because of potential involvement in the killings, but because they were alleged to have withheld critical information during the investigation, but no further information has yet been released.

ANGER-EXCITATION PLEASURE

The distinction between anger-retaliation rapes and murders and those involving anger-

VICTIMS

Claudio Stefanacci, Pia Rontini, Steffani Pettini, and Pasquale Gentilcore were all killed in a similar manner.

excitation attackers may seem a difficult one to draw, since much of the violence, including frenzied stabbing and mutilation, seems horrifically similar. But the fourth category of attacker meets one critical psychological requirement. Where an anger-retaliation criminal carries out his lethal violence to pay back women in general or, through them, one woman in particular whom he believes harmed or disrespected him in the past, the anger-excitation attacker has a simpler agenda. He is the true sadist, who is exhilarated by the suffering he inflicts on his victims. In other words, he is not paying off a score. He is not inflicting terror, pain, and suffering as part of a vendetta, but simply because he enjoys it, and this makes him perhaps the most dangerous of all criminals as a result.

After two male German tourists were murdered without mutilation it became clear to investigator Michele Giuttari (left) that the anger-retaliation serial killer was focusing his fury at women.

CASE

WHEN: 1979

WHERE: New York, USA

VICTIMS: Francine Elveson

CULPRIT: Carmine Calabro

CASE STUDY 31: FRANCINE ELVESON

Francine Elveson, a 26-year-old teacher of handicapped children, lived in the Bronx area of New York City, where her body was found on the roof of her apartment block on October 12, 1979. She had been strangled to death, but only after a terrible beating that broke her facial bones. Her wrists and ankles had been tied with her belt and stockings, and she had been left face up with her legs spread-eagled and an umbrella forced into her vagina. There were bite marks round her knees and on the inside of her thighs, and she had been stabbed numerous times with a penknife. In addition, the person who killed her had written messages on her skin challenging police to track him down, and defecated next to her body, covering it with items of her clothing.

THE PROFILE

FBI agent John Douglas produced a profile of the killer from the available evidence. He suggested this kind of killing was a crime of opportunity, which indicated the criminal was local and suffered from mental illness. The way in which his victim had been attacked with a combination of frenzied biting and brutal physical blows showed he was a disorganized killer who had probably developed his terrible anger-excitation fantasies over several years. He would also live near his victim, would be aged between 25 and 35, and probably be white, unemployed, and generally disheveled.

Police inquiries in the neighborhood soon turned up a suspect. Carmine Calabro was white, unemployed and aged 32, with a history of mental illness. In addition, while he did not live in the same apartment block as his victim, his father did. The suspect was asked to give a bite-mark impression, which he agreed to, and when this was matched to the marks left on his victim, the evidence helped convict him of her killing and earn him a life sentence. He learned too late that his impulses to inflict every kind of pain on the woman he killed had cost him his freedom. Significantly, before he could mount an appeal, which later proved to be unsuccessful, he had all his teeth extracted to prevent any further impressions being taken.

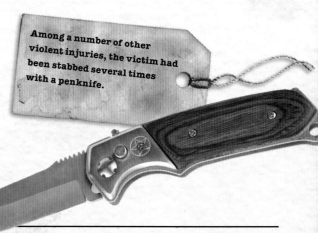

Among a number of other violent injuries, the victim had been stabbed several times with a penknife.

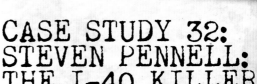

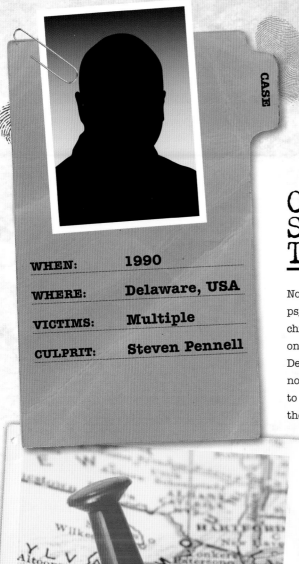

WHEN: 1990

WHERE: Delaware, USA

VICTIMS: Multiple

CULPRIT: Steven Pennell

Steven Brian Pennell, a ruthless and cunning serial killer, operated out of the state of Delaware.

CASE STUDY 32: STEVEN PENNELL: THE I-40 KILLER

Not all serial killers owe their terrible psychology to a tortured and oppressive childhood. Steven Brian Pennell became the only serial murderer in the small state of Delaware, yet not only seemed to enjoy a normal enough childhood, but tried very hard to join the state police force. However, even though he had taken courses in criminology at the University of Delaware, his applications were unsuccessful, and he finally turned to earning a living as an electrician, marrying, and settling down in New Castle.

A CHALLENGE TO HIS PURSUERS

If his childhood was normal enough, his marriage was not. He and his wife had two children, but his constant drive to control every aspect of his wife's existence created such tension that their son and daughter were sent to live with relatives. With them out of the way, and his wife browbeaten, he was able to leave home in his van to trawl the interstate highways I-40 and I-13 looking for prostitutes to provide his victims. Once he found a woman willing to join him in his vehicle, he would drive her to a suitably secluded site where he could rape and torture her as

Pennell carried a kit with various torture devices used during his attacks.

much as he wanted. However, he made life difficult for investigators and profilers by using his criminological knowledge to vary his routine as much as possible from crime to crime.

He might bind one victim hand and foot to remain in control while he raped and beat her with a whip he carried in his rape kit. In other cases he would beat his victim over her head with a hammer to render her unconscious. Sometimes he would take a pair of pliers from his kit to tear away a woman's nipples. In all cases, the end would be the same. Death by strangulation, followed by still more beating, before the lifeless corpses would be thrown out of his van to lie in full view alongside the highways that acted as his hunting grounds.

His first victim was Shirley Ellis on November 29, 1987. He killed three more women in the succeeding months, and the body of a fifth suspected victim was never found. Because the women had last been seen along the highways, and their bodies left a distance away from those last sightings, the killer must have been using a vehicle. The FBI profile had identified him as an anger-excitation rapist and killer, so that he was almost certainly in a reasonably stable relationship but abusing his wife. He would also be in a steady job, possibly one that provided the vehicle, and he would live in the northern Delaware area close to the roads from which his victims had vanished. Apart from this, the only hard evidence was a mass of blue fibers found on the body of one of the victims.

TRAPPED BY A POLICEWOMAN'S BRAVERY

In the end he was trapped by an extremely courageous female undercover police officer,

Renee C. Lano, who volunteered to pose as a prostitute and pretend to ply for hire along the I-40 highway. When approached she would open the door to the potential client's vehicle to negotiate terms, and grab a bunch of carpet fibers before seeming to change her mind, then slam the door and make her escape with a note of the suspect's vehicle registration number. In the end, it was Steven Pennell who pulled up in the hope of persuading her to join his toll of victims. By the time she had declined and run to safety, she had the vital fibers, which matched those found on the victim. Pennell was arrested and DNA matching showed he had raped at least two of his victims.

He was put on trial for these two murders and given a life sentence. However, in October 1991 charges were pending for two more killings when he announced he would not enter a plea. Although he still insisted he was innocent, he wanted to be executed to save his family further anguish. Nevertheless, his wife Kathy mounted a desperate attempt to save his life by declaring him mentally incompetent, but this was rejected by the Supreme Court. On March 14, 1992, the short and bloody career of the I-40 killer came to an end in a trailer parked in the grounds of Smyrna prison, where lethal injections were administered.

A female undercover police officer was able to connect Pennell with the murders after she matched fibers from his car to those found on one of the victims.

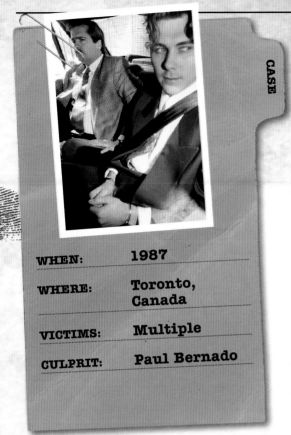

WHEN:	1987
WHERE:	Toronto, Canada
VICTIMS:	Multiple
CULPRIT:	Paul Bernado

CASE STUDY 33: THE SCARBOROUGH RAPIST

Sometimes a rapist or killer of a particular type may confuse profilers and others searching for him by progressing from one category to the next through an increasing level of violence. In the case of Paul Bernardo, he began his criminal career as a petty thief and receiver of stolen goods in the tough Toronto suburb of Scarborough, where he had grown up during the 1970s. He switched to sex assaults on May 4, 1987, when he seized a 21-year-old woman as she arrived home from a neighborhood bus stop at 1 a.m. He grabbed her from behind, pushed her to the ground and sexually assaulted her. Ten days later he repeated the routine with another victim.

SUSPECT NAMED, BUT MISSED

In October of that year he met a 17-year-old schoolgirl, Karla Homolka, who was eventually to become his willing accomplice. Because she let him make love to her, he showed none of the violence he meted out to those he attacked, even though these assaults were getting more and more violent. On December 16 he attacked a 15-year-old girl, subjected her to vaginal and anal rape and forced her to have oral sex with him as a way of further emphasizing her degradation. He then began banging her head against the ground in a battering that lasted a full hour.

During the course of the following year, he began to extend his control over his girlfriend by insisting on anal and oral sex, specifying how she should style her hair and what she should wear—including a dog collar during sex—while still attacking, raping, and beating strangers when the need arose to feed his increasingly sadistic appetites. FBI profilers were called in to produce a portrait of the Scarborough rapist, and they concluded the evidence showed the attacker was a young man in his 20s, probably living locally with his parents and showing progressively higher levels of violence that would almost certainly end in murder.

Paul Bernardo, pictured here, after being arrested and uncovered as the notorious Scarborough Rapist.

Bernardo's victims helped police produce an artist's impression of the criminal, and in May 1990 a woman who knew him reported to the police that he could be the person they were chasing. He was questioned by investigators and gave them DNA samples without hesitation. They were sent to the Toronto Forensic Sciences Laboratory where they languished for two years without result. In the meantime, Bernardo asked his girlfriend for a sinister Christmas present in the form of her teenage sister Tammy. She produced a strong animal anesthetic agent from the veterinary surgery where she now worked and between them they drugged the young girl in the basement of her parents' home on Christmas Eve. Bernardo then raped her and shot a video of her sister sexually assaulting her, after which they left her in a deep sleep, to choke on her own vomit, her death ascribed to an accident involving drink and drugs.

OUT OF CONTROL

Bernardo was now losing control as his sadism took over. He and Karla had moved into a new house together where he brought his next victim, 14-year-old Leslie Mahaffy. There they both sexually assaulted her before she was strangled with electrical cable and her body dismembered with a power saw, with the parts sealed in concrete. Soon afterward Bernardo and Homolka were married, but his sadistic killings continued, each one adding to the information available to profilers. On April 16, 1992, Kristen French, another 15-year-old, was taken back to their house for four days of concentrated physical and sexual abuse, ending only when she too was strangled. They then tried to divert suspicion: they dumped the body parts of Leslie Mahaffy in Lake Gibson, and washed the corpse of Kristen French and left it to be found in a ditch not far away, to suggest both had fallen victim to someone from that neighborhood.

EVENTUAL CAPTURE

On January 5, 1993, Karla left her husband after he beat her badly with a heavy flashlight, and on February 1 the forensic science lab finally announced his DNA matched the samples

Karla Homolka with her sister Lori and mother Dorothy. Homolka cut a deal with the defense and appeared as a Crown witness in the case against her husband.

Bernardo seen leaving the courthouse after seeking a court appointed lawyer for an appeal that would eventually fail.

Bernardo and Homolka disposed of Leslie Mahaffy's body in Lake Gibson, at some distance from their own home, in an attempt to keep the police from suspecting them.

from the Scarborough rapes. Tying him to the later killings was more difficult, but by questioning Karla carefully, they eventually persuaded her to admit he had killed the two most recent victims.

The final, most important piece of evidence was specified by the profilers: they were certain he would record material of him with some of his victims, and this would be hidden somewhere in their house. The searchers failed to find it after 10 weeks, but Bernardo told his attorney he wanted some tapes from the house and revealed exactly where they were hidden. The lawyer retrieved them, without telling the investigators. When he was replaced, the new attorney delivered the tapes to the police.

After a delay of 15 months, Bernardo was convicted of the murders and sentenced to life in prison, with no option for parole before 2020. Inquiries showed he had fitted the profile in nearly all respects. FBI profiler Gregg McCrary had predicted he would be in his late 20s, would work with an accomplice, would drive a sports car, and have a history of violence toward women stemming from some sexual problem in his past. When they spoke to a former girlfriend of Bernardo's, she revealed he could only produce an erection after frightening her or inflicting pain on her—a textbook specification for a serial sadistic rapist and murderer.

Bernardo's anger-excitation and sadistic demands included forcing Homolka to wear a dog collar when they had intercourse.

WHEN:	**1982**
WHERE:	**Louisiana, USA**
VICTIMS:	**Multiple**
CULPRITS:	**James Mitchell DeBardeleben II**

CASE

Roger Collin Blanchard, real name James Mitchell DeBardeleben II, was arrested in a mall near Knoxville, Tennessee.

CASE STUDY 34: MIKE DEBARDELEBEN

Many sadistic serial killers are defined by their terrible psychosis, as if their whole existence becomes dominated by the need to find, attack, threaten, and kill their victims, with little or no time for the routines of more normal lives. Perhaps the greatest exception to this rule was a man who first came to the notice of investigators as a counterfeiter of stolen money, and as police closed in, searching for evidence of his financial crimes, they stumbled without warning on a grisly record of rape and murder, buried beneath a multilayered cloak of conflicting information.

THE MALL PASSER

The case began with increasing numbers of forged currency being spent at shopping malls over a wide sweep of the United States. A mammoth operation was mounted to track down the counterfeiter responsible, known to law enforcement as the Mall Passer, and the first breakthrough came on a Wednesday afternoon, May 25, 1983, near Knoxville in Tennessee. A man had been arrested, apparently caught in the act of passing forged bills. He refused all cooperation, or even to give his name, but detectives found a driving license in the name of Roger Collin Blanchard. This proved as fake as the money, and when his Chrysler car was checked, it was found the license plates were stolen. The car was registered to a James R. Jones, but when detectives checked Jones' height, weight, and appearance with the Department of Motor Vehicles they proved to be identical to those of Blanchard. Clearly, Jones and Blanchard were the same person.

that they realized a bookmark in the pages relating to storage facilities might show where else the suspect kept his possessions. After phoning different storage companies they found Landmark Mini-Storage, where "J.R. Jones" had rented mini-storage locker number 230 six months previously.

Agents broke the locker open, and found police lights and a siren that could be attached to a car and powered from the cigar lighter connection, together with handcuffs, twine, a gun case and ammunition, and a ski mask. In other containers, along with printing plates they found fake IDs, articles of women's underwear, whips, and a dildo, together with more sinister articles they referred to as a "death kit," with a choker chain, laces, K-Y jelly, and more handcuffs. Even more disturbing was a collection of explicit pictures of very young women. They looked as if they were in fear of their lives, and showed signs of having suffered severe physical violence. Reinforcing this evidence was a set of audio tapes with recordings of women being subjected to such unspeakable torture that they begged for death to release them. It was clear that in addition to being a successful counterfeiter, DeBardeleben had, over the previous 18 years, been a bank robber and a kidnapper as well as a long-term sadistic serial rapist. However, his resolute and absolute refusal to cooperate in any way with

The police made a breakthrough when they discovered a storage unit in the area registered to one of DeBardeleben's pseudonyms.

BEHIND THE MULTIPLE IDENTITIES

In fact, both identities were false. When the suspect's fingerprints were checked with Secret Service records he was revealed to be James Mitchell DeBardeleben II, commonly known as Mike, a name well-known to the Service as that of a career criminal. He had been found guilty of passing fake 100-dollar bills in 1976, and had served two years in prison. Agents then searched his car, where they found a mixture of guns, pornography, drugs, stolen license plates, forged bills, and the merchandise they paid for. But to bring a case against DeBardeleben, they needed the press and plates used to produce the counterfeit currency.

They shifted the focus of the search to the Washington apartment given as "Jones'" address. After a day and a night sifting through stacks of material in the crowded rooms, they found nothing to provide a link to the forgery. It was only when one of the agents began searching through the telephone directories

Audio tapes confirmed that DeBardeleben's criminal career included anger-excitement serial rape.

the investigation meant that the number and identities of many of his victims may never be known.

DETAILING THE PROFILE

Nevertheless, investigators managed to find several women who had survived being seized by DeBardeleben when posing as a police officer. Once in his power, he would force them to let him film them while carrying out degrading sexual acts, and threaten them with publicity if they informed on him. In some of the notes found by agents, he spoke of the possibility of murdering one of his victims once he felt he was ready for it. FBI profiler John Douglas studied the accounts of his surviving victims and drew up a profile of a subject who had grown up with a weak father and a domineering mother, who had problems adjusting to others while at school and later when doing military service. Though careful and clever, he was likely to be interested in the police and their operations. He would have difficulty with females in general, and if married he would be prone to degrade his wife, possibly carrying out his sadomasochistic fantasies on her. He would also believe his victims enjoyed what he did to them, and might stalk them to relive the experiences.

DeBardeleben's background matched the profile closely, with some detail differences. His father was a soldier and a strict disciplinarian, while his mother was an alcoholic whom he began to beat up during his adolescence. He entered the military but was court-martialed and discharged. He was married five times. His first marriage lasted only three weeks, and he tried to control and degrade each succeeding spouse more and more.

Finally, in 1982, he crossed the boundary from sadistic attacks to full-blown murder. Posing as a Dr. Katz, he called a real-estate agent in Louisiana and made an appointment under a false name to be shown some houses for sale. Jean McPhaul went to meet him, and disappeared. Her body was found in one of the empty houses, hanging in the attic, with no sign of sexual assault, but dead from two puncture wounds to the heart. He was later suspected of being responsible for the murder of another female real-estate agent. Agents found evidence from other attacks and kidnappings and at least two murders, and he was finally put on trial for what they firmly believe to be but a small fraction of the killings he had actually carried out.

HOW MANY MORE MURDERS?

Believed by many who came into contact with him to be the ultimate sadistic killer, the charges of which DeBardeleben was found guilty probably represent the topmost tip of a bloody and terrifying iceberg. Some investigators worked through his obsessively detailed notebooks to deduce he must have been involved in more than 60 killings in all, though he has steadfastly refused to cooperate with them. Nevertheless, he was given a total sentence of 375 years in prison, before he can even be considered for parole. For a man who despised spontaneity and strove to control his criminal activities as well as his sadistic priorities, every aspect of his life is now ultimately under the control of others. For a self-styled criminal mastermind like Mike DeBardeleben, this is perhaps the ultimate nightmare, and perhaps the only real justice his manifold victims will be given.

Debardeleben recorded his conquests obsessively in notebooks that were eventually confiscated by the police.

CASE STUDY 35: THE WEMMER PAN KILLER

WHEN: 1996

WHERE: Johannesburg, South Africa

VICTIMS: Multiple

CULPRIT: Cedric Maake

Sometimes serial killers can shift between multiple targets and motivations to suggest to investigators and profilers alike that their murders are carried out by two entirely different individuals.

TARGETING COUPLES

The Wemmer Pan is the site of a dam near the city of Johannesburg in South Africa, where couples would often meet after work to make love before heading to their separate homes. Unfortunately, the seclusion that made it ideal as a meeting place also brought it to the attention of a determined killer with a routine eerily similar to the Monster of Florence (see Case Study 30). Time and again police would find the bodies of couples, with the man shot to death and the woman raped before being shot in turn. He would rob his victims of cash, clothing, and valuables, and sometimes he would let one or both of his victims escape. He killed his first victims in April 1996, and within just 16 months he had killed another 24 people. On one occasion, when he traveled farther toward Johannesburg, he passed a couple walking along the road. He shot the man dead and hit the woman in one knee, before dragging her into the bush and raping her. Later that same night he killed two more couples in what seemed like an uncontrollable blood lust.

Police profiler Elmarie Myburgh considered the killer must be local to the area to know the spot where he found his victims and their reasons for being there. She also believed he was in his 30s and might well live in the neighboring community of La Rochelle, possibly

The serial rapist and murderer operated in an area outside Johannesburg where couples were known to meet for sexual liaisons.

The second string of murders were all directed toward male tailors, leaving the police, understandably, unaware that the two sprees were connected.

working as a gardener, which would allow him enough time off to plan and carry out his crimes. But the killings ceased abruptly after September 1997, with police having no real idea of who they were looking for.

DIFFERENT KINDS OF VICTIMS

In the meantime, another criminal began attacking a very different kind of victim, this time in the Jeppe district of central Johannesburg. The first victim was a tailor working in his shop, who had been badly beaten with a hammer. A whole series of similar assaults followed, all directed against male tailors working alone, and all delivered with a hammer. Some of the victims died, some survived, though often with severe brain damage, and the attacker would escape with clothes or money from those he targeted. By August 1997 there had been 10 attacks, and profiler Dr. Micki Pistorius studied the details of the attacks before drawing up a description of the man responsible.

Most victims had been attacked in the mornings, so she assumed the criminal worked on night shifts that left him free during the day. He must be able to speak both English and Zulu, and might well be staying in one of the workers' hostels in the area, and was probably aged

between 25 and 30. He did not take large amounts of money from those he attacked, so he probably had a salaried job, but not one that paid well enough for him to have his own transport. Given his concentration on one particular occupation, it was almost certain he had a furious and bitter grudge against tailors in general, possibly because of having worked for one who had treated him badly. It was also clear he had taken the trouble to wipe his fingerprints at the crime scenes, which suggested he had spent time in prison and might appear on police records. His driving force was revenge, which suggested he would treat his wife and family badly, suppressing resistance to what he wanted.

TWO CRIME SERIES SOLVED

Police were planning to stake out premises of other potential victims in the area, when the story appeared in the newspapers, warning off the criminal. For a time it seemed the trail had gone cold, but on December 23, following a tip-off, Captain Piet Byleveld stopped to speak to a suspect he saw waiting at a taxi rank. This proved to be one Cedric Maake, who was a 35-year-old plumber living in La Rochelle who had plenty of free time during the day to carry out crime. He also proved to have a criminal record, but the answers he gave to police questioning revealed the astonishing truth that he was not only the Wemmer Pan killer but also the man who had been attacking tailors in their shops in the city. Another surprise was the sheer scale of his crimes. In March 2000 he was found guilty of 27 murders, 26 cases of attempted murder, 41 violent robberies, and 14 rapes, as well as firearms offenses. He was sentenced to 1,835 years and three months behind bars. When asked by the man who caught him why he had committed his crimes, he merely said that he did not like people, and thereafter steadfastly refused to explain his conduct.

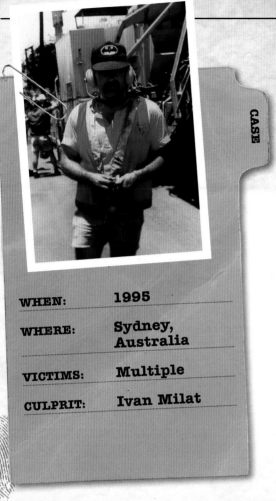

CASE

CASE STUDY 36: IVAN MILAT

WHEN:	**1995**
WHERE:	**Sydney, Australia**
VICTIMS:	**Multiple**
CULPRIT:	**Ivan Milat**

Police found remains of young hitchhikers and backpackers who had gone missing in the countryside to the south of Sydney.

After a series of young hitchhikers and backpackers from the United Kingdom, Germany, and Australia had gone missing in the countryside to the south of Sydney, Australian police were appalled to find traces of bodies and body fragments at different sites in the Belangalo State Forest region. The first had been found by orienteers on a run through a secluded part of the woodland close to the precipitous cliffs of Executioner's Gorge on Saturday, September 19, 1992, but it was not long before more and more of the missing were identified by clothing and possessions and, in some cases, dental charts. There were some common factors that were puzzling, with several body sites being close to crude fireplaces built from bricks and stones. Others were all too straightforward, in the form of bullets from a Ruger sporting rifle that had killed the victims together with wounds from a long sharp knife. In some cases the knife wounds were deep enough to have severed the spinal cord to render the individual totally helpless. However, because some of the bodies were badly decomposed and others skeletal, it was impossible to be certain whether

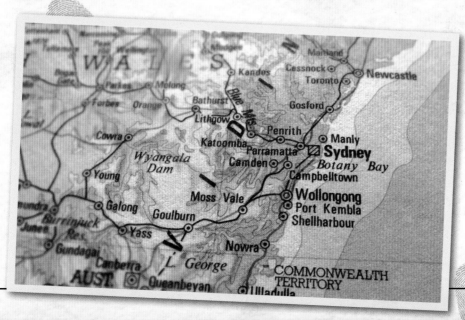

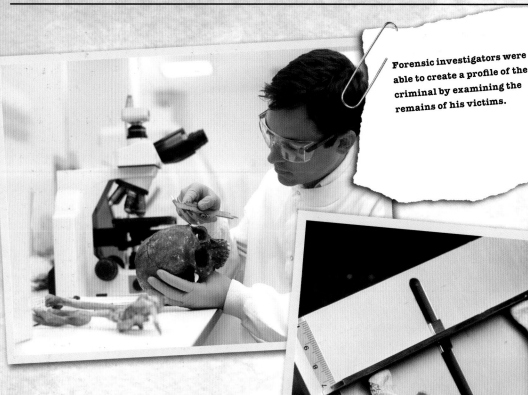

Forensic investigators were able to create a profile of the criminal by examining the remains of his victims.

they had been raped or sexually assaulted, apart from clothing being disarranged in suggestive ways. In one case, the victim's skull had been found some distance from her body, in a posture suggesting she had been forced to kneel down before being beheaded.

A PROFILE IS WORKED OUT

Working from the available evidence, forensic psychologist Dr. Rod Milton drew up a profile of the man who had carried out the killings. He saw him as a man with local knowledge of the forest who probably lived not far away, in a semi-rural area on the edge of a larger urban center. He was a killer who carefully planned his attacks and in one case the fact that a victim had had her head covered with a cloth was an attempt to depersonalize her as he forced her to kneel and then shot her in the head as a ritual execution. In other cases the attacks were clearly more frenzied, with multiple deep stab wounds beyond those needed to subdue or kill the victim, suggesting an escalating level of anger-excitation in an

otherwise organized killer. He was also probably in his mid-30s, working in a semiskilled, outdoor job, and would have a history of homosexuality or bisexuality, and disputes with authority including possibly a criminal record, and would also possibly be in an unstable or unsatisfactory relationship.

SETTING A FALSE TRAIL

In one case, two victims were identified as a couple missing since 1989, but thought to have headed in the opposite direction from Sydney after some of their possessions had been found at the roadside well to the north of the city. It was clear the killer had transported them there to lay a false trail, which had previously seemed convincing. Their skeletons showed evidence of lethal and disabling wounds, at least one of which could only by inflicted by someone with considerable physical strength. Furthermore, when the last victims were discovered, including the woman who had been beheaded, it was clear the killer was taking more time to carry out the killings and the sadism was becoming more and more pronounced.

At one stage, police were delighted to receive what seemed to be clear and positive evidence. A campaign aimed at the local gun club to track down owners of Ruger rifles had resulted in a tip-off that one member had seen something odd in the forest the year before. The man had given a statement of having been passed on a forest road the year before by two vehicles, each one containing men with a gagged woman. He gave detailed descriptions of the occupants, and signed his statement "Ivan Milat."

More information came in about a British hitchhiker called Paul Onions who had been given a lift on a journey looking for work, by a man with a moustache who said his name was "Bill." During the drive the man became more and more threatening and finally produced a length of rope and a gun, at which point Paul managed to open the door and leap out of the vehicle. Bill had tried to grab him, but Paul managed to flag down an approaching vehicle and persuade the driver to drop him at the nearest police station. This was back in 1990, and the statement he had made had been mislaid and so had played no part in the investigation. That is, until two more calls were made to the inquiry team.

Ivan Milat, pictured here holding a rifle, first called in to police to give a false witness statement.

Australia's notorious serial killer Ivan Milat being led from court during his trial in Sydney July 8, 1996.

NARROWING THE SEARCH

One call was from the woman who had given Paul Onions, now back in England, a lift to the police station. The other call was from a woman whose boyfriend worked with a man he thought should be checked out, a man by the name of Ivan Milat. Early in 1994, the police decided to talk to the employers of Ivan Milat, who apparently worked alongside his brother Richard. When they checked the timesheets of both men, they found Richard had been at work at the times of the killings but Ivan had not.

They also checked the criminal records, which revealed that Ivan Milat had a long history of mainly petty crime. The one exception was much more significant. In 1971 he had been arrested for picking up two female hitchhikers and raping one of them. The women had spoken of his carrying a large knife and a length of rope, but the prosecution had failed for lack of evidence and he had been freed.

Bit by bit the evidence was mounting. Checks on the Milat family revealed they had owned a property on the fringe of the state forest, and the owner of a four-wheel-drive vehicle he had

One of Milat's brothers admitted that he thought it likely that Milat had killed as many as 28 victims in total.

bought from the Milats showed police a cartridge he had found beneath the seats. It was a Ruger .22 cartridge identical to cases found at the murder sites. Paul Onions was contacted and flown back from England to identify the man who had threatened him. "Bill" turned out to be Ivan Milat.

Finally, at 6:30 a.m. on Sunday, May 22, 1994, police raided the Milat home, and brought out Ivan and his girlfriend. When they searched the premises they found weapons, together with items belonging to several of the victims, including a camera and camping gear. Though Milat insisted he was innocent, he was found guilty of seven murders on July 27, 1995, and sentenced to life for each one, with an additional six years for the attempted abduction of Paul Onions. He was sent to a prison in Maitland, but was involved in a failed escape attempt. He was then transferred to maximum-security confinement in Goulburn jail with his fellow would-be escapee, one George Savvas, who was later discovered hanged in his cell. Milat was later found to have concealed a hacksaw blade in a packet of biscuits and claimed he intended to escape at the first opportunity. In the meantime, one of his brothers had admitted he thought it likely that Ivan Milat had killed as many as 28 victims, with the rest still concealed in the forest.

CHAPTER 7

FINDING THE SIGNATURE

In all the cases covered in this book, profilers use the physical evidence found at crime scenes to reveal different aspects of the psychology and motivations of the suspect they are seeking. They then use that information to narrow down the search to a small enough population for police to close in on their adversary. In one sense, all these signs and pieces of forensic evidence add up to the signature of the person responsible. However, the word also has a much more specific meaning, relating directly to the insight a profiler develops into the personalities of those he confronts psychologically.

As physical evidence is compiled in a case, profilers are able to deduce psychological meaning.

SIGNATURE FOR A PROFILE

In order to explain the distinction between signature and profile, profilers often say that the study they carry out into the methods used by a criminal to commit a crime—how the site and the victim were targeted and approached, how the attack was carried out, what kinds of weapons were used, what precautions were taken to destroy incriminating evidence as far as possible, how the criminal left the scene, and so on—all relate to the criminal's modus operandi, or "MO." Essentially this means how the crime was carried out. The "signature" of the crime in profiling terms relates to why that particular crime was committed: in other words, the motivation of the criminal, the thing that drives the perpetrator to take the considerable personal risks posed by their criminal activities. Analyzing these aspects of the criminal involves exploring their inner compulsions, their innate behavior, and their thinking, which tends to change little even over a long period. Where the MO—the methods a criminal uses in committing his crimes—changes with increasing experience and increasing awareness of police methods and techniques, the signature will not, and signs that reveal this unchanging routine will say much about the kind of criminal responsible, and in some cases even help reveal their identity.

So what exactly is this signature? It usually reveals itself in aspects of the criminal's behavior, over and above what is needed to carry out the crime. For example, do they invariably engage in a specific sexual activity when they have the victim under their control? Do they achieve the total control they need by restricting the victim's movements with a specific type of binding? Do they inflict a similar type of injury to each victim? Do they mutilate or torture their victims in a particular way, or carry out a particular ritual at each crime scene, especially where this seems unusual, bizarre, or even senseless to those analyzing the scene? Do they display the victim's body in a particular way so as to shock those who find it, or in order to complete their personal ritual? Any of these feature can help generate a profile as individual as a handwritten signature from the criminal involved.

DIFFERENT TYPES OF SIGNATURE

Though the criminal's basic signature does not tend to change, since it is created by the real reasons they continue to commit the crimes, the details can develop and intensify as they attack more victims. For example, a power-reassurance rapist (see Chapter 7) may develop a script he uses to talk to his victim and try to create a closer bond between them. He may try to excuse his conduct and even apologize for it. Alternatively, he may ask her to agree that she enjoyed the experience, or that he treated her well and even gave her pleasure. If this ritual relates to his compulsions to carry out the rapes—his overriding need for reassurance—then with growing confidence his lengthening conversations may reveal more and more about himself. The need remains the same, but the time he takes to feed that need becomes greater and greater.

Investigators are constantly trying to discover a criminal's modus operandi.

The way a criminal leaves a crime scene tells as much about their motives as how they committed the actual crime.

SEPARATING THE SIGNATURE AND THE MO

Sometimes, inevitably, the boundary lines between the criminal's signature and their method of carrying out the crime can be blurred, making it difficult for investigators to decide where one ends and the other begins. FBI profiler John Douglas used two examples to help illustrate how the two factors differed in two different types of crime.

If a rapist, for example, broke into a house to assault a female victim and found her partner there as well, then to carry out the crime he clearly had to ensure the male witness could not overpower him or call for help. One way of achieving that would be to threaten him with a weapon and lock him away in another room to prevent either possibility. That would enable him to carry out his crime, though he would presumably have preferred to have found the woman on her own. However, if the criminal did not simply immobilize the victim's partner, but made him watch the rape being carried out, this would be a different kind of signature. It makes little difference to the chances of him being able to carry out the crime and get away afterward, but it makes an enormous difference from the point of view of the victim and her partner. The added infliction of pain, distress, anger, and helpless humiliation may give the criminal a powerful additional satisfaction over and above that derived from the rape, and would therefore be a vital part of any repeat crimes involving a couple rather than a single victim.

Douglas' second example related to a bank robbery, where again the criminal who carried out the crime might need to delay the possibility of bank staff calling the police too quickly for him to make his escape. One way of doing this might be to force them, at gunpoint, to strip off all their clothes. Apart from the resulting

At the opposite end of the spectrum, the anger-excitation rapist may kill his victims once the rape is completed and then continue to feed his inner demands by mutilating their bodies after death. This need will probably remain as part of his psychological makeup, but may require more and more sadistic acts to satisfy it. There will of course be exceptions, where a particular killer may not carry out the ritual to the full. However, these omissions are more often due to the danger of discovery, or an interruption from some cause outside of the criminal's control, or an unexpected response from the victim.

embarrassment, this would delay their response while they retrieved their clothes and dressed themselves before contacting the police. This would make little difference to the criminal's inner needs, but it would simply help him carry out the crime and then make his getaway. But what if forcing the bank employees to strip becomes a ritual of its own? What if the criminal not only makes them undress, but adds to their humiliation by making them pose in suggestive or embarrassing positions and photographs them? That would add nothing to the direct value of postponing their actions in finding their clothes, dressing and calling the police after he leaves. What it would do is feed his own fantasies of power and control, and therefore would be part of his signature, rather than his MO.

FIRE RAISERS AND BOMBERS

Signature can manifest itself in all kinds of ways. Investigators analyzing a burned-out building will look for where the blaze started, and what kind of accelerant was used to intensify the flames and establish the fire. Facts like these will explain how the criminal set the building alight, and from where the conflagration was started, and perhaps suggest what the arsonist's priorities were. However, signs of a ritual carried out by the arsonist before they had to escape the flames, such as objects deliberately smashed, or signs of defecation or urination inside the premises, relate to the criminal's own motivation and become part of his signature.

Similar dividing lines can be drawn in analyzing those who detonate bombs for different reasons. These may be to destroy property, make a political point that cannot be made so emphatic by any other means, or to repay a wrong. In that case the bomb itself, the type of explosive, the way in which it was detonated and how it was placed to achieve the objective all relate to the MO. But where the bomber modifies the device to increase the death and injury it inflicts on the victims of the blast, by fitting a stronger casing to intensify the blast, or by filling it with nails and metal fragments to create a shrapnel effect, then he is feeding his own inner compulsions to cause more pain and suffering through his actions, and these actions become part of his signature.

RELATING SIGNATURES

Individual signatures can also be recorded as part of the background to an individual crime and fed into a criminal records database. This enables investigators to decide whether a new crime is actually part of a series carried out by the same long-term criminal or even, where the signature behavior is sufficiently unusual, to point the way to an individual or a group of potential subjects. Significantly, when the FBI's Roy Hazelwood interviewed a group of male sexual sadists, he found they were happy enough to discuss matters relating to their violent crimes. Once the conversation shifted to their own sexual acts, needs, fantasies, or rituals, they became much more reluctant to cooperate. These were seen as much more personal matters, relating to their own personal signatures, which revealed how they thought and behaved.

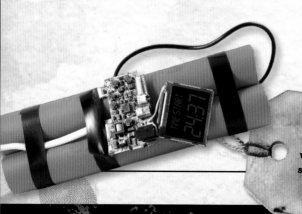

Much like an arsonist or rapist, a bomber can make modifications to their crimes to fulfil their own wants and desires, adding to their signature.

CASE

WHEN: **1990**

WHERE: **Washington, USA**

VICTIMS: **Multiple**

CULPRIT: **George Russell**

CASE STUDY 37: GEORGE RUSSELL

During the summer and early fall of 1990, three women were found murdered in a matter of weeks around Bellevue, in Washington State. Apart from the violence which each victim had suffered and which ended their lives, each of the bodies had been carefully posed to suggest some kind of message that must have been important to their killer, but which made no real sense to investigators. To profilers, the purpose was clearly part of the killer's ritual signature, and perhaps this bizarre window into his personality would also offer a route to identifying him and catching him.

FINDING THE BODIES

The first victim was 27-year-old Mary Ann Pohlreich, whose naked body had been dumped in an alleyway separating a local restaurant, the Black Angus, from a branch of McDonald's, early in the morning of June 23, 1990. She was found by the McDonald's counter clerk on his way to empty trash into the dumpster located at the back of the alley. Police arrived and found she had almost certainly been killed elsewhere, since her body showed abrasions from being dragged after death from the place of her murder to where her body was found. She had been left in open view, lying on her back, with her legs partially crossed and her left foot lying across her right instep. An empty food container was placed over her right eye, and in her hand was a large fir cone. She had been violently raped and stabbed in the anus by a sharp object, and death was almost certainly due to a blow that had cracked her skull. Other blows, including one that ruptured her liver, and signs of strangulation, were revealed at her post-mortem examination to have almost certainly been inflicted after she was dead. They were part of the same ritual that posed her remains with such precision.

The next victim was Carol Beethe, a divorced single mother of two young daughters aged 9 and 13, who worked behind the bar of a

Bellevue, Washington, was the site of three murders committed in a very short time span in 1990.

singles restaurant called Cucina Cucina. She had spent the evening of August 9 in another bar, the Keg, chatting to the barman whom she knew well. She left at 2 a.m. and drove home, where a neighbor walking his dog saw her enter her property at around 2:30 a.m. Her elder daughter Kelly found her body when she went to wake her, and called the police.

The police found that Carol Beethe had suffered several heavy blows from a weapon that left unusual Y-shaped wounds in her face and skull. She was lying on her side and her head had afterward been covered with a thick plastic clothes bag, and a pillow from the bed. Her nightdress had been taken off and she was left naked apart from a pair of red high-heeled shoes, pushed roughly onto her feet. A shotgun which she kept in the property for protection had been pushed with considerable force into her vagina and her torso was covered with marks showing the efforts the killer had gone to to inflict pain and degradation on his helpless victim.

THE QUIET KILLER

There were several detail differences from the way the first victim had been killed and then displayed. In particular, Carol Beethe had been left in her own bedroom. But this in itself

The first victim was discovered in a dumpster behind a McDonald's restaurant.

focused attention even more closely on the killer's true priorities beyond the taking of his victim's life. All the time he had been torturing and killing their mother, two young girls had been lying asleep in an adjacent room. Not only had he taken the risk that either daughter might have woken up and caught him in mid-attack, but he had carried out his routine slowly, carefully, and quietly. Aside from the savage blows that rendered his victim helpless and finally killed her, he had concentrated on the deep inner satisfactions provided by his ritual.

A SERIAL KILLER'S SIGNATURE

Local police were still reluctant to assume this was the work of a serial killer, given the differences in MO. But to a profiler, there were three unmistakable indications of the murderer's signature: the extreme sexual perversion shown in both attacks, the sadistic determination to show as much contempt for the victim as possible in both attacks and in the display of their bodies afterward, and finally the element of taunting implicit in the way no attempt had been made to conceal the bodies from the investigators.

The matter was proved beyond doubt with the third killing. On September 3, 1990, the corpse of 24-year-old Andrea Levine—known to friends and colleagues as Randi—was found on her blood-soaked bed in her ground-floor apartment. She was last seen in the Maple Gardens Restaurant four days earlier, and it was likely her killer had managed to break in and kill her while she was asleep. Once again she was posed to shock and challenge those who found her, but even more bloodily and elaborately than the earlier victims. Like them, she was naked. The back of her skull had been smashed in, and a blood-drenched pillow covered her face. A vibrator had been forced down her throat, her legs were spread, and a copy of a book called *More Joy of Sex* was gripped in her left hand. The whole of her body was marked by more than 250 stab wounds from what appeared to

be a table knife. As with the other victims, there was no sign of the weapon that had been used to kill her.

TRIGGERS FOR MURDER

By now it was all too clear from the common factors relating to the killer's signature that all three women had been killed by the same sadistic murderer. But what else did they have in common? They lived in fairly close proximity to one another—Carol Beethe lived and died 1½ miles from where the first victim had been found, and 4 miles from the home of the third victim. All had spent much of their leisure time in bars in the area, where detectives assumed they could have met the man who took their lives. But when they spoke to friends of the dead women, another vital factor emerged in the common personalities of two of them. Carol Beethe was known to enjoy the routines of flirtation, in appearing to suggest to a male acquaintance that she might welcome his advances. She would then retreat, leaving him confused and possibly frustrated if he lacked the confidence to continue the game with a suitable response. Randi Levine was described as having a caustic wit, prone to sarcasm and the devastating put-down. Both these women posed

The second victim's body was found wearing nothing but a pair of red, high-heeled shoes.

no problems to men with enough confidence to be at ease with them, but to a deeply angry person with a grudge against women, their behavior could provoke the most lethal violence.

But what about the first victim, Mary Ann Pohlreich? Investigators were convinced that her killing and the display of her body might be a result of the criminal's anger reaching the level where he turned to killing for the first time. The signs were it had not been premeditated to the same level as the others, so perhaps killer and victim had made a date, and something had happened while they were together that provoked him into such a violent rape and murder. Instead of fantasizing about being able to repay the women in his life by killing them

and degrading them, he had realized for the first time he could turn those fantasies into reality. When he did so twice more, he became more ambitious in the violence and the display, revealing more of his nature on each occasion.

THE SUSPECT REVEALED

The search for suspects had so far only turned up one: John Comfort, barman at the Keg where Carol Beethe had spent the last night of her life. At the end of the evening she had helped him close the bar, then gone to his car to make love, before she headed home. Police kept him under surveillance until a solid alibi at the time of the third murder had taken him off the list. But had the real killer been watching them both in the bar, and afterward?

At last the investigators had the breakthrough they so badly needed. On the night of September 12, 1990, a call came in to report someone prowling around the caller's property. A patrol that was sent out to drive around the neighborhood spotted a lone figure walking along one of the roads. They stopped him and found he could give no clear reason for being in an area far from his own address at that time of night. They took his name to check his record. He was a young black man named George Waterfield Russell, and slowly the pieces slotted into place. He was a burglar and drug supplier, and more significantly the woman who had made the call turned out to be a friend of Randi Levine, and she revealed that both she and the victim knew him as a familiar figure on the bar and restaurant scene of the area.

In fact, Russell's background read like an ideal specification to fit a serial sadistic killer. Born in Florida 32 years earlier, his mother had abandoned him at the age of 6 months. His father was unable to cope and the boy grew up being shuttled between his aunts and grandmother. When he was 6, his mother reappeared with a new husband and eventually the three of them moved up to the

Russell is believed to have met his victims at a singles bar in town.

The skyline of Bellevue, Washington, where all the murders took place.

Northwest to live in a well-heeled Seattle suburb. Then, when he was a teenager, his mother decamped once again. His stepfather tried to cope with the young man's succession of arrests for burglary, drug trafficking, or vandalism offenses. Finally, at the age of 17 he was abandoned again as his stepfather remarried, to a wife who refused to live with someone so constantly in trouble.

It was then that George Russell moved to the Bellevue area where he would eventually find his victims. He lived off handouts and the proceeds of petty crime, though his previously wealthy background enabled him to fit into this raffish society so long as his growing anger remained carefully concealed. When detectives began talking to his friends, they found other gaps in the picture being filled in: one had lent him a pick-up truck on the night of the first murder. They found bloodstains on the vehicle's carpet, which were the same type as that of Mary Ann Pohlreich. Others recalled him in the company of Carol Beethe, behaving angrily and threateningly and later referring to all the murder victims as "whores" who deserved their fate. More significantly still, regular visitors to the bars produced pieces of jewelry that Russell had sold to them, and that had belonged to his victims. Most damning of all, the sperm found in his first victim's body was a positive DNA match. Together with the perfect fit of the killer's profile, and the signature evidence at the crime scenes, this hard evidence was enough to sentence him to life imprisonment.

The killer's third victim had been stabbed over 250 times.

POLICE DEPT BATH, OH
0-07-81
81 120
21 - 6 0 - 200

WHEN:	**1978**
WHERE:	**Ohio, USA**
VICTIMS:	**Multiple**
CULPRIT:	**Jeffrey Dahmer**

CASE STUDY 38: JEFFREY DAHMER

Jeffrey Dahmer's terrible reputation as a serial killer seems to have originated with a pathological fear of being left on his own, carried to the point where he would kill to prevent this happening. The first time it happened was when he was still living with his parents in Richfield, Ohio, in 1978. At the age of 18 he had recently graduated from high school and had been left at home alone while his parents were away. With the house to himself, he was able to plan a little excitement. He picked up a hitchhiker, 19-year-old Steven Mark Hicks, who accepted his invitation to come and have a beer. The two young men then had sex, but Hicks was anxious to continue his journey. Determined to stop this happening, but unable to control Hicks, Dahmer picked up a heavy piece of weight-training equipment and hit the other on the head with it. It was enough to kill him, leaving Dahmer with the problem of disposing of the body before his parents returned. Calmly and carefully he went about the task. After first

This fenced vacant lot was the site of the apartment building where serial killer and cannibal Jeffrey Dahmer lived and mutilated his victims.

NO TRESPASSING

Tony Hughes, one of Jeffrey Dahmer's victims.

burying the corpse outside the house, he dug it up some weeks later, chopped it into pieces, stripped the flesh away from the bones and dissolved it in acid. Finally he smashed the bones into small pieces that he then concealed in the woods near the house.

THE START OF SOMETHING

Having coped with the result of his first killing, he decided to repeat the experience again and again. Over a total of 13 years he would pick up a succession of compliant young men. Once they had had sex, and once his temporary companions showed signs of wanting to leave, he would kill them in a wide variety of ways before carrying out all kinds of strange rituals with their remains. In 1988, the 28-year-old Dahmer moved into his own apartment in Milwaukee, where he was able to turn his combination of sex and murder into an assembly-line process. He bought large freezers in which to keep the bodies and body parts of his victims, and a large vat full of acid in which to dissolve their remains, all secure behind the protection of a series of bolts and security locks.

As he became more adept at this terrible routine, he was able to modify it to suit his indelible internal priorities. He was careful to pick up only young men who were transients without links to the local community or to people who would notice their disappearance. When in their company, he would be careful to avoid being seen by anyone who knew him. He would persuade them to go back to his home, promising to pay them to pose for photographs. Once back in his apartment and behind the locks and bolts, he would drug them, sometimes have sex with them and finally strangle them. Then, at last, Dahmer would have the complete control over his victims that could alone ease his fears of abandonment. Not only could he have sex with their lifeless bodies, but he could dismember them, eat parts of their flesh, and even wear their body parts around the apartment. He would display the severed heads of his victims as trophies on shelves. Naturally, all this took time, so he would try to operate to a timetable, finding his victims at the end of the working week to have the entire weekend to carry out his rituals of sex, death, dismemberment, and cannibalism.

Jeffrey Dahmer poses for booking photographs at the Milwaukee County Sheriff's Department after a 1982 arrest for indecent exposure. It wasn't until 1991 that he was finally arrested on charges of murder.

LETHAL BRAIN SURGERY

His ultimate aim became to control his victims while they were still alive. After drugging them to render them unconscious, he would drill holes in their heads and inject acid into the frontal lobes of their brains to try to modify their behavior. The first victim on whom he tried this died as a result. The next two regained consciousness, but complained of crippling headaches so he killed them anyway. Things went badly wrong from Dahmer's point of view with his fourth experiment, when the victim escaped from the apartment in a highly confused state. Neighbors called the police, who could not understand what the victim was trying to tell them, so they accepted Dahmer's offer to

take care of him, whereupon he took the boy back to his flat and injected his brain with more acid, which finally killed him.

GRUESOME FIND

This had been a narrow escape for Dahmer, but when another victim escaped on July 23, 1991, the game was truly up. Tracy Edwards, a young black man, stopped a police car, claiming he had been attacked. He gave them Dahmer's address, and when they checked their records, police found that Dahmer was already on parole for an earlier sexual assault. As he had clearly been drinking when they called at his apartment, he was technically in breach of his parole conditions, so they entered his property to put

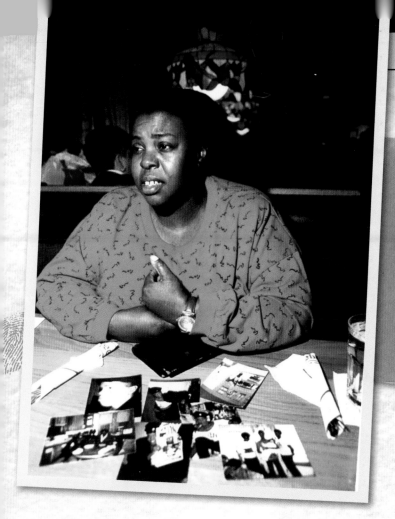

Theresa Smith, the sister of one of Dahmer's victims, Eddie Smith, displays pictures of her dead brother.

him under arrest. They found an appalling spectacle of heads and body parts, some displayed and others in a large drum in the bedroom, together with photos of his victims before and after death and an all-pervading stench of decomposing flesh.

DAHMER'S SIGNATURE?

Even now experts differ over what Dahmer's signature actually consisted of. Some insist he was too inconsistent in his methods, victims, and priorities to display a discernible signature, while others insist his lifelong preoccupation with preventing his victims from leaving him, dead or alive, amounts to the most unmistakable signature displayed by any serial killer anywhere in the world, at any time. Ironically, his obsession with not being left on his own was to result in him leaving the rest of the human

race behind. After being given a life sentence, he was murdered by another prisoner on November 28, 1994.

Ohio

WHEN: 1994

WHERE: Johannesburg, South Africa

VICTIMS: Multiple

CULPRIT: Moses Sithole

CASE STUDY 39: DAVID SELEPE AND MOSES SITHOLE

Sometimes, in a minority of cases, signature evidence can be misleading, and lead to confusion between different killers with identical psychological priorities. In the summer of 1994, South African police realized a serial killer was at large in the Cleveland industrial area of Johannesburg. By late September the bodies of 10 victims had been found dumped alongside the highway running through the district. They were adult women in their late teens or early 20s, who happened to be out of work. Some of the victims had been left half naked, others completely naked; all had been raped, then strangled with items of their clothing. In one case, two months after a victim's body was removed by police from the location where it was found, another victim's body was found on the same spot. Two weeks after that too was taken away, a third body was left on exactly the same spot. Before surveillance could be set up, the story of what happened appeared in a local newspaper, and the killer moved elsewhere.

GATHERING INFORMATION

In the meantime, Dr. Micki Pistorius had drawn up a profile of the killer. Based on the ages of his victims, he was probably aged between 23 and 30. It was clear the victims had been transported from their own home area to the places they had been attacked and killed, so he clearly not only owned a car, but this was

While showing investigators where he had dumped the bodies of his victims, David Selepe was released from handcuffs, and took the opportunity to try and escape, only to be shot by a police officer.

Maps show the area in which Selepe operated along highways running through Johannesburg.

presumably relatively new and well maintained, so that women would feel safe in accepting a lift from the driver. Likewise, it would be normal to assume he was articulate enough and confident enough to have reassured them he presented no threat whatsoever. However, in one case, the killer had written a message on the legs of his victim, which might indicate that he had difficulty communicating with women at a deeper level. He also referred to a victim as a "bitch," which hinted at an underlying anger toward women in general, which could mean the recent string of murders might have been triggered by a rejection on the part of one particular woman in his life.

During that fall two more bodies were found in the countryside around Atteridgeville near Pretoria, showing the same methods as the earlier killings. Two more were discovered later in October, again showing the same signs of rape, followed by strangulation with their own clothing. But more leads were turning up following the identification of the victims through publication of pictures and facial

composite portraits. Several of their friends and colleagues recalled the last time they had seen the victims alive was when they were about to meet someone about a promised job. In one case they saw the person the victim was going to meet, and described him as a black man, aged 25 to 30, who could speak Zulu. Others had been approached by a man with job offers, and they agreed with the description and helped in the drawing up of an artist's impression.

A CONFESSION

Detectives soon had a suspect in mind. David Selepe was the black owner of a computer college, training young women who wanted to find jobs with local companies. He drove a Mercedes and lived in Boksburg, which was close to both Johannesburg and Cleveland. He was said to dress well and have a confident manner, while one witness claimed he had offered her a job but then tried to rape her. Police were ready to arrest him, but found he had moved out of South Africa altogether. He

Moses Sithole, the second killer, attacked an officer with an ax before being taken into custody.

was tracked down to Maputo in neighboring Mozambique, where he was trying to raise cash by selling his car. He was arrested and taken back to South Africa. There he confessed to killing 15 women, but refused to make and sign a formal statement. However, he did agree to take police to the places where he had left the bodies. On Sunday, December 18, the second day of this operation, he was released from his chains and handcuffs to show police where he had buried a victim's underwear. While one of the team was trying to find the evidence, he was hit over the head by a branch wielded by the suspect, who then made his escape, only to be shot by one of the police. He was taken to hospital but died later from a gunshot wound to the head.

THE SAME SIGNATURE?

The resulting controversy over how the operation had been handled smoldered on for weeks. Then, on February 13, 1995, the body of a young black woman was found near Village Deep some 6 miles from Cleveland. To the dismay of the police, there were signs suggesting she might have been raped. What was certain, however, was that she had been strangled with her own underwear. She was identified by her brother, who confirmed she had last been seen late in January, a month after Selepe had been shot. There must be a new killer on the loose, with an eerily similar signature.

Soon a whole succession of victims was discovered, some in the area around Pretoria, others at Atteridgeville and Boksburg, and one near Cleveland. Ominously, once some were identified and their backgrounds checked, it seemed they had vanished after going to meet

someone about a job offer. When Dr. Pistorius drew up a profile of the killer, it was clear that the signs pointed to someone very similar to David Selepe. Once again, the women were mostly in their mid-20s to early 30s, were smartly dressed and well-enough educated to be looking for attractive job opportunities. In this case, however, when she studied the victims in the order in which they had been killed, whoever was responsible was clearly changing his method of operation. The early victims had not been tied up, but as the killings continued the suspect had tied their hands in front of them with a piece of their clothing. Then he had progressed to tying their hands behind them to keep them further under his control. Even the method he had used to kill them had developed with increasing experience. First he had strangled his victims with his bare hands, then he had used an item of the victim's clothing, and finally he had used a stick or some similar object to tighten the ligature into a garrote to provide the ultimate in control over their life and death.

This added up to a sadistic serial killer, with a similar signature to that of the late David Selepe. Profiles drawn up by Dr. Pistorius and the FBI's Robert Ressler agreed he was possessed by an abnormally high sex drive, and would be prone to treat women as objects purely for his own pleasure. He would masturbate after a successful killing and probably take and keep trophies from his victims. He would enjoy being able to charm women into letting him get the better of them. In particular, Dr. Pistorius considered he was a self-employed and moderately successful black man in his late 20s or early 30s, he would be outwardly charming, wear flamboyant clothes and jewelry, and probably be married or divorced. Almost certainly he was already known to the police, probably from crimes of fraud or robbery, and would have been exposed to violence when young.

TRAPPING THE SECOND KILLER

But who was the unknown killer? At one crime scene, near Boksburg, the bodies of 10 victims were found in close proximity.

It seemed likely his later victims would see the bodies of their predecessors and know what awaited them. Here police found a handbag with an identity card inside. This belonged to Amelia Rapodile, and those who knew her recalled she had vanished after leaving for a job interview with Moses Sithole, who ran an organization called Youth Against Human Abuse. The name of this group had been linked to other victims, and police decided to arrest him. Their opportunity came when he contacted his brother-in-law to buy him a firearm for his own protection. Police set up a rendezvous for October 18, 1995, but when Moses Sithole turned up, he realized one of the people at the spot was a policeman and attacked him with an ax, only to be shot in the leg and stomach. He was taken to hospital and charged in his absence with 29 murders just five days later.

His trial began almost exactly a year afterward. In spite of denying any involvement in any of the killings, he was identified by his earliest rape victims, who had met him in connection with his spurious job opportunities in the late 1980s, and for which he had served three years in jail. Other witnesses who knew his later victims identified him as the man seen with several of them immediately before they disappeared. Fellow prisoners had even recorded an apparent confession from him before his trial, and despite doubts over its admissibility as evidence, it helped convince the jury. The case was finally reinforced by DNA evidence linking him directly with several of the victims. On December 5, 1995, he was found guilty of 40 rapes, 38 murders, and six robberies, and sentenced to no less than 2,410 years in prison, with no possibility of parole until at least 930 years had passed.

Though repeatedly questioned about any possible link with David Selepe, Sithole has continued to deny any connection. Nevertheless, both men had strikingly similar backgrounds. Sithole's father died during his childhood, his mother deserted him and his siblings, and he told several of his early rape victims that he had been mistreated by women in his life, in particular one who wrongly accused him of raping her in 1989. Some links were even closer: when Selepe took police to the place where he admitted killing Amanda Thethe, he tried to escape and was shot. But when detectives were assembling the case against Sithole they found Amanda Thethe's missing bank card had been used by Sithole after her death and—even more inexplicably—DNA analysis showed that semen found inside her body belonged to Sithole and not Selepe. So far, this additional mystery remains unsolved.

David Selepe was eventually taken into custody in Mozambique after fleeing South Africa.

SUFFER THE LITTLE CHILDREN

The majority of people would agree that the most terrible crimes are those carried out against children, from suspected molestation at one end of the spectrum to sadistic murder at the other. The criminals involved vary widely. At the most violent extreme, there are serial sadistic killers who see children as the ideal prey, because of their relative weakness and frailty and the ease with which they can be persuaded to put themselves at the mercy of their abductor, rapist, or killer. To profilers, this suggests the criminal was abused by adults in their own childhood, and so may well have abused their own children in turn. If they have no children, or if they have lost contact with them through divorce, imprisonment, or other restrictions on their freedom, they may then try to abduct or abuse the children of others as a means of payback. If, on the other hand, the criminal's attitude to children is perverted rather than violent, seeing them as objects of affection or even potential sexual partners rather than prey for their own sadistic impulses, then the children themselves may be in less immediate physical danger from the criminals who have them temporarily at their mercy.

The most terrible crimes are those that involve children. They are often carried out by criminals who were themselves abused during their childhood.

INNATE FANTASIES

Most references to criminals who threaten children describe them as pedophiles or child molesters. In many ways these terms are used in the media on a largely interchangeable basis. But there are several different types of child attacker, each with their own description, their own psychologies and their own ways of dealing with their feelings for children. For example, a pedophile is technically a person who has sexual feelings for children who are below the age of puberty. In many cases these feelings remain repressed, and if this is the case, then they are breaking no law. They may never encounter a situation where their feelings are expressed, nor one where they present a genuine threat to a single child, so they do not appear on a sex offenders' register. In the same way, a person who conceals feelings of violent hatred against certain individuals or people from a particular sector of society, up to the point where they may even fantasize about attacking them or killing them or inflicting fearful pain on them, do not actually break any law. They may be tortured by their own internal anger, and they may well need serious psychiatric treatment, but as long as their desires and fantasies remain secret, they present no threat.

Clearly, once these fantasies and desires are translated into action, the picture changes completely. This is where the knowledge and understanding of the criminal profiler becomes an essential weapon in the campaign to identify, track and arrest criminals who target their real or potential victims. In the case of pedophiles, realizing their desires can either involve a sexual threat to the young targets of their obsession, or a need to carry out sadistic torture and murder on their helpless prey.

Italian Gianni Bisoli is seen during an interview with Reuters in Verona on April 8, 2010. Bisoli is one of a group of former pupils of an institute for the deaf in Verona demanding justice for sexual abuse carried out by priests from the 1950s to 1980s.

SITUATIONAL CHILD MOLESTER

When a person switches from an innate pedophile to an active one, they become a child molester. How serious a threat they then present depends on their particular type. Lowest in terms of threat level is the situational child molester, who has experienced a challenging or threatening event in their own life that triggers a desire to molest someone from a highly vulnerable group within society. In different circumstances, this could involve victims who are old, ailing or disabled, or children. Where children are involved, there are three different types of situational child molester: the regressed child molester, the morally indiscriminate child molester, and the inadequate child molester, all with different reasons for their conduct.

Regressed

For example, a regressed child molester could well be involved in a normal adult sexual relationship, until some life-changing event threatens that previously stable state, such as divorce or even the loss of a job. These changes can destroy self-esteem to the level where the sufferer begins to see children as an easier

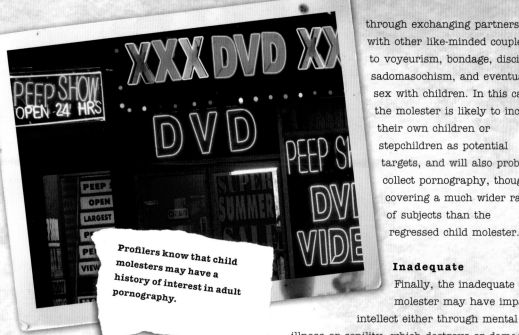

Profilers know that child molesters may have a history of interest in adult pornography.

through exchanging partners with other like-minded couples, to voyeurism, bondage, discipline, sadomasochism, and eventually sex with children. In this case the molester is likely to include their own children or stepchildren as potential targets, and will also probably collect pornography, though covering a much wider range of subjects than the regressed child molester.

Inadequate

Finally, the inadequate child molester may have impaired intellect either through mental illness or senility, which destroys or damages the normal moral mechanisms to help tell right from wrong, and which prevents them from forming normal adult sexual relationships. In fact, they may present less of a physical threat to their victims, since they may want limited contact, such as holding, kissing, and fondling, rather than full sexual intercourse. They are also much easier to spot, because their limitations cause people who know them to see them as "odd" or "strange," but not necessarily threatening. Other key signals are that they tend to live on their own, or with members of their immediate family. If they collect pornography it will be similar to that of the regressed child molester, in that it will invariably feature adults as its subject matter.

prospect for a sexual relationship, particularly if their situation affords fairly easy access to children in any case. In profiling terms, this suggests that a regressed child molester will not only have this recent trigger in their life story, but will tend to target children whom they do not already know. If they have access to children of both sexes, then they will usually approach girls rather than boys. In terms of their wider background, they will tend to be, or have been, married, and may well have lived in their community for some time. Earlier evidence of sexual leanings may show up as an interest in pornography, but with adult subjects rather than children.

Morally Indiscriminate

Morally indiscriminate child molesters operate to different imperatives. In their case there is no need for a challenge or threat to trigger the change to targeting children for sexual purposes. Their motivation tends to develop from the safety of a stable sexual relationship into a desire to experience more and more unusual sexual practices to maintain the necessary level of excitement. They may progress, for example,

PREFERENTIAL CHILD MOLESTERS

In ascending order of danger, the situational child molesters, of whatever type, occupy a level below those belonging to the other main subtype, the preferential child molesters. These fall into two classifications rather than three: the fixated child molester and the mysoped child molester. The major difference that separates both types from situational child molesters is that they do not see children as substitute sexual partners, for whatever reason, for adults. Instead, they actually prefer children as a conscious choice. As a direct consequence of this, they will tend to look for pornography that features children—possibly together with adults—as a constant theme.

Fixated Child Molesters

Fixated child molesters, as the name implies, are subjects who identify so closely with children that they essentially think of themselves as children. They try to live like children and behave like children as much as possible, and they feel much less comfortable in the presence of people of their own age. Consequently they will lack an adult partner, and focus all their affection and longing on the children they feel are their true equals. This means they will approach the objective of a fully sexual relationship with a child to whom they feel particularly attracted in the same way as a normal person would approach another adult to whom they felt attracted. They would approach them, bond with them, get to know them, woo them, and finally try to seduce them. Two facts follow from this psychology: the molester will know the victim, since the whole relationship has been aimed at producing an ever-closer relationship, and secondly the victim is in relatively little direct physical danger, especially in the early stages. If events result in a

sexual relationship, it is likely to begin with oral sex and only proceed to full sexual intercourse over the longer term. Furthermore, although most of these molesters are heterosexual by nature, most victims are boys, possibly because at their early stage of development, they are easier to approach and persuade.

Most Dangerous of All: Mysoped Molesters

Of course all molesters present children with dangers of different kinds and at different levels of threat. But mysoped child molesters suffer from a psychology in which children are potential targets for their own heightened feelings of anger and longing to inflict extreme violence. As such, their whole conduct is entirely different from the other types of child molester. They will search for victims as coldly and dispassionately as any predator, trawling schools, public playgrounds, and shopping malls where children can be found. When the opportunity arises for them to abduct the victim without alerting anyone presenting a security threat, they will simply seize the child and remove it into their power with overwhelming physical force.

They will not worry about causing shock, pain, or distress, since this is what excites them and what they want to draw from the incident. They usually set out to harm the child, and often the crime ends with the death of the young victim. Afterward they may mutilate and occasionally even eat part of the child's body as a macabre part of their signature. Roy Hazelwood, an experienced FBI profiler, has said that these extreme types of child molester closely resemble sadistic serial killers of adult victims. Both tend to show strong signature elements in their crimes, carrying out complex rituals with the bodies of those they harm and kill. While these invariably differ quite markedly from one criminal to the next, they

TO THE

FOR THAT

THIS FATHER LOST
LIFE IN THE FIG
WITH PEDOPHILES

UŽ VAIKO
AŠARAS
ie sumokėjo
savo
KRAUJU

FATHER IS GONE, HE
US SAVING

Protestors line up outside the Lithuanian Embassy in support of Drasius Kedys in 2010. Kedys shot pedophiles who molested his four-year-old daughter.

The Paulsgrove estate in Portsmouth, U.K., exploded into violence when parents discovered a child sex offender was living in their community.

usually remain fairly consistent for each individual over a whole series of crimes.

In profiling terms, they tend to be antisocial individuals, seeing themselves as outcasts from conventional society. They rarely stay for long in one neighborhood since each crime creates such a hue and cry that they feel compelled to move to escape being caught. In many cases they will have an existing criminal record, often involving violence such as assault or rape. Other common factors often include a history as a victim of abuse in their own childhood, which may well be the source of their catastrophic anger. They are often vain and easily bored, especially in terms of sex, and derive such pleasure from their violent acts that they may well try to keep souvenirs or record evidence of them in some other way, so they can relive them from time to time. They are highly likely to abuse their own children, and they can rarely be reformed to avoid repeating their deadly offenses.

Unfortunately, they are often able to present a reassuring front to prison authorities, so there is a danger they may be released on parole to threaten additional victims. Since more publicity has been given to high-profile child murders, abduction, and pedophile approaches, public pressure has resulted in much stricter rules governing where convicted pedophiles can live, and the right of others in the vicinity to be kept informed of their presence. The problems multiply when this information becomes known

to the wider public and demonstrations and vigilante action results in the criminals in question disappearing. Usually, they manage to evade the authorities and go underground where their increasing experience at disguising the threat they represent can make it possible for them to surface in another location with a completely new identity. In cases where their conduct is so dangerous that their presence is eventually revealed by another terrible crime, skillful profiling is an essential weapon in the armory of law enforcement to ensure they are quickly identified, apprehended, and brought back within the legal system.

KIDNAPPERS AND ABDUCTORS

Of course one most extreme crime against children, and occasionally adults, is that of deliberate kidnapping. This differs from all the others in that sexual questions scarcely arise. Deliberate kidnappings fall into two distinct types. Some sad cases result from the extreme anguish that may be caused by the loss of a child or an inability to produce children, developing to the point where sufferers feel they have no alternative to spiriting away someone else's child and raising it as their own. In this case, the last thing they want is publicity, or any contact with the authorities, since this would effectively make their objective of bringing up their new child in a stable home completely impossible. Tracking them down may well prove difficult, except by trying to seek out individuals or couples with failed applications for adoption or fertility treatment, or other warning signs in official records. Furthermore, the children they snatch will almost certainly be infants, and possibly newborn babies, since they would see these victims as far more likely to accept their new situation without intense and continuing distress. In addition, their ultimate objective means the abducted child is unlikely to suffer physical danger, provided they can be found and returned to their own family with the minimum of delay.

The victim is the person most useful to profilers.

Ransom Kidnappings

The other type of deliberate kidnapping, of adult or child, is for the individual kidnapped to act as a weapon, or a lever to exert on those from whom the kidnapping took place, to pay a ransom in return for their safe return. This is an extension of the crime of extortion, covered in Chapter 10, and entirely different rules apply. At one level, where the need for the ransom to be paid is genuine, then the kidnapper has a strong incentive to return the victim unharmed once they have received the payment. Unfortunately, most kidnappers realize the payment of the ransom is the part of the crime that presents the greatest personal threat to themselves in particular. As a result, they are likely to kill the victim immediately before or after the payment is handed over, not least because a released victim is the person most likely to be able to help identify them afterward.

Sadistic Kidnappers

Unfortunately, while ordinary kidnapping crimes impose deadly danger on the victim, there are other kidnappers who never intend to release their victims in the first place. Where sadistic rapists and killers carry out their crimes in order to achieve the highest possible levels of control over their chosen victims, kidnapping offers control of a different kind, not only over the victim but also over their families. To derive the greatest possible satisfaction from their crime and the resulting control over those closely involved, they will often devise detailed and elaborate schemes for the paying of the money and the release of the victim, to raise hopes among the families. Then by not bothering to collect the money and reveal the location of the victim's body, they can feed their own sadistic impulses by the grief and disappointment they inflict on their helpless targets without ever having to meet them.

Profiling Kidnappers

In profiling terms, these two types of kidnapper present different challenges. Kidnappers who want to extort the money have to communicate with those searching for them in order to pass on their instructions over the ransom payments. Consequently, every detail of these messages, whether phone messages or handwritten or printed notes, replaces the conventional crime scene as the source for information on the criminal and their background, education, work, and family roles, and existing criminal record.

On the other hand, profiling the kidnapper who never intends to release his victim but to inflict the maximum pain on family and friends before revealing their loved one is already dead is basically similar to the profiling of any other sadist, rapist, or killer. The method may be different but the overriding priorities are exactly the same, and the hope is that existing insight can be used to reveal the person responsible.

CASE

WHEN: **1994**

WHERE: **Nottingham, U.K.**

VICTIM: **Abbie Humphries**

CULPRIT: **Julie Kelley**

CASE STUDY 40: ABBIE HUMPHRIES' ABDUCTION

New baby Abbie Humphries was born to parents Roger and Karen Humphries on July 1, 1994, at the Queens' Medical Centre Hospital in Nottingham in the United Kingdom. However, within hours of her birth, Karen left Abbie in the care of her husband and the baby's 3-year-old brother while she went to phone her mother to tell her about their good news. While she was away, a nurse appeared at her bedside, and took Abbie away for a hearing test. Crucially, when Karen returned, she immediately suspected the worst. As a midwife she knew only too well that it was not normal to test babies' hearing so soon after birth, and she raised the alarm. The hospital was equipped with a network of CCTV

cameras, and it was a relatively straightforward exercise to find images of the nurse carrying Abbie through the corridors before changing out of her uniform into ordinary clothes and making her escape.

WHO AND WHY?

Profiler Paul Britton was called in to advise police on how to track the kidnapper down. He said the person responsible was probably aged between 20 and her early 30s, and had sufficient familiarity and confidence in a hospital setting to appear convincing to the baby's father and overcome any doubts or questions he might have raised. On the other hand, the CCTV images suggested a degree of panic as she approached the hospital boundaries, which suggested she had carefully planned the actual abduction, but not its aftermath. This conclusion was supported by her failure to bring baby clothes or blankets to add to the impression of a normal mother and baby leaving the hospital.

Why had she done it? One possibility might have been that she was deluded into believing the baby genuinely belonged to her, but her behavior suggested she was well aware she was stealing someone else's infant. Another might be to pay back a grudge against Abbie's parents, a

Kelley eventually admitted she had feigned a pregnancy and stolen Abbie from the hospital where she had just been born.

theory that floundered on the fact that mother and baby had been switched from a different ward at short notice. Equally, a grudge against the hospital would normally produce a different threat at a different target.

Finally, the explanation that made the most sense was that she had taken the baby to help mend a long-term relationship where the lack of a child was perhaps proving a problem. If this was the case, Abbie was in little immediate danger, since the abductor would probably have made everything ready at home for the new baby, including preparing a cover story to explain its sudden arrival. However, it was still urgent that investigators find Abbie before her kidnapper bonded too closely to release her when challenged. Consequently, police began a campaign aimed at the abductor, emphasizing the extreme distress her disappearance was causing her parents.

THE BABY THAT NEVER WAS

A total of 4,700 calls came in from the public, many of them inevitably false leads. However, several drew attention to a house in the

One theory profilers had was that the abductor had everything ready at home for Abbie's arrival.

Julie Kelley, the woman accused of abducting baby Abbie, arrives at Nottingham Court in 1994.

Woolaton district of the city, which motor mechanic Leigh Gilbert shared with his mother and his long-term partner Julie Kelley, 22-years-old and a former dental nurse. Police called at the address, but were disconcerted to find an apparently normal family celebrating the birth of a new baby in an entirely blameless way. More calls were received hinting that there was something suspicious about the household, and a midwife eventually checked the birth records to find that no live birth had been linked to that address.

Police returned to arrest Julie, Leigh, and Julie's mother, and retrieve baby Abbie. Julie Kelley admitted abducting her from the hospital, to try to prevent Gilbert transferring his affections to someone else. She had told him she was pregnant, bought things for the expected baby, decorated a room as a nursery, worn increasing amounts of padding under her clothes, claimed to have suffered food cravings and morning sickness and even attended the hospital for feigned antenatal appointments. She had then abducted Abbie wearing her old dental nurse uniform while her mother and boyfriend were out, and claimed to have given birth before they returned.

CASE

WHEN:	1978–90
WHERE:	Russia
VICTIMS:	Multiple
CULPRIT:	Andrei Chikatilo

41: RUSSIAN SERIAL CHILD KILLER ANDREI CHIKATILO

It began with the finding of the skeleton of a young girl in a strip of woodland near Novocherkassk in southern Russia in 1982. From her bones it was possible to deduce she had been stabbed numerous times, and her eyeballs gouged out. She was finally identified as local 13-year-old Lyubov Biryuk, but there was no evidence that could be used to lead to her killer. All the same, it was an unusual crime for the area: most killings were the result of an angry or drunken dispute with another family member, or in furtherance of a robbery. Yet another victim was found two months later not far away, once again a female skeleton with evidence of multiple stab wounds and gouged-out eyeballs, and a third a month after that with the same terrible signature, and then a fourth.

CLUES AND CONFUSION

The fifth victim was a 10-year-old girl, Olga Stalmachenok, who had not returned from a piano lesson in the town of Novo Shakhtinsk on December 10, 1982. Her naked body was found on April 14, 1983, in a field belonging to a collective farm a few miles from the music school. Because she had been killed in the depths of the Russian winter, her body was fresh enough to display the wounds inflicted on her. She had been stabbed about the head, chest, and stomach with particular damage to her sexual organs and her eyes had been removed with a knife. At last, some conclusions were emerging to guide police as to the type of criminal they were hunting. He must have had a car to take her all the way from the music school to the site where her body had been found, and he must have been reassuring enough and plausible enough to persuade her to accept a lift. He was confident enough to leave his victims on public view, and yet shrewd enough to leave no evidence, but showed an insane level of sadistic violence in his killings and mutilations.

Andrei Chikatilo as a boy.

Investigators preparing for the trial of Chikatilo which took place in Rostov on April 14, 1992.

The total increased with more and more bodies being found. This caused a measure of confusion, since it was believed sadistic serial murderers focused on the same type of victim, while here the bodies of young boys and middle-aged adults also showed up with similar signatures. A potential suspect confessed to the murders, but while he was in custody more victims were found. By the end of the year the total reached 10, and the latest victims showed more mutilation: one young girl had had her nipples torn off, and her bowels eviscerated, while another had been completely disemboweled. The tenth victim was 14-year-old Sergei Markov, who had been stabbed 70 times in the neck, anally raped, and had his genitals cut away and removed altogether.

MORE KILLINGS—AND NEW VARIATIONS

More false suspects confessed to these crimes, but none of them matched the semen found in Markov's body. During 1984 still more victims turned up. Several female bodies had sperm on them that matched the samples from Markov, and the killing of 10-year-old Dmitri Plashnikov in October showed a new variation on the pattern. His penis and the tip of his tongue had

been cut away, and the semen on his shirt contained the same AB antigens as the other victims. However, this time someone had seen the boy with a tall man who wore glasses, had hollow cheeks, and walked stiffly. They had also seen a white car, but could not suggest the identity of the person they had seen.

As more and more victims were found, the pattern changed again, with the killer removing the victim's nose or lips, and leaving them in their open mouths. Yet in spite of the escalating violence, he seemed to make no mistakes. Profilers decided they were looking for a tall, well-built man aged between 25 and 30, with above average intelligence, and verbally convincing. He would probably live with his wife or mother and might have a history of substance abuse, medical experience, or have spent time as a psychiatric patient.

FIRST SIGHTING ENDS IN DISAPPOINTMENT

An undercover police officer, Major Zanasovsky, spotted a tall man in Rostov bus station talking

Evidence given at the trial of Andrei Chikatilo.

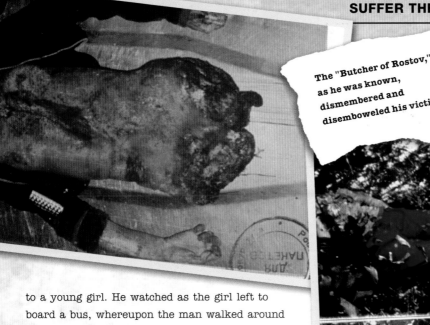

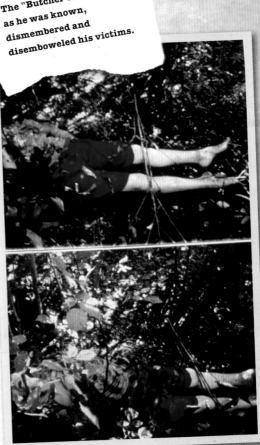

The "Butcher of Rostov," as he was known, dismembered and disemboweled his victims.

to a young girl. He watched as the girl left to board a bus, whereupon the man walked around and sat down next to another young girl. The major approached him and he gave his name as Andrei Chikatilo, manager of a machinery supply company and a former teacher, who simply enjoyed talking to young people. The officer watched him board a bus and followed him. When he saw him talk to different women and eventually persuade a prostitute to give him oral sex under his coat, he arrested Chikatilo and looked through his briefcase to find a jar of petroleum jelly, a grubby towel, a piece of rope, and a sharp kitchen knife. This was promising, but blood tests revealed Chikatilo had type A blood, so could not apparently be the killer.

Psychiatrist Alexander Bukhanovsky drew up another profile of the probable killer. He would be aged between 25 and 50 and be about 5 feet 10 inches tall, and would be sexually dysfunctional. He would remove his victims' eyes to prevent them from looking at him, and could only be aroused by giving full vent to his sadistic preferences. He could clearly draw up a plan and follow it, so was not schizophrenic or retarded, and would be a loner. But this still did not bring police any closer to their quarry.

WORTHLESS EVIDENCE

Then the killings seemed to stop. Perhaps the murderer was dead, or had moved somewhere

Evidence submitted at Chikatilo's trial showed victims of different sexes and ages.

else. A body found in October near Moscow, some 600 miles to the north, showed an exactly similar signature to the earlier victims. The killer must have moved, and this was confirmed when evidence emerged of three young boys killed in the same area, all of them raped and one decapitated. After that the killer was back in the Rostov region, with the discovery of the body of an 18-year-old girl with colored threads and a strand of gray hair found on her body, and traces of sweat containing AB antigens.

At the end of the year, investigators received the most bitter of shocks. Apparently the discrepancy between the blood group of suspects and the antigens in the killer's semen was not conclusive, since laboratory errors or defects in the theory could result in these apparent mismatches. Faced with the possibility of having to reinterview all their suspects, the police mounted a surveillance operation at railway stations, since so many of the victims seemed to disappear after a train journey. No one was seen behaving suspiciously with potential victims, but names of passengers were recorded, and one was seen emerging from nearby woodland to wash his hands at a nearby pump. He had red smears on his face, a cut finger, and twigs on his coat. He had been questioned and cleared in 1984, but he was now back in the frame. His name was Andrei Chikatilo.

THE FULL STORY

Over days and days of detailed, painstaking questioning the full story emerged. He had grown up in Ukraine before the war, where famine made cannibalism and murder commonplace, and as he reached adolescence found he could not produce an erection, but could ejaculate with ease. This lost him girlfriends and eventually his wife, and nurtured in him a corrosive fury against women, for humiliating him, and men for enjoying what he could not. Only when he inflicted pain could he feel arousal, and this took over his life. He had worked as a teacher but had been dismissed for fondling girl students, and he was dismissed from the machinery company for not returning from train trips with the parts he had been sent to fetch. Instead he had been busy killing. Eventually, he was found guilty of five acts of molestation and no less than 52 murders. On February 15, 1994, his final appeal was dismissed and he was taken out and shot.

Homicide chief Viktor Burakov had 220 evidence books against Andrei Chikatilo, who murdered and cannibalized 52 people.

Chikatilo grew up during a famine, which had made cannablism and murder commonplace.

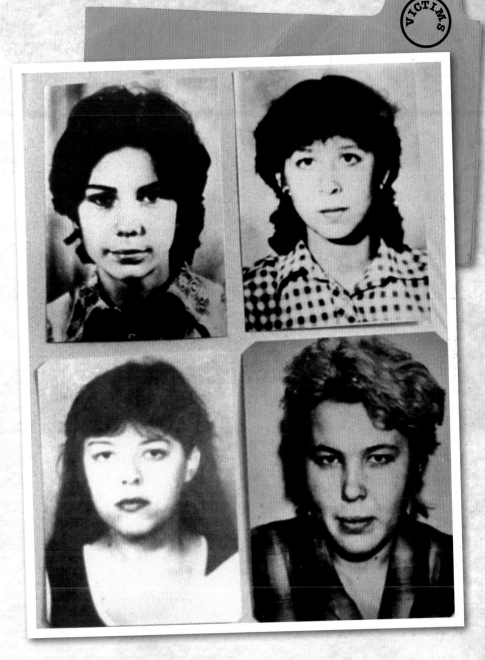

Chikatilo discovered that only when he inflicted pain, could he feel arousal. He possessed a corrosive fury toward women and anger toward men, so his 52 victims were from both sexes and were made up of many ages.

CASE STUDY 42: SURENDER KOLI

WHEN:	**2000s**
WHERE:	**Kithari, India**
VICTIMS:	**Multiple**
CULPRITS:	**Surender Koli and Moninder Singh Pandher**

For two years the inhabitants of the small satellite town of Nithari, which borders the Indian capital of Delhi, had been suffering a series of tragedies as one by one their young children had disappeared. In the main, their parents were the hard-working urban poor—rickshaw operators, manual workers, servers at roadside stalls, or domestic servants in the houses of the well-to-do in the adjacent developments. Complaints to the police seemed to bring no action, and yet from 2004 to 2006 more than 38 children, most of them girls, had apparently vanished without trace in this single community.

TECHNOLOGICAL LEAD

One of the few adults among the missing was a 20-year-old call-girl who went under the name of Payal. However, she was known to have possessed a cell phone that was still being used in the fall of 2006, even though it appeared the SIM card relating it was inactive. Using digital technology to trace the location of the signal, Indian police were able to find the whereabouts of the phone and the name of the rickshaw puller who had sold it on, following the girl's disappearance. The trail

ABOVE AND RIGHT Nithari borders the capital, Delhi.

A rickshaw puller had sold the cell phone of one of Koli's victims, which was still giving a signal.

led to the large and luxurious house of 55-year-old Moninder Singh Pandher, who was taken in for questioning on December 26, but who could shed no light on the missing girl's whereabouts. The next day they turned their attention to Pandher's servant, 38-year-old Surender Koli, who to their surprise not only confessed to killing the girl, but took detectives to what he said was the location of her body, which was in a drain behind Pandher's house.

MASSACRE OF THE INNOCENTS

Police began digging two days later to find the victim's body, but instead they found an entirely different set of remains. One by one they uncovered 17 skeletons of young children, 10 girls and seven boys, and finally managed to identify 15 of them—10 by Koli when shown photographs of the missing, and another five by family members when they were shown the children's belongings also found at the scene.

The torsos of the victims were missing, which led to suspicions of illegal trafficking in organs, but this was later refuted.

An official inquiry into police negligence finally resulted in the suspension of two superintendents and six rank-and-file policemen for dereliction of duty, and the case was finally passed to the Central Bureau of Investigation (CBI). Pandher and Koli had been charged with the murder of the numerous victims, and were taken to CBI headquarters in Delhi on January 11, 2007. Koli had already confessed that he had killed the children one by one

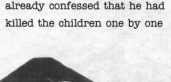

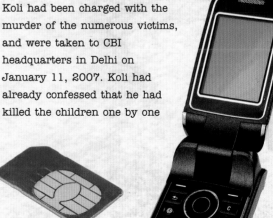

by strangulation. Once each child was dead, he would rape them and then carry the bodies through to his personal washroom in the Pandher house, where he would chop them up. He insisted that his employer was distracted by women troubles and had been completely unaware of what had been going on behind his back and inside his own house. Further searches of the drains around the house revealed the skulls of three more children, some torsos, and different body parts. Many of the torsos missing from the original skeletons were found in the drains, sealed in polythene bags to prevent them being found.

PROFILE OF THE KILLER

It appeared from questioning the suspects that Koli himself was a serial child killer who had no compunction about killing, abusing, and dismembering his tiny victims. Given their ages,

he showed the profile of a mysoped child molester carried to its extreme, with the added horror of the way in which he could enjoy the ultimate possession of those he killed, by eating their flesh and internal organs. Both men were put on trial for the murders, Koli for all of them and his employer for six, and the cases were being heard one by one.

The first charge involved the rape and murder of 14-year-old Rimpa Haldhar, and was heard in a court in Ghaziabad in 2009, resulting in both men being sentenced to death on February 13. However, the Allahabad High Court overturned the verdict on Pandher since he was held to have been in Australia at the time of the killing. More recently charges have been heard relating to the rape and murder of 8-year-old Arti Prasad, daughter of a taxi driver, and a pupil at a local kindergarten who had vanished on September 25, 2006, on her way to visit her grandfather's house for a promised chocolate.

Crowds gather outside the house as police and forensic experts discover bones and other remains of the many child victims.

Crowds gathered in horror as the brutal acts of the most sadistic killer of children in a small community were revealed.

Many of the torsos of the children were discovered sealed in polythene bags in the drains around the house.

Her disappearance was reported to the local police, who took three months to file a charge sheet, and her remains were found in the drains around Pandher's house. At the time of writing both men face the possibility of the death sentence and legal arguments are continuing. Whatever the outcome, there seems little doubt that Surender Koli represents the most sadistic killer of young children within a small community yet recorded.

GETTING IT IN WRITING

Much profiling work depends on analyzing evidence found at the crime scenes to help narrow down the search for the person responsible. In these cases the search for information and the reasoning involved varies little with the type of crime carried out. The crime scene is where the criminal and his or her victim's lives collided, often with violent and sometimes fatal results. Therefore that is the prime source of data that can reveal the criminal's thinking and planning, their background and development, psychological needs, and the reasons why the crime was committed in the first place.

However, where crimes of extortion, kidnapping, or abduction are concerned, the balance between criminal and profiler is tilted in entirely the opposite direction. With crimes of violence, the criminal will either want to conceal their presence at the scene of the crime, by removing the smallest scraps of information they may have left that will tie them to the attack, or they will want to stage the scene to point the authorities in the wrong direction altogether, or to feed their fantasies and need for power in challenging investigators to track them down and make a case. However, for an extortioner or kidnapper to collect a ransom or inflict damage on the victims and their families, they have to make and maintain contact with the people to whom they are making these demands, or to the police if they are involved in negotiating arrangements for the payment and handover.

Here the perpetrator faces two powerful threats. In merely making contact, they risk revealing something that will eventually lead police to their door. In negotiating the arrangements for the ransom to be paid, they run a much greater risk in that any flaw in their plans, or simply an error in passing them on to the other party involved, may mean that they end up being arrested rather than paid.

Sending threats, demands, or ransom notes to police leaves the perpetrator vulnerable.

COMMUNICATION LINKS

Each of the usual communication channels presents both risks and opportunities. The criminal may telephone the family of a kidnap victim, to confirm they have successfully seized the person in question and to warn against any attempt to contact the police. Often the initial call will also try to set up the payment arrangements, or these may be detailed in a follow-up call. Here the criminal can assume the time when contact is made presents a very real personal danger, so they want to shut down communications as quickly as possible. On the other hand, forcing the victim's family to wait for more information, anxious as they must be about the condition and fate of the hostage, adds to the pressure on them to agree to a deal speedily, and without asking too many awkward questions. Moreover, the same priorities face the criminals involved in using extortion rather than a kidnapping, as their means of pressing an organization rather than a family into handing over money to prevent a tragedy.

Even in making these demands, the criminal is effectively handing over more information on who they are and how they think than they would otherwise prefer to give. For example, how big is the sum of money demanded? Is it large enough to be credible, in terms of what the family might be able to raise in the time available? If it is too low to be convincing, it suggests an amateur who has seized on this high-risk means to raise money to meet some desperate and unpredictable need. This at least offers investigators the hope that whatever means are laid down for the handover of the cash will be sufficiently flawed to allow them to trace and follow the kidnapper and release the hostage before they can be harmed.

On the other hand, what seems a carefully chosen and researched level of ransom is an indication that the people behind the abduction are seasoned professionals. As a result, there is perhaps more reason for hope, in that it is in the kidnappers' interests to return the hostage unharmed, and they are more likely to have taken extreme care not to reveal their identities to the hostage. This allows them to carry out the release of the victim without feeling so threatened that they have to kill them to eliminate the most vital source of evidence open to those hunting them.

The most dangerous and dispiriting kind of ransom demand to receive is of course none at all. This may show the crime was intended from the beginning to result in the death of the hostage as its primary objective, and the additional grief caused to the family is simply a bonus for the abductor involved. On the other hand, these criminals sometimes communicate with the family or the police without ever issuing a credible ransom demand or arrangements for payment, since this extends

Even the size of the ransom demand gives valuable information to investigators.

A criminal may demand a ransom under the threat of poisoning the food or medicines of ordinary shoppers.

payback was involved, opening up possibilities for careful detective work to help identify the person or persons responsible.

EXTORTION FOR FINANCIAL GAIN

Many of these priorities and possibilities will also apply in cases of extortion. In a sense, these are basically the same crimes as kidnaps for ransom, except that the threat imposed to produce the ransom payment is not the life of someone in the kidnapper's hands, but of something the kidnapper might do if the ransom is not paid. Very often, given the character of modern shopping systems, the threat hinges on the possible contamination of food or pharmaceuticals on store or supermarket shelves in a way that normal security systems would not pick up in advance. Therefore, should the store or the company operating a chain of stores not pay the ransom, customers are going to buy the food and suffer poisoning as a result. At its most extreme, these extortion attempts are backed by the ultimate threat: a poison lethal enough to cause the death or serious injuries of customers who buy the product in good faith, without realizing the hidden threat in what they are eating.

From the extortionist's point of view, this kind of crime has massive advantages over kidnapping. The targets are more plentiful and less heavily guarded than families wealthy enough to cope with a massive ransom demand. With huge numbers of individual store outlets, policing them to the level needed to spot someone switching jars on a particular shelf would be virtually impossible. This makes it possible for the criminals to confirm the seriousness of the threat they present in a way totally impossible for kidnappers. Where a claim that the son or daughter of a rich family was

their control over those involved without adding greatly to the risk they face. In cases like these, where negotiations appear to be continuing, police will often ask the abductors to provide some proof that the hostage is still alive and well. In the past this has often meant showing photographs of the hostage holding the clearly identifiable current issue of a daily newspaper, or replying to questions asked over a telephone line.

Once the communication link has been established, police experts can monitor the demands and responses made by the kidnapper, which can reveal much about their state of mind, and with it the serious chances of achieving the release of the hostage. Do the arrangements made for payment add up to a credible plan by someone with experience in this type of crime, or do they reveal the muddled thinking and lack of confidence of an amateur? Does anything the kidnapper say reveal why they carried out the abduction, and why that particular person was seized—were they simply easily accessible, were they chosen on the spur of the moment, or were their movements carefully tracked for weeks on end to make the operation as smooth and risk-free as possible? If they believe the victim was deliberately chosen because of who they are, rather than the wealth of their family, this could also indicate some element of grudge or

One ransomer demanded that payments be sent to an account and the card sent to multiple addresses.

distinguished from the normal contents had been added, and the can resealed. Cans like this would be placed on the shelves of five different supermarkets every day, effectively destroying the company's business. The only way to prevent this was to pay $150,000 each year into specified bank accounts over a five-year period. The ATM cards and PIN numbers for each account were then to be mailed to a large number of accommodation addresses, so that the police could not stake out each one. This would leave the criminal free to withdraw the ransom payments from any of each society's ATM machines, with almost negligible risk to himself.

about to be snatched would fail, simply because the obvious response would be to improve security to the point where the crime became impossible, retail operations could only achieve that level of security by shutting down their entire operations, which would almost certainly cost them many times the sum actually demanded. So all the extortionist needs to do is carry out the contamination of the chosen products and place them on shelves of as many different individual stores as possible. Once these are found and recognized for what they are, then the threat becomes all too real.

In one notorious extortion case in the United Kingdom in August 1988, the criminal actually made the threat in the most direct and confident way possible, by sending a can of contaminated dog food to the company who made it. With it was a letter that claimed the can had been opened, toxic chemicals that could not be

Police advised the company to delay the ransom payments, blaming the banking bureaucracy. The criminal's reply was to add more threats and a demonstration consisting of leaving three cans of dog food at different supermarkets, marked as "contaminated." When tested, these were found to contain fragments of razor blades concealed in the meat. By March the following year the campaign had reached an impasse. The criminal was now demanding $1.9 million and had left a total of 14 contaminated cans, following a telephone warning each time. When the demands stopped it seemed the company's policy had paid off.

Fragments of razor blades were found in cans of dog food left by the ransomer.

STAINLESS

BABIES IN THE FIRING LINE

On March 22, 1989, a letter similar to that originally sent to the pet food manufacturer was received by the Heinz food company. With the letter was a jar of Heinz baby food, outwardly normal but in fact found to contain caustic soda, an odorless and colorless chemical that could inflict terrible burns but that was easily obtained in drain-cleaning agents. The company decided not to deal with the blackmailer, but this time no warnings were given before a mother suffered burns when opening a jar of contaminated baby food and an infant suffered a cut lip from razor blade pieces in a container of yogurt.

So far the criminal had conducted a highly professional extortion operation, and the company was forced to set up the bank accounts needed to pay the ransom demand. But the contents of the communications and the details of the plan were already telling profilers a great deal about the type of person they were dealing with. He was clearly mature enough to think and plan exactly how to achieve his objectives with minimal risk, reasonably well-educated and of average or above average intelligence. The clever method for securing the payments suggested he had been a policeman who would have been aware of how ransom payments were watched to catch the person responsible, but profiler Paul Britton suspected an even closer link. The first time this payment method had been used was in a murder threat campaign, and clearly the present perpetrator had copied it. However, the most significant feature of that earlier example was that the criminal had set up a clever system but had made the mistake of revisiting a small number of ATM machines in his own vicinity. Police had monitored the transactions and eventually been able to target the machines in question, ultimately capturing the person behind the crime.

Inside Information

In this case, the criminal made no such mistake. In fact, he seemed to know when the police

Poisoning and tampering with prepared baby food caused widespread panic among mothers and shoppers.

targeted a particular area to watch ATM machines, whereupon he avoided them with ease. This strongly suggested he had contacts with the investigation, possibly because he was recently retired from the force and might know many of those still involved. A small team was put together to work out whether there was any pattern in the cash machine withdrawals, without telling anyone on the wider team, and this smaller unit began watching individual ATMs. At last, on October 21, 1989, officers saw a tall bearded man walk over to an ATM in Enfield, north of London. When they approached him, they recognized him as Rodney Whitchelo, a former member of the London Regional Crime Squad, who had actually been part of the investigation until taking early retirement on the grounds of ill-health, which was intended to give him more time to run his extortion campaign. On seeing his former colleagues, he fainted. Late the following year, he was sentenced to 17 years in jail. He had also triggered a revolution in the food and pharmaceuticals industry, forcing makers to produce tamper-proof packs that showed clearly when they had been opened, and which were impossible to reseal.

GRIEVANCE EXTORTION

Rodney Whitchelo failed to fit the normal profile for extortionists operating this kind of blackmail, in that he was clever and closely involved with the operation set up to catch him. In most cases extortionists are motivated by anger directed toward the company that makes the product they target, or the company that retails it, or against the wider target of society in general. Individuals who fit this profile usually have a long history of personal failure in areas such as education, work, social life and personal relationships. Other common factors include a difficulty meeting women of their own age and educational level, and may also include a measure of disability or mental or physical limitations. There is also a significant tendency to opt for jobs as low-level authority figures such as security guards, which would give them a closer knowledge of how retail operations work. They may also have served in the armed forces, generally in the less technical branches, and their records may show evidence of psychiatric and behavioral problems.

COLLATERAL DAMAGE

Also worthy of note is the possibility of extortion camouflaging another offense. One case in particular involved the criminal using an extortion attempt to hide a straightforward case of murder. This began as two suspicious deaths a week apart. The first involved 40-year-old Susan Snow, a Seattle bank employee, who was found dead on her bathroom floor on June 11, 1986. She showed symptoms of cyanide poisoning, shortly after suffering a headache and taking extra-strength Excedrin painkilling tablets. A few days later, police were called by Stella Nickell to report that her husband Bruce,

who had died two weeks earlier, apparently from emphysema, had also taken these painkillers just before he died. She was convinced they had been contaminated and intended to sue the makers for compensation in a wrongful-death campaign.

Police checked out both claims, and found nothing sinister in the sad death of Susan Snow. In the case of Bruce Nickell, the figures failed to add up. After checking all the stores in the area selling these tablets, they found only five had contaminated products on their shelves. Yet the Nickell household had two bottles of contaminated tablets, which Stella claimed had been bought from different stores on different occasions. The chances against both being contaminated on a random basis were truly astronomical, and they examined the tablets more carefully. Mixed in with the deliberate contaminant were traces of an accidental contaminant of a completely different kind, intended to exterminate algae in tropical fish tanks.

Police found an assistant at a local pet store who had sold the algae exterminator to Stella Nickell for the couple's fish tanks, along with a pestle and mortar used to grind up the cyanide tablets to add the powder to the painkillers. They also found large insurance policies on Bruce's life with Stella as the sole beneficiary. She had a history of fraud, forgery, and child abuse, and was facing imminent bankruptcy. Finally on May 9, 1988, she was sentenced to 180 years in prison for two murders—her husband's and that of the entirely innocent Susan Snow, whose role was to add reinforcement to the idea of a botched extortion attempt rather than a genuine murder.

Poisoned painkiller packets caused seven deaths, including three members of the same family.

CASE

WHEN:	1982
WHERE:	Chicago, USA
VICTIMS:	Multiple
CULPRIT:	James William Lewis

CASE STUDY 43: THE TYLENOL BLACKMAIL CASE

One of the most notorious product tampering cases in the US was centered in the Chicago area in the fall of 1982, and related to the popular painkillers Tylenol Extra Strength. In this case, though, the criminal responsible did not mount a demonstration to press producers to pay his demands without harming anyone. Instead, he simply laced glass bottles of the tablets with lethal potassium cyanide and placed them on the shelves of different drugstores and pharmacies without telling anyone of his plans. The results were soon plain to see. In three days, at the end of September, no less than seven people in the area, including three members of one family, a 12-year-old girl, and the mother of a newly born baby took the

tablets to cope with pain, only to collapse and die.

Faced with a threat of this magnitude, the authorities acted quickly. The product was taken off the shelves immediately, and people with Tylenol in their houses were asked to bring the tablets to their local police stations so they could be checked out.

In the meantime, closer inspection of the contaminated tablets revealed some highly significant factors. The tablets were made in two different plants a long distance apart, so it was highly unlikely they could have been contaminated at source. The cyanide was corrosive enough to break down the gel coating sealing the tablets, so the tampering would soon become obvious. This, together with the fact that only a single contaminated bottle was ever found at each store targeted, suggested the extortionist had chosen Tylenol Extra Strength because the bottles could be opened and closed in seconds. In other words, he had approached a store he wanted to target, had taken a bottle of the product off the shelf, opened it, added a contaminated tablet, closed the bottle, and left, without alerting anyone's suspicions.

The painkiller poisonings centered in the Chicago area in 1982, and only required a few tampered bottles to be effective.

The President of the makers of Tylenol warned the Senate Committee that there is no such thing as a "safe" package.

TYLENOL TURN-IN ←

Boxes of Tylenol were recalled to try to prevent further poisonings.

FINDING THE POISONER

The ransom demands took a long time to arrive. The first was from a person claiming to be the poisoner and demanding a payment of $100,000, but he was caught and unmasked as Vernon Williams, an unemployed opportunist from New Jersey who had read details of the campaign in the papers and wanted to cash in. The real ransom demand was for a total of $1 million to prevent future poisonings. It was clear from the text that the writer, who signed himself Robert Richardson, knew exactly how the drops of the tampered tablets were made. Moreover, other letters by the same hand had been sent to newspapers in the area, demanding that police reopen the investigation of the murder of Raymond West four years earlier.

FBI profiler John Douglas had already drawn up a profile of the criminal responsible, based on the usual extortionist makeup, but with some additional factors. He was likely to be prone to writing angry and threatening letters to high-profile public figures to redress some grievance he would claim to have suffered. He would also be unable or unhappy to contact his intended targets face to face, preferring instead to carry out impersonal killings at random.

In the end it was the letters to the papers that provided the breakthrough. Since these were all postmarked in New York City, and since the crimes had been carried out in Chicago, Douglas reasoned the criminal would want to keep in close touch with what was happening in the investigation in his home city. This would mean him paying regular visits to a New York reference library that put Chicago papers on public display. When police and FBI staked out these libraries, looking for figures who resembled those captured on CCTV footage in stores where contaminated tablets had been left, they found their quarry on December 12, 1982. He was 36-year-old James William Lewis, a former Chicago accountant. Murder victim Raymond West had been one of his clients, and he felt that a sloppy police investigation had placed suspicion on him, though no charges had been made. He fitted the profile closely, even having written to President Reagan, threatening to kill him if he did not make changes to the tax system. However, because there was no direct evidence to show he had placed the poison in the tablets, he was never charged with murder. He was charged with extortion and sentenced to 20 years in jail, and once he was locked up, the poisonings stopped.

A worker checks the newly implemented safety seals on Tylenol bottles.

CASE

WHEN: 1992

WHERE: New Jersey, USA

VICTIMS: Sidney Reso

CULPRIT: Arthur Seale, Jackie Seale

Exxon Mobil's Las Flores Canyon oil processing plant, where Exxon were accused of committing environmental crimes.

CASE STUDY 44: THE EXXON KIDNAPPING

When Sidney Reso, President of Exxon International, was abducted on the way to his office on the morning of Wednesday, April 29, 1992, it seemed at first glance to be a reasonably professional operation. He had left his New Jersey home at 7 a.m., but never made it beyond the end of his drive, where his VW station wagon was found with its driver's door open and the engine still running. The kidnappers made contact the next day, when a female voice on the telephone revealed that a message would be left in a shopping mall in the neighboring town of Livingstone. This was a note instructing the family not to contact the police but to open a cell phone account that would allow the kidnappers to contact them once they had placed an advertisement in a local paper to inform them of the cell phone number.

PHONE CONTACT

This was their first mistake. They had planned the abduction very carefully, knowing from watching their target that he always stopped at the end of his drive, out of sight of the house, to pick up his morning paper that would have been left on the grass verge. On the morning of the kidnapping, they simply moved the paper to the other side of the drive, forcing their intended victim to stop the car, climb out and walk to pick up the paper, when they had seized him and made off at speed. But their lack of experience let them down: they were completely unaware that calls made to cell phones could easily be traced by police.

There followed a series of calls from the kidnappers to the police cell phone, to claim a total ransom of $18.5 million and to set up arrangements for it to be paid. All the calls were made from public payphones in the area, but attempts to catch the kidnappers in the act of phoning came to nothing. They claimed to demand the money to account for the environmental crimes Exxon had committed, but checks with local environmentalists soon revealed this claim was false, and simply made to mask a straightforward extortion.

SCRAPS OF PHYSICAL EVIDENCE

Gregg McCrary of the FBI profiled the kidnapper as having some kind of direct connection with the victim and the company he ran: was the kidnapper someone who had worked for the company, and who suffered from some real or imaginary grievance as a result? For the moment, all they could do was examine the ransom note as closely as possible, since this remained the only physical evidence available to them. Two things stood out. First, a hair identified as belonging to a golden Labrador was stuck to a page, which suggested the abductors were not desperate down-and-outs but people

more comfortably off. Secondly, some of the text was highly significant, with terms such as "surveillance" confirming a possible background working in security, the police or the military, a normal factor in this type of crime.

The events that followed reinforced the combination of cool professionalism and amateur incompetence. Originally the kidnappers set up an arrangement for the ransom to be paid on May 3, but failed to make contact again as promised to give more details of how, when, and where the money was to be handed over. More messages were received by phone and by letter to set up another arrangement, to be confirmed by coded messages published as small ads in local newspapers. All this took time, though, and it was not until June 18 that the payment operation finally went into action.

RANSOM PAYMENT THAT FAILED

The investigators were ordered to drive the victim's family's station wagon with the ransom and the cell phone used for communications carried with them. They were called by the kidnappers from a succession of public payphones to direct them along a complex route intended to evade any pursuit. At the same time, other agents were watching the most promising local phone boxes to try to catch one of the calls actually being made. They finally struck lucky at 10:40 p.m., when they spotted a white male using a phone box in a shopping mall in the town of Chester to make a call that was picked up on the cell phone. The surveillance team followed the caller when he left the box, and saw him board a hired car and drive

Protestors against oil-giant Exxon. The kidnapper claimed to be one of them, but this was shown to be false.

off—but not before they had noted the license number.

At 11:16 p.m., another surveillance team caught a white female in a public call box, this time in the town of Gladstone, making another call to the cell phone. This was followed by a series of calls sending the ransom vehicle round the whole district before finally sending it to the Far Hills railway station. As they waited in the station parking lot, they saw the hired car with the first caller pull in, wait a few minutes and then drive away. Though it was later spotted by another team, they lost track of it, and the opportunity seemed lost.

SUCCESS—AND FAILURE

However, investigators failed to account for the naiveté of the kidnappers. The FBI traced the license number to the hire depot that supplied the car. They went to the depot after midnight to check the records. To their unbounded surprise, the car they had lost drew up outside at 12:45 a.m. The kidnappers had given up on the payment attempt and called to return the hire car. They were arrested and taken for questioning, when their identities were revealed as Arthur and Jackie Seale. Arthur Seale was a former policeman, who had later worked as a security guard at the Exxon headquarters, where he had devised the idea of kidnapping Sidney Reso to raise a large enough ransom to pay off all his considerable business debts. They had stalked their intended prey to discover his routine, and devised the simple means of using his morning newspaper pick-up as a way of getting him out of his car in a place free from surveillance, where they could order him at gunpoint into their van.

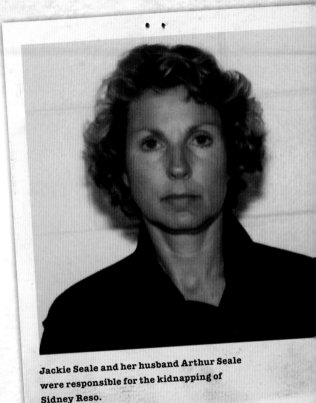

Jackie Seale and her husband Arthur Seale were responsible for the kidnapping of Sidney Reso.

Sadly, long before they had tried to collect the ransom, their victim was already dead. As early as May 4, while Sidney Reso was gagged and blindfolded and shut up in the confines of a wooden box, he had suffered a fatal heart attack from all the stress he had undergone. This was made worse by the Seales' gun having gone off accidentally during the actual abduction, wounding their victim in the arm, and by him not being given enough to eat or drink during five days in close confinement. He had been buried in a shallow grave in a forest at the southern end of the state. All the indications were that the kidnappers intended to return him unharmed once they had collected the ransom, but he had died as a consequence of their own bungling rather than a deliberate, cold-blooded murder. Nevertheless, Arthur Seale was sentenced to life imprisonment and his wife to 20 years for extortion.

CASE

WHEN: 1989

WHERE: Florida, USA

VICTIMS: Multiple

CULPRIT: Oba Chandler

CASE STUDY 45: THE BODIES IN THE BAY

A sailing party returning to Tampa Bay in Florida following a trip to Key West on June 4, 1989, were passing under the Sunshine Skyway highway bridge when they saw a body floating in the sea. A second body was discovered 2 miles off the harbor pier in St Petersburg, to the north of the first discovery, and as the coastguards were retrieving this body, a call came in to report a third body a few hundred yards to the eastward. All three bodies were female, with their hands and feet bound and ropes tied around their necks to concrete weights. All three were gagged with sticky tape, and they were naked below the waist.

FLORIDA VACATION

Post-mortem examinations revealed all three had been alive when they were dropped into the water. The victims were 36-year-old Joan Rogers and her daughters, 17-year-old Michelle and 14-year-old Christe, who were vacationing in Florida while husband and father Hal Rogers ran the family dairy farm in Willshire, Ohio. They had left home on May 26, and reached Florida on June 1.

The Harbor Pier in St Petersburg, Florida, where the bodies of Joan Rogers and her two daughters were found in the water.

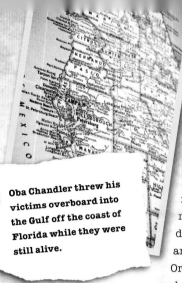

Oba Chandler threw his victims overboard into the Gulf off the coast of Florida while they were still alive.

On June 8, a housekeeper at the Days Inn motel had noticed their beds had not been slept in, but nothing else in the room had been disturbed. They had arrived from Orlando on June 3 and checked into the motel in the early afternoon, and had last been seen alive at the motel restaurant that evening. Their car was found parked at a boat dock on the Courtney Campbell Causeway, and when experts compared the timeline from their disappearance to the point where their bodies had been discovered, they said it was certain they had been dropped overboard from a boat, and not from anywhere on land.

KILLER AND VICTIMS: HOW DID THEY MEET?

Unfortunately there was almost nothing in the way of evidence to link the victims to their killer. Given how their bodies ended in the water, the most likely scenario was that they had taken a boat trip, during which the boatman had sexually assaulted them, then thrown them in the water to prevent any repercussions. But how could the man be found? Time dragged on with no progress in the case, until detectives decided to use the one tenuous link between killer and victims. Investigators had assumed they had died at the hands of a disorganized killer who had unexpectedly found himself with three attractive women under his control and had acted violently, lethally, and on impulse. The chances were high that he would have attempted rape before, and maybe carried it through, though not necessarily killing his earlier victim.

How had the women met their killer? One explanation might well have been that, as strangers to the Tampa Bay area, they had found difficulty finding the motel, and had stopped to ask directions from a local who happened to own a boat. Possibly the boatman had offered them an evening cruise in the bay, and their acceptance had led to their deaths. Certainly this theory was borne out by the discovery in their car of a brochure containing handwritten directions to the boat dock, and a brief description, jotted down by Joan Rogers, of the boat they were to look for.

EARLIER ATTEMPTS

Finally, after a long delay while the case had apparently gone cold, it was decided to publish the handwriting samples on billboards all around the area, together with details of the victims and the known facts about the case. They soon received a response from someone who identified the writing as being that of a neighbor, one Oba Chandler. To prove his assertion, he provided a work order written by Chandler, and the handwriting proved a perfect match. Chandler himself was a native of Ohio, having been born in Cincinnati, and grown up only 100 miles from the Rogers' farm. He had suffered a disturbed childhood blighted by the suicide of his adored father. By his early teenage years he had been involved in a variety of petty

Agreeing to an unofficial cruise tour may have cost the Rogers their lives.

The Sunshine Skyway highway bridge where the Rogers' bodies were found floating in the water.

Anna Maria Island, where Chandler is suspected of committing a previous rape and murder.

crimes, including breaking and entering, kidnapping, and armed robbery.

He was also found to have approached two female Canadian tourists two weeks before the Rogers' murders, showing that he felt confident enough to approach more than one potential victim at a time. In fact one of the women, Barbara Mottram, refused to go on his boat for a trip, although her friend Judy Blair agreed. Chandler had raped her, but knowing that her friend remained aware of the trip, he was forced to drop his victim back on dry land.

One of the employees in his aluminum building business testified Chandler had bragged to him about dating three women on the night of the murders, and finally his own daughter revealed he had told her about killing the three women, which is why he had moved his family away from Tampa to avoid the hue and cry.

At his trial, Chandler insisted on conducting his own defense and constructed an elaborate set of alibis based on the women not having

turned up for the booked trip, and on his having gone fishing on his own, only to have suffered engine failure that delayed his return to land. He claimed to have called the coastguard and the Florida Marine Patrol only to find they were too busy and subsequently repaired the fault himself. These were refuted by official phone records and expert testimony on the engine installation of his boat. He was found guilty of the murders on November 4, 1994, and remains on Death Row while lengthy and complex appeals are conducted. Nevertheless, profilers are convinced that in taking on three victims at once, he must have gained confidence from having succeeded at a similar crime beforehand. He remains an official suspect for the rape and murder of a woman whose body was found floating in the water off Anna Maria Island in 1982, but as he is already under sentence of death, he has not been formally accused of this crime.

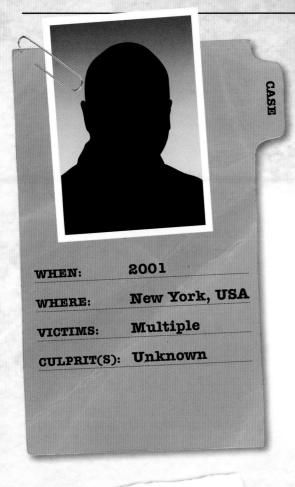

CASE

WHEN: 2001

WHERE: New York, USA

VICTIMS: Multiple

CULPRIT(S): Unknown

CASE STUDY 46: THE ANTHRAX LETTERS

In the horrified aftermath of the Twin Towers tragedy of September 11, 2001, the US security service were on a heightened state of alert in case further terrorist attacks, possibly of an entirely different kind, should follow soon afterward. The next threat was not long in arriving, in the form of letters laced with anthrax bacilli, and addressed to two senators, a worker at NBC and the New York Post Office. Apart from minutely detailed analysis of the anthrax they contained, FBI profilers were limited to the information they were able to deduce from the letters, their content and the handwriting of the person who had sent them. However, this added up to a surprisingly detailed profile of the person responsible, and though no more letters have been received and the person has not been identified, the information remains on file to help target the perpetrator if more attempts should be made.

HANDWRITING QUIRKS

First of all, the profilers noticed the writing on the letters and their envelopes was entirely in capitals. The one slight inconsistency was that the initial letter of the first word of each sentence was written as a slightly larger capital letter, which indicates that the writer may well be uncomfortable writing lowercase characters.

Letters containing the anthrax virus were sent to New York through the postal system.

The New York anthrax case sparked fear across the United States, not just in New York.

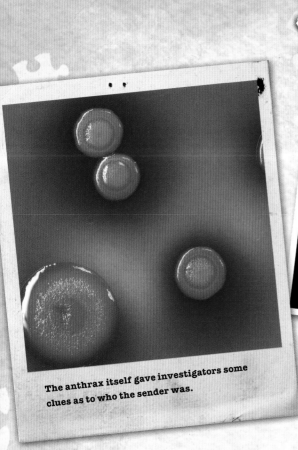

The anthrax itself gave investigators some clues as to who the sender was.

Another significant sign was the way the writer set down dates as 09-11-2001 rather than the more common 09/11/2001. Each line of writing tends to tilt downward from left to right on a consistent basis, and the writer uses the words "can not" rather than the more common "cannot." Finally, the number "1" is written with a definite angled downstroke at the top of the main vertical line, rather than the simple single vertical downstroke on its own, which is the more common form outside continental Europe. So far, this information is only of limited use in terms of profiling the person responsible. However, these idiosyncrasies do provide a set of recognizable symptoms that can be compared with any other letters received as part of a similar campaign in the future. Should all these features be present, the chances are high that they are all written by the same person.

PROFILING THE SENDER

Much more helpful in profiling terms is the contents of the letters—the use of anthrax to pose a deadly and pervasive threat. This suggests a much more detailed portrait of the person behind the campaign. For example, profilers believe he will be an adult male, whose work (if he is employed) will not tend to bring him into close contact with the public. Given his apparent confidence with such a potentially deadly agent, he may well work in a scientific laboratory and have either scientific qualifications or a keen interest in this branch of science.

He will also have a source of supply of anthrax, and has the knowledge, the experience, and the skill to refine it to the standards of the samples found in the letters. He will have taken the necessary precautions to remain safe in close proximity to the anthrax, which may include antibiotics or an anthrax vaccination. He will also have access to the necessary laboratory equipment, including a microscope and centrifuge. Finally, his behavior tends to categorize him as a rational organized individual capable of planning his actions and carrying them out.

He must also have direct or indirect contact and familiarity with the Trenton area in New Jersey, where the letters were postmarked, and must also be comfortable traveling in and around that area. His victims were all specifically targeted, including the use of the right address and ZIP code, which probably means the recipients are important to the suspect, and may well represent a pattern of real or imagined grievances, which to him demand payback of this kind.

KILLING AT A DISTANCE

The type of crime also shows the person responsible is not confrontational, preferring to carry out his attacks from a distance and anonymously. He lacks the personal skills needed to tackle people face to face, and will probably have tried this tactic before, though not necessarily with anthrax, but by sending threatening letters to people against whom he bears a grudge. He will either be a loner, or if in a relationship, there will be an element of some exploitation.

Before sending the letters, those close enough to him may have noticed behavioral changes and a greater tendency toward secrecy. He may show disinterest in media coverage of the terrorist threat, and he may have begun taking antibiotics unexpectedly as part of becoming mission-oriented. After the mailing of the letters he is more likely to show mood swings, with greater levels of anxiety and absenteeism, marked tendencies to withdrawal and preoccupation, and changes in sleep patterns and eating routines. So far, the suspect has not been identified, but the greater insight resulting from careful profiling will be of help as soon as anyone is apprehended with connections to this campaign in the future.

A pond drained at Frederick Municipal Forest, Maryland, to investigate the anthrax poisoning case.

The process of cleaning up the anthrax attack required specially trained personnel.

QUESTIONS AND ANSWERS

The most dramatic benefits of profiling are usually linked to understanding the kind of person who committed a crime or series of crimes, from studying evidence left at the scene, or signature aspects of the criminal's psychology, experience, development, and background as an aid to identifying and capturing the person responsible.

But this insight into the criminal's motivation and priorities can be crucial even after the moment of arrest. Because profilers have uncovered the perpetrator's aims and objectives, strengths and weaknesses, drives and desires, they make it possible for investigators to fine-tune their tactics for questioning the criminal to overcome their natural reluctance to admit to a crime, and persuade them to confess what they did, and how and why they did it. Experience shows that each approach has to be tailored to its target to be effective. A strategy that works with one type of crime and one individual suspect may prove to be entirely wrong with another suspect for the same crime.

Investigators scrutinize detained criminals as they are interviewed, in an attempt to piece together a profile from their behavior that may shed further light on evidence left at the crime scene.

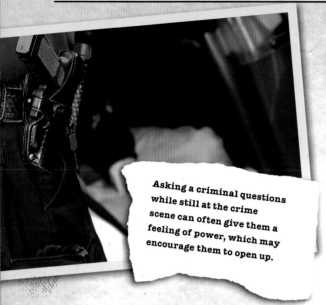

Asking a criminal questions while still at the crime scene can often give them a feeling of power, which may encourage them to open up.

A VITAL CHANGE OF TACTICS

In some cases, with additional background information on a particular person, investigators can switch tactics to adopt a more effective approach, to capitalize on the personality of the person being questioned. One particular case in point was a double shooting of a high-school girl and her boyfriend from a Midwestern community, each shot to death in the boyfriend's car. The prime suspect was the girl's stepfather, the local football coach, who had a frightening reputation among local people as a demanding and threatening control freak. Although he had made a significant admission under questioning that he had not killed the couple while in his right mind, he had then retracted the statement and challenged the questioners to prove anything different.

This was the kind of impasse that could easily have wrecked any case against the suspect. But profilers advised the questioners to change their aim. Instead of simply questioning their suspect, they should exploit his aggressive masculinity and need to control and dominate every situation by appearing to ask for his help in solving the case. Very often, investigators will try to use a picture or an object related to the crime as a trigger to remind the suspect of what actually happened and what their involvement was, as a background to the questioning. So the suspect was taken to a different interrogation room, where pictures of the crime scene had been put up on the walls. Here, against a background more closely related to the crime, they completely changed their approach.

Instead of pressing him to admit his part in the killings, they were now virtually admitting they were making no progress in finding out the truth, and any help he could give them to track down whoever had carried out the killings would be invaluable. This effectively placed the suspect in a position of strength, since instead of being the target of aggressive questions he was now seen as a trusted and respected adviser, who was simply adding his viewpoint as a stepfather who had lost his stepdaughter, to help capture those responsible. Before long, he was beginning to suggest to the police how they could direct their search for suspects, and was responding positively to what he saw as his increasing control over the proceedings.

Yet he remained unaware of the trap he was walking into. When he and the police had been positioned as adversaries, simple self-preservation had forced him to remain defensive and on his guard, which had paradoxically prevented him from confronting the truth of what he had done. Once they began behaving as allies in the campaign to catch his stepdaughter's killer, he was forced progressively to approach the undeniable truth, that he was the person they were all seeking for her death. Because they were discussing and reviewing the crime in the smallest details, he was being brought up short, time and again, to face the consequences of his actions, and slowly the increasing pressure began to erode his control over the situation in which he found himself. It took eight hours to bring him to the point where he finally broke down and wept. Even then he was left to bring his emotions under control, but when his collaborators resumed their review, he decided he could take no more, and finally confessed he had killed both victims.

QUESTIONING METHODS

FBI profiler John Douglas has made an extensive study of this vital stage in the investigation, and how to approach the prime suspect in the right way to persuade them to confess. He found it expedient to plan the route along which the suspect would be guided after being brought to police headquarters and taken to the interrogation room. This would be arranged so suspect and questioners would have to walk through the room occupied by the investigators actively pursuing the crime. By emphasizing the number of different people, the pace of the questioning, the stacks of files and papers left on desks and the pictures pinned to the walls, the intention is to imply a huge amount of effort by expert and dedicated people to find out the truth.

Whatever pictures or CCTV footage exist of the suspect at large would be playing, to suggest the police already know all the material facts, and therefore the only sensible tactic would be to confess and reduce the likely sentence. Another way of emphasizing this is to have large and legible wall charts showing the different penalties likely to be imposed in the event of a not guilty plea being disbelieved by the court. Extra psychological pressure can be placed on suspects by questioning them out of normal working hours, when they would normally expect to be relaxing. Questioning them early in the morning or late at night suggests two inferences: the investigating team are dedicated enough and energetic enough to carry on until they find the truth, and that there are no conventional social limits to bring the questioning to an end, like lunchtime or the end of the working day.

Finally, there are specific ways of approaching and questioning specific types of criminal. Disorganized criminals do not usually have the social skills needed to relate to other people for prolonged amounts of time, so that simply keeping up a lengthy conversation with the suspect adds to the pressure. Usually they respond well to questioners who seem to accept their stories at the beginning of the session, which gives the investigators the chance to speed up the pace of the conversation and then introduce a sudden vital query that has real relevance to the case, to break the suspect's confidence and throw them on the back foot, making a damaging admission that much more probable.

Organized criminals march to a different psychological rhythm. They think of themselves as primarily competent and professional, and respect and empathize with those qualities in their questioners. This allows them to be more clearly adversarial, but the onus is on the investigators to be ruthlessly consistent in the information they present to the suspect as genuine. If they have hoped or assumed something about the crime is true without it being a proven fact, the danger is that the suspect, because of their direct role in the crime, may know it is not in fact the case. That vital flaw would boost the suspect's own confidence that they remain in control, and may mean they will be even more determined not to admit anything incriminating.

CAPITALIZING ON WEAKNESSES

In other cases, profilers have to look for the suspect's weaknesses and use them to their own advantage. In the case of a power-reassurance rapist, the key is to play on his need to reassure himself of his own masculinity, and his lack of animosity toward his victim. So questioners will try to add to the necessary reassurance on both counts, especially by

Ensuring crinimals see stacks of files left out on desks as they enter the police station gives them the impression that a large and dedicated team of police are on the case.

appearing to believe he had no wish to harm his victim beyond the minimum needed to subdue her to his will. In some cases, questioners have been able to build up such a rapport with the suspect that they not only admit to the crime for which they are being questioned, but have even owned up to earlier, hitherto unsolved crimes as part of the confession process.

Anger-retaliation rapists are much more driven by their hatred of women, so questioners have two possible routes. Either they can ensure the interrogators are male, to suggest an identification between questioner and suspect, or they can use one female questioner and one male. If the suspect seems to dislike the woman questioner, her male colleague can persuade her to leave the room, and subtly signal to the suspect that with this distracting presence out of the way, they can make real progress. With more violent criminals, such as power-assertive and anger-excitation attackers, the professionalism of the questioners and the completeness of their information and the case they are building from it are essential. They need to convince the suspect that they already know he has carried out the crime and can actually prove their accusations. In the meantime, though, they just want to check out some of the smaller details, and in putting over this tactic, they are effectively appealing to the suspect's respect for accuracy and precision. Of course, if he then confirms even the most trivial of matters, he is actually admitting he only has the information as a result of having carried out the crime.

Finally, in many individual cases, the suspect will have a weakness over and above those typical of the criminal type they belong to. In the case of the British serial sex killers Fred and Rosemary West, Fred was all too clearly a sadistic psychopath, who could normally be expected to deny his own involvement in all the crimes for which he was suspected and charged. In fact, he surprised his questioners by admitting his guilt, though in such a way as to ease the burden of blame as much as he could.

The home of the Wests in Gloucester is searched for evidence of the rapes and murders they carried out on at least 12 women over a period of 20 years.

What he refused to admit, with the utmost tenacity, was his wife's role in the killings.

Since the investigators knew Rosemary must have been happy to take part in the abuse, torture, and murder of their many victims, it was vital this should be revealed. They took Fred slowly and carefully though the crimes to which he had admitted, revealing his wife's participation little by little. During this time she maintained her blanket denial that she had known or been involved in any of the violence that took place in their small terraced house, a clear impossibility. As part of this defense strategy, she effectively turned her back on her husband, refusing to acknowledge him in court or reply to his letters. He was clearly so shaken that profiler Paul Britton regarded him as a suicide risk, and so it proved. He hanged himself in his prison cell, but this did not prevent his wife being found guilty of 10 charges of murder on November 22, 1995, and sentenced to life imprisonment.

The ten girls with whose murder Rosemary West was charged.

Fred and Rosemary West, pictured together in the mid-1980s, two decades after the murders began.

Fred West pictured as a child. Profilers discovered that incest was a daily occurrence in both Rosemary and Fred's childhoods.

Rosemary West, pictured in 1995.

CASE STUDY 47: STEWART WILKEN

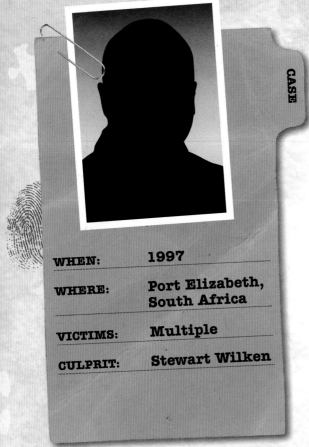

CASE

WHEN: 1997

WHERE: Port Elizabeth, South Africa

VICTIMS: Multiple

CULPRIT: Stewart Wilken

In the main, serial killers tend to confine their crimes to one particular type of victim. This is usually because one kind of victim has the attributes that attract either their lust or their hatred. For example, those whose anger dates back to an abusive mother, will tend to attack more mature victims than those who are simply trying to obtain payback for insults or injuries originally inflicted by their own contemporaries. This is the reason why victimology, or studying the type and background of the victims selected by an individual criminal, is such a vital part of the profiling routine, in order to develop an understanding of how the suspect operates, and how he can be isolated and caught.

In rare cases a serial killer whose psychological development has been more complex may target more than one type of victim, perhaps entirely different from one another. Whenever this occurs, profilers and investigators have to be careful not to be misled into assuming the crimes were committed by two or more killers. On the other hand, this double imperative can help when the time comes and the suspect has been caught and is about to be questioned, since it can provide a direct route into the mind of the suspect.

TWO TYPES OF VICTIM

One of the many serial killers operating in South Africa during the 1990s was murdering victims around the city of Port Elizabeth. Detectives found that his victims fell into two quite distinct groups: young boys and adult female prostitutes. But finding the offender was proving difficult, and it was not until January 1997 that investigators had their first positive lead. A 12-year-old boy named Henry Bakers

Port Elizabeth turned from a beautiful port into a crime scene in the 1990s when it became the haunt of serial killer Stewart Wilken.

Superintendent Jan Swart, the head of the Child Protection Unit in Cape Town, South Africa, runs a special police unit dealing with sexual abuse cases against children.

marital problems. However, Sergeant Ursula Barnard of the Child Protection Unit knew Wilken had some sinister issues of his own. Not only did he not have a fixed address, but his own daughter Wuane had disappeared three years earlier, and he was facing possible sodomy charges relating to the two sons of his second wife.

On January 28, 1997, Sergeant Barnard found Wilken and arrested him on suspicion of involvement in Henry Bakers' disappearance. He admitted he knew the boy and had seen him six days earlier on the day he vanished, but Wilken insisted he had spent that night with a woman friend. Police checked the alibi and finding it false, rearrested Wilken three days later. The police Child Protection Unit contacted Sergeant Derrick Norsworthy of the Murder and Robbery Unit, who had been taught psychological profiling by Dr. Micki Pistorius, with particular attention to advanced questioning methods. They hoped he could persuade Wilken to admit what had happened.

RACKING UP THE PRESSURE

failed to return home on Wednesday, January 22, and at first his mother simply assumed he had gone to stay overnight at his grandmother's home, which was within walking distance.

When he did not return on the Thursday, she walked to her mother's house on the Friday morning, only to find her son had been there on the Wednesday afternoon, but had not stayed overnight. Inquiries revealed that he had been playing with a friend, but the friend had to run an errand, and had last seen Henry with a man called Stewart Wilken. He had asked Henry where he was going, and Wilken had said it was none of his business. Ironically, both of Henry's parents knew Wilken, and he had even stayed at Henry's grandmother's house while having

When Wilken arrived in Norsworthy's office, the sergeant told him to sit down in a particular chair. This had been positioned facing a snapshot of Norsworthy's own daughter, who was a similar age to Wilken's missing daughter Wuane. He left him alone there for several minutes and when he came back to the office, he found Wilken staring at the picture. Norsworthy then pointed out the framed certificates on the office wall, showing his qualifications for investigating serial murders. When he saw Wilken turning back to the picture of his daughter, the sergeant said firmly that he knew Wilken had killed Henry and Wuane, and that he had returned to the scene to live out his fantasies and have sex with their bodies. Wilken stared into the distance and then admitted he was a bad man, and that he had indeed killed both children.

Once the psychological dam had burst, more and more revelations emerged. He had carried out the killings to send the children to a better world, protecting his daughter—who he said was no longer a virgin—from sexual exploitation, and the boy from what he alleged was physical abuse by his parents. He also owned up to having killed at least eight more victims, all adolescent boys or adult female prostitutes.

Since then, details emerged that revealed his own tragic upbringing, which might have contributed to his attitudes to his two types of victim. Effectively orphaned through desertion

by his parents while still a baby, he and his sister were taken in by a man who abused them cruelly, and he was only saved by being adopted by neighbors, Mr and Mrs Wilken, at the age of 2. When he went to school he proved slow to learn and was bullied by classmates, and he assaulted both his teacher and his adoptive mother, for which he was beaten. At the age of 9 he was raped by a deacon after Sunday school, and during that same year his adoptive father died. His adoptive mother, unable to cope with him, had him transferred to a reformatory where he was abused by the older inmates. He was married twice but both relationships failed because of his insistence on painful sex and his tendency to violence, after which he lived rough in the bush, with no one to witness his escalation to murder.

Stewart Wilken killed children around Cape Elizabeth in South Africa because he thought he was sending them to a better world.

Wilken was abused repeatedly as a child, and failed in his personal relationships before his mental state deteriorated.

CASE

WHEN:	1985
WHERE:	Utah, USA
VICTIMS:	Multiple
CULPRIT:	Mark Hofmann

CASE STUDY 48: MARK HOFMANN: THE MORMON BOMBER

On October 15, 1985, two different people in Salt Lake City, Utah, each took delivery of a large brown paper package. When opened, the packages exploded with lethal violence. The first recipient was killed instantly, while the second, Steve Christensen, was grievously injured and survived for only a short time. Both packages had contained pipe bombs, which had been packed with nails to increase their killing power. The next victim was Kathleen Sheets, wife of Christensen's former business partner, Gary Sheets. In this case the package was addressed to Gary,

but when she picked it up from the front of their property, it detonated and blew her apart. Finally, on the next afternoon, a bomb exploded in the sports car being driven by Mark Hofmann, an apparent victim linked to the other three. He had been supposed to meet Steve Christensen the previous day to finalize an agreement over a collection of rare documents relating to the Mormon church. He survived in spite of losing a finger and a kneecap, and sustaining burns down one side.

Once experts examined the car, and his injuries, their findings told a very different story. Far from being an innocent victim, they declared he had prepared the bomb, and the detonation had been an accident. When his background was investigated, it transpired he had been dealing in rare documents that were mainly his expert forgeries, and frequently aimed to damage the Mormon Church. Facing an almost certain guilty verdict and a probable death sentence, he admitted his crimes, though he insisted the fourth bomb had been intended to enable him to commit suicide, and he began a long prison sentence on January 23, 1987.

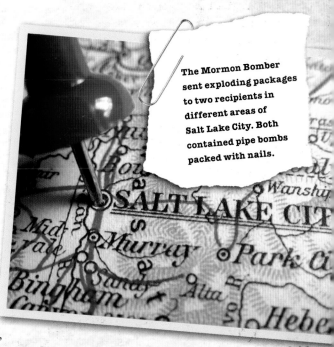

The Mormon Bomber sent exploding packages to two recipients in different areas of Salt Lake City. Both contained pipe bombs packed with nails.

EXPLAINING THE CRIME

Hofmann's guilty plea meant that the FBI had had almost no chance to find out how and why he had planted the bombs in the first place. So in this case, profiler Gregg McCrary from the Behavioral Science Unit, working with a partner, set out to interview the killer in prison. While this was very different from an interrogation to establish guilt, it was still an attempt to reveal information that had been carefully concealed by a defendant who had refused to say anything about his crimes. All that was known about him, including his ability to lie easily and convincingly, his cruelty to animals, and his indifference to the suffering of others—before his trial he had said he did not care that his bomb aimed at Gary Sheets had killed his wife instead—pointed to psychopathic tendencies. This would mean they would have to be very careful in the way they questioned him to obtain the information they wanted.

However, the fact that he was a convicted prisoner did give them one advantage. He could not refuse to see them, and he would not know

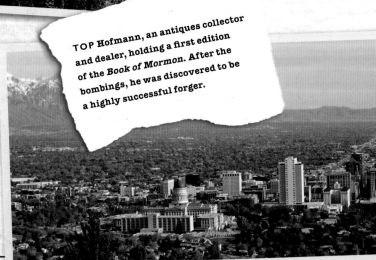

TOP Hofmann, an antiques collector and dealer, holding a first edition of the *Book of Mormon*. After the bombings, he was discovered to be a highly successful forger.

Salt Lake City is the headquarters for the Church of Jesus Christ of Latter-Day Saints. Hofmann, a successful forger, is especially noted for his creation of documents related to the history of the Mormon Church.

in advance that they were coming. On the other hand, the signs were not promising, since the prison staff said he never talked to anyone at all, spending all day and night on his own, apart from the one-hour exercise period when he simply walked round and round the prison yard. Nevertheless, the two FBI men persuaded the guards to let them speak to the prisoner, and to post a guard outside the door instead of in the small interview room with them. They also arranged the chairs so that Hofmann would sit next to the door, and would feel able to leave at any time.

FERRETING OUT THE DETAILS

When Hofmann met the agents he refused to talk on the grounds he had been told not to speak to investigators. They replied by saying in that case they would talk and he could listen, and they would talk about whatever he wanted. Then followed a long period where he spoke about his business and the difficulties it had faced, and in particular the stress this had imposed on him. As this suited his psychopathic attitude to the vital importance of anything that affected him in particular, he was willing to unbend and speak of the problems he had faced. Nevertheless, the interviewers watched Hofmann's body language very carefully.

As soon as he showed signs of the slightest boredom, they would switch the subject to something that reawakened his interest.

At last the continuing assumption that he had done what he did as a consequence of the stress, and out of a need to help his wife and children, rather than as a conscious and deliberate crime, had the desired effect. When the agents spoke with respect about the skill that must have been needed to construct his convincing forgeries, they were able to steer him on to the reasoning for his violent antipathy toward the Mormon Church. He had become a member of the church and expected his baptism would change his life for the better, and when nothing seemed to change, he damned the church for what he called its hypocrisy. It was then he started faking documents that, had they been genuine, would have completely discredited the Mormons. Unfortunately, his forgeries were about to be revealed, and when he felt his world beginning to unravel, he decided to set off the bombs to divert attention.

He then told the agents what they wanted to know about how he had bought the parts and constructed the bombs. As he did so, McCrary noticed that he became agitated and excited as he spoke about the procedure in detail and how he'd carried out the killings. But from start to finish, he insisted the third bomb had been meant only for him. Though the agents had managed to collect most of the information they wanted by tailoring their questions and tactics to suit their adversary, on this question at least, he refused to give any ground at all.

Hofmann told detectives that he had sent the bombs to divert attention away from the discovery of his forged documents.

CASE

WHEN:	1979
WHERE:	Georgia, USA
VICTIM:	Mary Frances Stoner
CULPRITS:	Darrell Gene Devier

Local witnesses told police that a tree-trimming crew had been working outside the Stoner property on the day of Mary's disappearance.

CASE STUDY 49: MARY FRANCES STONER

One of the most effective uses of profiling to persuade a killer to admit his guilt was in the case of the rape and murder of 12-year-old Mary Frances Stoner on the afternoon of November 30, 1979, in rural Georgia. She had taken the bus home from Adairsville High School, and been dropped 100 yards from her home, but she never completed the last stage of her journey. Her body was found the following day in woodland close to the neighboring county boundary. She had been raped and her skull crushed by heavy blows delivered with the aid of several bloodstained rocks found close to her body. Though she was fully dressed, one of her shoes was unfastened and there were signs she had dressed in a hurry.

THE EVIDENCE

Surprisingly, the conventional part of the investigation proved straightforward enough. Witnesses recalled that a tree-trimming crew had been working along the road that ran past the Stoner property, and had finished the job on the afternoon of the girl's disappearance. One of the members of the crew testified that a colleague named Darrell Gene Devier had seen Mary alighting from the school bus earlier in the week and referred to her as "good-looking," and said how much he would like to have sex with her.

Two more witnesses mentioned seeing a dark-colored Ford Pinto with alloy wheels parked off

the road 50 yards north of the Stoner home at the time the school bus was due to appear from that direction. They said the driver was a white man with a beard and long hair. A student on the bus who alighted at the next stop after Mary also saw a dark Pinto with alloy wheels, but this time it was backing out of the Stoner driveway with two people on board.

Police checks revealed that Devier owned a black Pinto with alloy wheels, and he was arrested on suspicion of rape and murder.

Within days, the local police enlisted the aid of the FBI, who called in John Douglas, specialist in exploiting profiling to persuade suspects to admit their guilt. On studying the evidence, Douglas was convinced that Devier had forced or persuaded

LEFT Devier was arrested on suspicion of rape after a colleague testified he had expressed a desire to have sex with Mary and his car was seen leaving the family driveway on the day of her murder.

RIGHT Devier was part of the timber crew working on the street outside Mary Stoner's house.

the girl into his car, then driven off with her to the site where her body had been found. There he stripped her and raped her in the car, before letting her out to get dressed. When she still showed signs of extreme distress, he must have panicked and realized for the first time the danger he was in. Deciding she would have to be silenced, he tried to strangle her, but only managed to render her unconscious. He then picked up several rocks, the largest of which weighed almost 50 pounds, and smashed them down on her head violently enough to crack her skull and take her life.

Local police called in John Douglas, a specialist FBI profiler, to persuade the suspect to admit to his guilt.

OUTFLANKING THE KILLER'S DEFENSES

Reconstructing the crime was a step forward, but for the time being Devier had decided that since no one had actually seen him attack his victim, he could simply refuse to cooperate in any way. Douglas decided the way to crack his defense was to probe for his weaknesses. He

Devier panicked when his victim was still extremely distressed after being attacked and raped, so he picked up some rocks nearby to crack her skull.

was clearly a disorganized killer who had seen the girl's predictable appearance on the day his work had finished as an opportunity too great to ignore, without thinking of the consequences. He was clearly a local man, since he knew the spot where he had left her body, which would not have been familiar to anyone visiting the area.

On the other hand, it must have dawned on him once the rape was over that it would have been only too easy for his victim to identify him, especially since he had been working outside her home for the better part of a week. On this basis, killing her was more likely to seem to him an unfortunate necessity, rather than the additional pleasure of a sadistic killer, who would have brought a weapon with him instead of having to look for one at the crime scene. So reminding him, in the most graphic way possible, of what he had done might be the way to jolt him out his noncooperation.

THE WEAPON IN THE ROOM

Douglas and his team prepared for the questioning very carefully. The questioners were drawn from the local police and the state FBI office, to stress the importance and professionalism of the investigation. Files were stacked in the interrogation room, with Devier's name written in large bold characters, even if some of them were only filled with blank sheets of paper.

The questioning would begin in the evening, with the lighting dimmed, to suggest a relaxed and informal atmosphere, and lead the suspect to drop his guard. The questioners would start by concentrating on the question of blood spatter, which was almost inevitable with this kind of killing, and would almost certainly have stained his hands and clothing. Another part of the tactic was to appear to shift blame onto the victim, suggesting the girl might have led him on, but the killer punch was placed a few feet away from where Devier would sit, and below his line of sight. This was the heavy, bloodstained rock with which he had delivered the death blows.

As soon as he was brought into the room, he was clearly transfixed by the rock, and unable to deflect his eyes as he cowered away from it. The questioners added to the pressure by picking it up and placing it on the table in front of him. They continued to explain that they realized he had not originally intended to kill his victim, otherwise he would have brought a weapon with him, instead of using a rock. At that point his resolution cracked, and he admitted what he had done. Not only that, but he also admitted raping another girl, Linda Gail Elrod, on June 2. He was put on trial, found guilty and sentenced to death. The sentence was finally carried out, after a succession of appeals, on May 17, 1995, in the electric chair at the state prison. He had been due for execution two days earlier, but a local thunderstorm cut the power to the chair moments before he was strapped into it. Since the storm also cut the phone lines, the state Attorney General had to drive out into the country with a cell phone to find a signal and call to check that there had been no last minute stay of execution.

Police checks revealed that Devier owned a black Pinto with alloy wheels.

WHAT PROFILING CAN DO

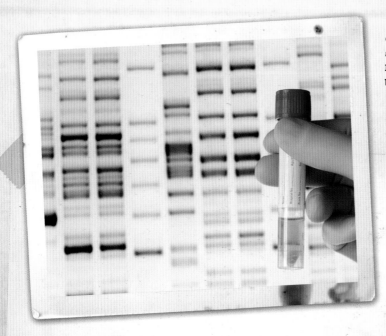

DNA comparison can help to convict a suspect, but profiling helps to find them before they kill again.

For all the undoubted value of criminal profiling, it remains vital to remember that it is still much more of an art than a science, at least at this stage of development. Where DNA comparison, for example, will give a match or a nonmatch between genetic material found at a crime scene and that of a potential suspect, profiling deals with psychology and personality, difficult to pin down in cold scientific terms. As experience grows, and with the help of more comprehensive statistics on crime and criminals, many of the assertions made by the original profilers can now be viewed with greater confidence. Nevertheless, while profiling can be an extremely valuable tool to investigators, it can occasionally throw them off the scent, with damaging results for those most closely involved.

OCCASIONAL FAILINGS

Fortunately, even these occasional lapses can usually be traced to factors quite outside the basic information involved in drawing up a profile and the accuracy of its conclusions. Some of these have been covered already, but additional examples are particularly important.

At the time of the 1996 Summer Games, bombs were placed in the Centennial Olympic Park in Atlanta. There was immense pressure to track down the bomber before some outrage caused major casualties, and an early suspect was harassed and investigated, to the extent that growing evidence pointing to the real perpetrator was effectively being ignored.

In the Washington Beltway sniper attacks (see Case Study 51) a profile was drawn up identifying the man responsible as a middle-aged white male. The truth was that two men were involved, both black, and one was only 17 years old. The problem here was the basic limitation of profiling in that it deals with probabilities, and this was a case of behavior so unusual it failed to fit the normal rules.

In fact, very few cases stretch or break the boundaries in this way. A much more serious problem is where some of the vital evidence essential for an accurate profile is left out of the reckoning, either because it was missed in the initial collection of evidence or because it was rejected as unimportant by those in the investigation not actually experienced in profiling. But the most serious failure of all is where the result of the profile needed to catch the real criminal is skewed as a direct result of deliberate tampering to make it accord with a suspect already assumed to be guilty.

Pressure to find the Atlanta Olympic Games bomber led to evidence being ignored while police followed a profile.

The body of one of the victims following the bomb explosion at the AT&T Pavilion in the Centennial Olympic Park.

Immediate aftermath of the pipe-bomb explosion where two people were killed while attending a concert during the 1996 Games.

Police attend the scene of the concert pipe-bombing to gather evidence.

VALUE—AND LIMITS—OF PROFILING

Occasional failings like these have caused opponents of profiling to question its value to investigators. In particular, they have pointed out that many experienced FBI agents and profilers do not have formal qualifications in psychology, though their track record does suggest that the technique still works well in the great majority of cases. In the United Kingdom, three university psychologists have criticized the whole assumption that any weight should be given to assessing a suspect's personality traits under the unprecedented circumstances of carrying out a violent crime, while others insist that it is only under such unique conditions that it is most difficult for the suspect to hide or repress these personality characteristics.

What does seem to suggest a real need for caution is the possible use of profiling information as a form of evidence at a trial, since conclusions drawn from them can occasionally be false or misleading. Even more controversial is so-called "active profiling," a development of the method to include the setting up of conditions likely to provoke a suspect into revealing more of their underlying psychology without being aware of this. Current laws barring entrapment or even suspect harassment tend to make any evidence obtained in this way inadmissible in a trial anyway.

In the final analysis, the true value of profiling remains, as always, as an intermediate stage between finding the crime and analyzing the evidence at the scene, and the eventual

arrest of a suspect. If profiling can lead the law officers to the suspect, then the rest of the case depends on the normal priorities of detection and collection of evidence and the mounting of a case to secure the conviction of the guilty. The examples reviewed in this book have looked at many different types of criminal and shown how profiling was able to help find each of them. However, the one factor that most have in common is that the profile acts as an additional tool to traditional police skills, but does not replace them.

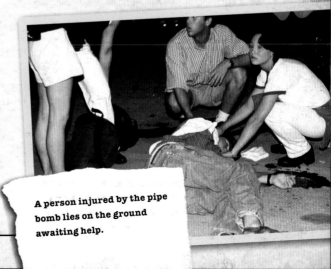

A person injured by the pipe bomb lies on the ground awaiting help.

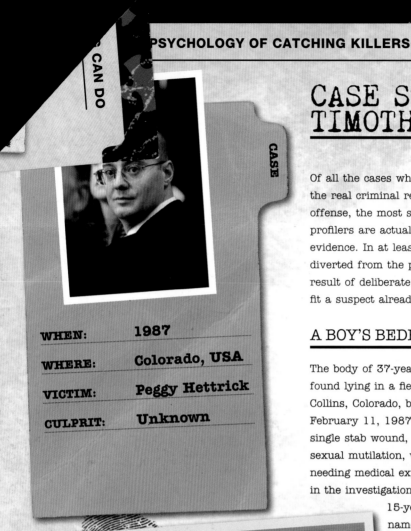

CASE STUDY 50: TIMOTHY MASTERS

WHEN: 1987

WHERE: Colorado, USA

VICTIM: Peggy Hettrick

CULPRIT: Unknown

Of all the cases where profiling fails to deliver the real criminal responsible for a particular offense, the most serious has to be where the profilers are actually misled by withheld evidence. In at least one case, attention was diverted from the person responsible as a direct result of deliberate tampering to make evidence fit a suspect already assumed to be guilty.

A BOY'S BEDROOM

The body of 37-year-old Peggy Hettrick was found lying in a field near the town of Fort Collins, Colorado, by a passing cyclist on February 11, 1987. She had been killed by a single stab wound, but had also been subject to sexual mutilation, which a doctor certified as needing medical expertise to accomplish. Early in the investigation, police determined that a 15-year-old high-school student named Timothy Masters had passed the spot on his way to classes that morning, but had not reported the body because he thought it was a shop-window dummy placed there by someone as a practical joke.

Lacking any other potential suspects, the police homed in on Masters and his home was searched. In his room and among his possessions they found written material and pictures that hinted at a preoccupation with violence, together with a knife collection and cuttings from the local newspaper describing the finding of the body. However, there was no direct evidence to link him with the victim—

Mountains near Fort Collins, Colorado, where Peggy Hettrick was murdered.

hairs found on her body did not match the suspect, nor did fingerprints on her purse. Claims were later made that Masters had spoken of the mutilation of the victim's body to schoolmates. When he was told of this, he claimed a fellow art student had helped the police search the crime scene and had given him details of what was found there.

The investigation stalled for 10 years, by which time Masters was serving in the US Navy, but the police investigator covering the case called in a California-based criminal psychologist. He drew up a profile based on the materials recovered from Masters' room, without ever speaking to Masters himself. This seemed to show quite clearly that he could have carried out the crime, and that by extension he probably did. Expert opinion from FBI specialist profiler Roy Hazelwood that contradicted this finding was ignored, and though Masters protested his innocence throughout, he was arrested, charged with Peggy Hettrick's murder, and sentenced to life imprisonment in 1999.

THE CASE FINALLY REEXAMINED

A succession of appeals finally resulted in a new defense team being appointed in 2004 to reexamine the case. They found much of the evidence used in the earlier trial was inadmissible, and that key items such as hair samples and fingerprints that might have contributed to establishing his innocence had been lost. They also alleged that the prosecution had suppressed potential evidence relating to another suspect, a Dr. Richard Hammond. In 1995, before Masters' original trial, Hammond had been arrested for secretly photographing the genitalia of female members of his family while they used the toilet. Pornography found at his home testified to an obsession with this part of the female anatomy, and the window of his

Dutch DNA experts sit with Tim Masters during a party held for him after he was released from prison.

Hair analysis and fingerprint evidence that might have aided Masters' defence was lost before his trial.

room overlooked the field where the victim's
body had been found. Furthermore, he spent the
morning of the murder at home, despite
a crowded surgery schedule, and had the
specialized expertise needed to carry out the
mutilation of the body—all pointers that would
have contributed to a proper killer profile.

Hammond himself had been released on
bail, but several days after his original arrest,
his body was found in a Denver motel with a
syringe containing cyanide embedded in his leg,
and a note referring to the media's "thirst for
blood." The defense team insisted that the police
investigators withheld this information at
Masters' trial and did not pass it on to the FBI
or their own profiler. A former boyfriend of the
victim was also implicated by DNA evidence
found on her body, though he had been ruled out
by investigators. Finally, DNA testing revealed no
trace of Masters' DNA at the scene, and a
Colorado judge finally ordered him to be released
in January 2008. The prosecuting lawyers were
censured by the Colorado Supreme Court for
failing to pass on information from the police
to the defense team, even though it might have
helped exonerate the defendant, and Masters
himself accepted a settlement of just over
$4 million compensation.

Masters said he did not report the body because he thought it was a shop mannequin placed in the position as a joke.

Masters' fingerprints did not match any found on Peggy Hettrick's possessions.

The investigation stalled for 10 years,
and Masters had joined the Navy.

Masters accepted a settlement
of around $4 million from the
county after his wrongful
imprisonment.

The city of Fort Collins settled
with Masters for a figure closer
to $5.6 million.

CASE

WHEN:	2003
WHERE:	Maryland, USA
VICTIMS:	Multiple
CULPRITS:	John Allen Muhammad, Lee Boyd Malvo

The Washington Snipers covered a large area with alarming speed and created widespread panic.

things the victims had been doing when they unexpectedly became targets for an unseen killer. Two men were killed in separate shootings when filling their cars with fuel, a woman was wounded when loading her vehicle at a shopping mall, and a teenager was hit at his school. The only common factor seemed to be that they had been shot by a skilled and accurate sniper, and yet no witnesses at any of the scenes had seen anything or anyone out of the ordinary.

FLOUTING ALL PROBABILITIES

A huge investigation was set up by Maryland Police, aided by the FBI and other specialist agencies, to try to profile and arrest the person or people responsible. However, the problem was that the crime occupied an area that remains an inherent weakness of profiling. Essentially, the art involves classifying criminals by the probabilities and patterns of how they think and operate, to

The snipers struck in Washington, DC, killing ordinary people as they went about their daily routines.

CASE STUDY 51: THE WASHINGTON SNIPERS

Over a three-week period in October 2003, a series of killings along the route of the I-95 highway in the areas around Washington, DC and adjacent neighborhoods of Maryland and Virginia, caused widespread panic. The first victim was a man shot while crossing a parking lot in Wheaton, Maryland, on October 2. This might have seemed a random and senseless killing, had it not been followed up so quickly by a whole string of shootings: including five on the very next day—four more in Maryland and one in DC. This was bad enough, but what made matters worse was the ordinary, everyday

Using Interstate 95, the snipers moved quickly through Virginia, Maryland, and Washington, DC.

draw conclusions about what this reveals of their background, their life and the reasons for their offending. Unfortunately, this crime was so unusual there was little in the way of other crimes and criminals to which it could be compared.

Using conventional profiling techniques, it was logical to assume the sniper was white, since most lone snipers in previous cases had been white. It also seemed sensible to assume he operated with a white van, since one witness had reported seeing a white van at the scene of a shooting, and using a van rather than a car would allow the weapon to be kept concealed more easily. Unfortunately, with so little hard data on which to base a profile, the investigators could only deal in probabilities, each of which could be right, or wrong, in this particular case. Geographical profiling for example was of limited use, since clearly the person responsible was using the highway to cover long distances quickly, and tying the scenes of the shootings to a possible location for a base would be unlikely to succeed. It also emerged later in the investigation that the killer was basing his plans around what the media revealed about the police approach—for example, after someone observed he did not shoot children, he shot a 13-year-old, and when another pointed out he killed no one at a weekend, he remedied that omission almost immediately.

MAKING THE VITAL MISTAKE

In the end, the killers effectively trapped themselves by their own over-confidence, which resulted from the patent lack of progress made in tracking them down. As with many serial killers, a wish to taunt the police eventually became too powerful to resist.

Hillandale Beer and Wine, one of the sites where an innocent victim was killed by the Washington Snipers.

On October 17, with nine killings to date, the most recent being FBI analyst Linda Franklin, shot while leaving a home-improvement store in Falls Church, Virginia, a call came through on the information line. The voice identified himself as the killer, and claimed to have killed two women while robbing a liquor store in Montgomery, Alabama, in September.

Immediately, the investigators checked the claim. It emerged that there had indeed been a robbery, though only one of the women had actually been killed. The most important fact for the hunt for the sniper was that there was both fingerprint and ballistic evidence relating to the robbery. Prints found were identified as those of Lee Boyd Malvo, with an arrest record in Washington State, and when that file was

Attempts to track down the killers were unsuccessful despite organized man-hunts.

Victim Linda Franklin was an Intelligence Operations Specialist for the FBI and was killed by the snipers with a single gunshot wound as she returned to her car in the Home Depot parking lot.

The gas station where one sniper victim was murdered as he refueled his car.

Police stopping and searching Chevy Astor mini vans moments after the eighth sniper shooting.

Washington Sniper suspect Lee Boyd Malvo is shown in a booking photo taken November 9, 2003.

Boyd lived in a modest Tacoma duplex and gave neighbors no indication he was a killer.

checked, it revealed a reference to a John Allen Muhammad, who could be a possible second suspect. Moreover, it appeared that Muhammad was known to have a Bushmaster .223 rifle in his possession. Almost the final link in the chain was uncovered in the criminal records database that linked Muhammad to the ownership of a blue Chevy Caprice saloon bearing the license number NDA-21Z. Agents and the public were alerted, and within hours a report was received that the car had been spotted in a car park at a rest stop on the I-70 highway in Maryland. Quickly the scene was secured and the criminals arrested.

John Allen Muhammad arrives at the Prince William County courthouse in Manassas, VA, November 13, 2002, after being denied clemency.

During their killing spree the Washington Snipers killed ten people and critically injured three others.

They found the car full of evidence. A hole had been cut behind the back seat to allow a gunman to enter the luggage compartment. In addition, the rear paneling had a hole cut just above the license plate to allow the sniper to fire from inside the car without revealing himself. Inside the car was a Bushmaster .223 rifle, which was proved to be the one used in the killings, together with a telescopic sight and a tripod for precision aiming. There was also a laptop with maps of the shooting sites and details of approach and getaway routes, and the car handbook had impressions in it that matched the writing of one of the notes sent to police to demand a ransom for stopping the shootings. Both men were put on trial for the shootings in DC, Virginia, and Maryland, and both were found guilty and sentenced to life imprisonment. In addition, Muhammad, who was identified as the principal sniper, faces the death penalty in Virginia.

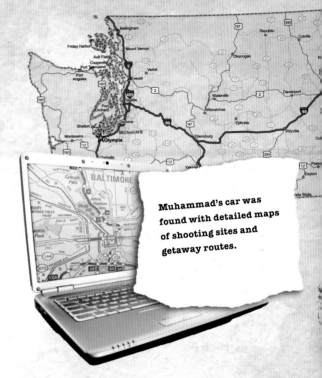

Muhammad's car was found with detailed maps of shooting sites and getaway routes.

Witness Gerald Driscoll points to a map of the murder trail as he testifies during the trial of sniper suspect John Allen Muhammad.

CASE

WHEN: 2003

WHERE: London, U.K.

VICTIMS: Michael Little

CULPRITS: Craig Harman

CASE STUDY 52: DEATH FROM A MOTORWAY BRIDGE

At about 12:30 a.m. on March 21, 2003, 53-year-old truck driver Michael Little was steering his 40-ton truck along the London-bound carriageway of the M3 motorway. Suddenly, with no warning, a brick crashed through the windscreen and hit him a crippling blow to the chest. This triggered a massive, and fatal, heart attack, but in his last moments of life he managed to steer his truck to a stop on the hard shoulder without colliding with other vehicles. Police found his truck and his lifeless body, and next to it the two halves of the brick, which, having been thrown from the bridge across the motorway close to that point, had undoubtedly caused his death.

Finding the person responsible seemed, on the face of it, to be impossible. There were traces of DNA on the brick that almost certainly belonged to the person who had thrown it, but at that stage it was impossible to match it to anyone already in the criminal database. All that could be concluded was that the person responsible was probably white. Profiling the criminal also suggested he would be under 35 years old, to commit this type of casual and apparently motiveless vandalism. He was almost certainly local, to be in that place at that time of night, which suggested it might be possible to carry out a mass DNA sampling of the local population fitting the limits of age and ethnic origin suggested by the profile. Unfortunately this revealed no clear suspect, so the police fell back on the relatively new technique of familial DNA matching.

They checked with the national DNA database and found a single match with the sample from

Harman and his companion tried to hot-wire a Renault Clio parked nearby.

The M3 motorway is a busy highway, and Little saved many lives by safely guiding his truck to a stop before passing away.

The Old Bailey in London, where Harman was tried and convicted of manslaughter.

This thrown brick split in half on its impact with Michael Little's vehicle.

the crime scene in 16 out of 20 areas, a correspondence that indicated a close family kinship. Follow-up checks revealed that the person whose entry was in the database was related to a 19-year-old shop assistant called Craig Harman. Police took a DNA sample from him and found it a perfect match with the DNA found on the brick and also on a Renault Clio car parked nearby, which Harman and his companion had tried to hot-wire to save them a long walk home after spending the evening drinking. Harman was put on trial at the Old Bailey, where he admitted to manslaughter and was given a six-year prison sentence.

WHEN:	Multiple years
WHERE:	Multiple
VICTIMS:	Multiple
CULPRITS:	Multiple

Surveillance footage showing suicide bomber Hasib Hussain with his backpack bomb at King's Cross station, London.

The explosive belts worn by suicide bombers are heavy and bulky enough to be recognized through clothing.

CASE STUDY 53: PROFILING THE SUICIDE BOMBERS

One of the most common factors in criminal profiling relates to working with information from scenes where crimes have already been committed, in order to catch those responsible and prevent them carrying out further crimes. But in one area profiling has recently acquired a new significance, in trying to prevent a crime being committed in the first place. This relates to the terrifying threat of the suicide bomber, who strikes without warning in crowded public places to cause panic by killing as many innocent and unsuspecting victims as possible. In some cases these attacks take place on the battlefield, where the perpetrators are dedicated fanatics who appear from concealment to wreak havoc in their last moments of life.

However, the majority of suicide bombers operate in spaces both civilian and public, where at the very least they have to move to whatever target they have been briefed to attack, or to approach whatever objective seems to them to represent a worthwhile sacrifice of their life. In facing up to this deadly menace, the Israelis have devoted much thought to the profiles of the bombers themselves, and the telltale signs that might reveal them as such. If these can be used to give even a few moments' warning, there is at least a chance that avoidance action can be taken to reduce the death toll they inflict.

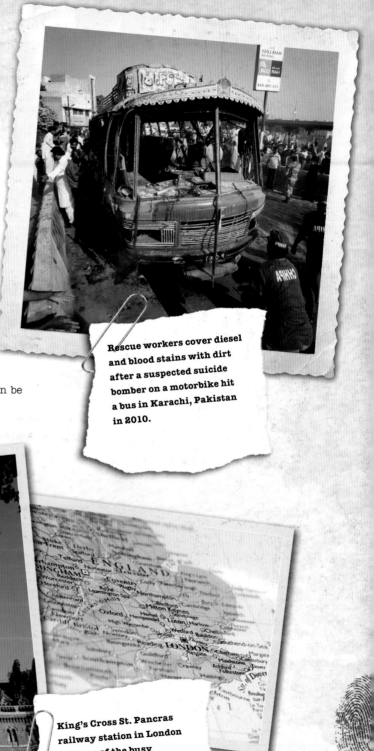

Rescue workers cover diesel and blood stains with dirt after a suspected suicide bomber on a motorbike hit a bus in Karachi, Pakistan in 2010.

King's Cross St. Pancras railway station in London was one of the busy commuter targets for the suicide bombers.

TELLTALE SIGNS

What kind of profile can be used to identify a suicide bomber? In most cases, a male suspect will be Muslim, and of a traditional enough persuasion to normally wear a beard. Many suicide bombers prepare for their imminent martyrdom by a ritual cleansing that includes shaving most of the body, including the beard, and a recent shave might be revealed by paler skin around the chin and cheeks. However, the real giveaway with all suicide bombers is the extra weight and bulk of the belt carrying the explosives they plan to detonate. With a filling of explosive, augmented by nails or ball bearings to increase the killing effect of the charge, all sewn into a tough canvas wrapping and carried by braces over the shoulders, the belt could easily weigh in at 40 pounds or more, heading for the kind of weight carried by a postman on a busy delivery round.

An attaché case with 9 pounds of explosives and over a thousand screw nuts was found in a cave near Tul Karem in 2003.

Abed al Basit Mohammed Qasem Odeh, the suicide bomber who blew himself up in a hotel in Netanya, Israel, in 2002.

The four British suicide bombers responsible for 52 deaths on London transport in 2005.

This inevitable restriction has two effects. The bulk of the belt has to be hidden since it would be otherwise all too obvious to watchful army, police, or security men, so thick sweaters, overcoats, or fleeces may be worn to camouflage it. Seeing this kind of heavy clothing in warm weather is as good as a warning notice. In addition, the sheer weight of the belt forces the person carrying it to change their stance and walk, to carry it without making it obvious. In addition, many would-be martyrs suffer from last-minute doubts, whereupon those who send them will ensure they are sufficiently drugged to go through with their suicide, but not so heavily influenced they are unable to carry it out. This too is reflected in their gait, which will be exaggeratedly careful compared with a normal walk.

Many other signs relate to body language and stress. Suicide bombers commonly sweat from the burden they carry, but will also show nervous symptoms such as tics. Research shows

A forensic expert collects evidence at the scene of a suicide bombing near Sana'a airport in Yemen.

most suicide bombers are relatively eager to sign up to the campaign while their martyrdom remains fairly remote, and while surrounded by likeminded and sympathetic collaborators. As the moment of action comes, however, they lack the comfort of comrades alongside them. Their heightened sense of suppressed panic at what is about to happen to them creates almost intolerable pressure. Coping with this often involves staring straight ahead, without reaction to any of the outside events and sounds that would normally divert attention. Shallow breathing is another sign, as is the moving lips of a religious mantra being recited over and over again as a comfort and to stiffen resolve. The other signs depend on the type of detonator used to fire the explosive charges. Usually these involve batteries, often carried in a separate bag. If so, the bomber will most often

Suicide bombers often sweat from carrying the weight of explosives. They also usually carry a detonator in a separate bag, usually involving batteries.

Russian law enforcement agency officers photograph bodies in a train car after the Park Kultury bombing in 2010.

be trained to keep a hand in the bag with fingers on the button in case of a desperate attempt to take them down before the explosion.

HOW TO USE THIS INFORMATION

All this information has been painfully assembled from increasing experience with dealing with suicide bombers and their terrible after-effects. But what can this tiny additional warning time actually achieve? In the future, it may be possible to design security measures so that each person wanting to enter a restricted area comes under increased scrutiny for a longer time, either from protected viewpoints or from CCTV cameras, to extend the warning time before they actually reach enough people to constitute a target, and to increase the time under which they feel helpless under watchful eyes. Another prospect for the future would be to develop sensors that can pick up on the colossal internal stress endured by bombers, and to reveal it rather as airport sensors can reveal when people have contracted an epidemic disease fever, and stop them before they board a crowded airliner.

Russian investigators working at the site of the car bomb explosion in Kizlyar, Republic of Dagestan, Russia in 2010.

FURTHER READING

Applied Criminal Psychology: A Guide to Forensic Behavioural Sciences, Dr. Richard N. Kocsis, Springfield IL, Charles C. Thomas, 2009

Applying Psychology to Crime, Julie Harrower, London, Hodder & Stoughton, 1998

Beyond the Crime Lab: the New Science of Investigation, Jon Zonderman, New York NY, John Wiley & Sons, 1996

Catch Me a Killer: Serial Murders: A Profiler's True Story, Dr. Micki Pistorius, Johannesburg, Penguin Books, 2000

Catching the Killers: A History of Crime Detection, James Morton, London, Ebury Press, 2001

Crime Classification Manual, John Douglas, Ann Burgess, A. G. Burgess, and Robert Ressler, Lexington MA, Lexington Books, 1992

Criminal Psychology, a Beginner's Guide (2nd Edition), Ray Bull, Oxford UK and New York, Oneworld Publications 2009

Criminal Shadows, David Canter, London, HarperCollins, 1995

Criminalistics, Richard Saferstein, New York NY, Prentice Hall (various editions)

Dark Dreams: Sexual Violence, Homicide, and the Criminal Mind, Roy Hazelwood and Stephen G. Michaud, New York NY, St Martin's Press, 2001

Handbook of Psychology for Forensic Practitioners, G. J. Towl and D. A. Crighton, London, Sage, 1996

Hidden Evidence: 50 True Crimes and How Forensic Science Helped Solve Them (2nd edition), David Owen, London, Quintet Publishing, 2009

Hunting Humans: The Rise of the Modern Multiple Murderer, E. Leyton, Toronto, Canada, Seal Books, 1986

In the Minds of Murderers: The Extraordinary Science of Criminal Profiling, Paul Roland, Edison NJ, Chartwell Books, 2008

Killers on the Loose, Antonio Mendoza, London, Virgin Books, 2002

Men who Rape: the Psychology of the Offender, Nicholas Groth, New York, Plenum, 1979

Mindhunter: Inside the FBI Elite Serial Crime Unit, John Douglas and Mark Olshaker, London, Arrow Books, 1997

Offender Profiling—Theory, Research and Practice, edited by Janet L. Jackson and Debra A. Bekerian, Chichester UK, John Wiley, 1997

Offender Profiling and Crime Analysis, Peter B. Ainsworth, Portland OR, Willan Publishing, 2001

Practical Aspects of Rape Investigation: A Multidisciplinary Approach, Roy Hazelwood and Ann Burgess (editors), Amsterdam, Elsevier, 1987

Profilers: Leading Investigators Take You Inside the Criminal Mind, Don Denevi and John H. Campbell, New York NY, Prometheus Books, 2004

Profiling the Criminal Mind: Behavioural Science and Criminal Investigative Analysis, Dr. Robert Girod, Sr, Bloomington IN, iUniverse Inc, 2004

Profiling Violent Crimes: an Investigative Tool (3rd Edition), Ronald M. Holmes and Stephen T. Holmes, Thousand Oaks CA, Sage Publications, 2002

Psychological Methods in Criminal Investigation and Evidence, D. C. Raskin (editor), New York NY, Springer Publishing, 1989

Roadside Prey, Alva Bush, New York NY, Kensington, 1996

Serial Murderers and Their Victims, E. W. Hickey, California, Brooks-Cole, 1991

Sexual Homicide: Patterns and Motives, Robert K. Ressler, Ann W. Burgess and John E. Douglas, London, Simon and Schuster, 1993

She Must Have Known: the Trial of Rosemary West, Brian Masters, London, Corgi Books, 1998.

Signature Killers: Interpreting the Calling Cards of the Serial Murderer, Robert D. Keppel with William J. Birnes, London, Arrow Books, 1998

The Anatomy of Motive, John Douglas, and Mark Olshaker, London, Simon and Schuster, 2000

The Blooding, Joseph Wambaugh, London, Bantam Books, 1989

The Cases that Haunt Us: From Jack the Ripper to JonBenet Ramsey, the FBI's Legendary Manhunter Sheds Light on the Mysteries that Won't Go Away, John Douglas and Mark Olshaker, New York NY, Scribner, 2000

The Encyclopaedia of Forensic Science, Brian Lane, London, Hodder Headline, 1992

The Evil that Men Do, Stephen G. Michaud with Roy Hazelwood, New York NY, St Martin's Press, 1988

The Jigsaw Man, Paul Britton, London, Corgi Books, 1998

The Scientific Investigation of Crime, S. S. Kind, London, Forensic Science Service, 1987

The Unknown Darkness: Profiling the Predators Among Us, Gregg O. McCrary with Katherine Ramsland PhD, New York, HarperCollins, 2003

Understanding Sexual Violence: a Study of Convicted Rapists, D. Scully, Boston MA, Unwin Hyman, 1990

Whoever Fights Monsters, R. K. Kessler and T. Schachtman, London, Simon and Schuster, 1992

PICTURE CREDITS

All other images are the copyright of Quintet Publishing Ltd. While every effort has been made to credit the contributors, Quintet Publishing would like to apologize should there have been any omissions or errors—and would be pleased to make the appropriate correction for future editions of the book.

(T=top, B=bottom, L=left, R=right, C=center)

Alamy 145 © Peter Noyce LC / Alamy.

Corbis 21B © Alen MacWeeney; 25T © Underwood & Underwood; 31BR © Bettmann; 37B © Skyscan; 42 © MAPS.com; 44T © Bettmann; 49 © Bettmann; 56TL © MAPS.com; 64T, 64B © Gideon Mendel; 68T, 72, 73L, 77T, 77B, 81TL © Bettmann; 137 © Jerry Cabluck/Sygma; 148B, 150R, 151B © Bettmann; 184 © Megan Lewis/Reuters; 188 © William Whitehurst; 198 © Ralf-Finn Hestoft; 203 © Peter Groenendijk/Robert Harding World Imagery; 206 © Stringer/Italy/Reuters; 228 © Roger Ressmeyer; 230TL © Bettmann; 230B © Leif Skoogfors; 231T © Sygma; 232 © Bettmann; 233 © Sygma; 241 © Joe Skipper/Reuters; 253T © Ocean; 260T; 261T, 263BL © Rocky Mountain News/ Barry Gutierrez/Pool/Reuters; 267T © Ron Sachs/CNP; 272BL © Olivier Fitoussi/epa; 273TR, 275B © Akhtar Soomro/Reuters; 277 © NTV/epa.

Getty 14 © English School; 22B © Judd Mehlman/NY Daily News Archive; 23 © NY Daily News Archive; 63B © Per-Anders Pettersson; 85 © Walter B. McKenzie; 90B © William F. Campbell/Time Life Pictures; 92R © Thomas S. England/Time Life Pictures; 95T © Scott Troyanos/Time Life Pictures; 98BL © David Goddard; 126T; 126B, 127T © Baton Rouge Police Department; 128R, 129T © Mario Villafuerte; 129C © Erik S. Lesser; 151TL © Acey Harper/Time & Life Pictures; 151TR © Bill Frakes/Time & Life Pictures; 154 © Arthur Tanner/Express; 173T © Carlo Allegri/AFP; 175TL © Darwin Wiggett; 182T © Adam Gault; 196B © Steve Kagan/Time Life Pictures; 197 © Taro Yamasaki/Time Life Pictures; 199T © Steve Kagan/Time Life Pictures; 216T © Terry Smith/Time Life Pictures; 217 © Terry Smith/Time Life Pictures; 218T © Shailesh Raval/The India Today Group; 220 © Imtiyaz Khan/The India Today Group; 221T © Kalyan Chakravorty/The India Today Group; 238TR © Mario Tama; 239R © Stefan Zaklin; 243 © Alexander Hassenstein; 247 © Per-Anders Pettersson; 248L; 249T, 250T © Ben Martin/Time Life Pictures; 255 © SuperStock, Inc.; 258L © John Biever/Sports Illustrated; 258R © Pool; 268TR © Ron Wurzer; 268B © Joe Raedle; 270B © Andreas Schlegel; 271T © Tim Graham.

istock 3TR; 3C; 3B; 5TR; 8; 9T; 9BR; 11R; 15R; 26; 30R; 32TL; 33; 40; 41; 44B; 45; 46; 47R; 48L; 48R; 50; 52T; 53T; 53B; 54; 56B; 57; 58BL; 58BR; 60; 66; 67T; 69R; 70; 71T; 71B; 73R; 74T; 76; 78R; 79; 80; 81B; 88; 89T; 92L; 94C; 96T; 96B; 97; 98T; 98BR; 100CL; 100C; 103; 106L; 106R; 107TL; 109T; 109B; 119; 120R; 122; 123T; 124; 125; 127B; 129B; 130TC; 130TL; 130CL; 132; 133L; 133R; 135B; 136; 139T; 140; 141B; 144B;

A

abductions
  by mysoped molesters 208
  staged 87–9, 90–3, 98–9
  see also kidnapping
abuse victims, abusers as 64–6,
  162, 205, 209, 245, 248
Albert Victor, Prince 19, 20
Alderson, Anne 40
Aluffi, Sergeant 73
anger-excitation rapists 33, 157, 168–9
  Bernardo 173–5
  Calabro 170
  DeBardeleben 176–8
  Florence group 166–9, 179
  Pennell 171–2
anger-retaliatory rapists 33, 157, 162
  Spencer 163–5
animals, cruelty to 42–3, 70, 250
anthrax letters 237–9
applied criminology courses 31
arrogance, 149, 150
arson 42
Ashworth, Dawn 144–5
Asperger's syndrome 111
Atlanta Olympic Games bomber 258

B

baby food extortion case 227–8
backgrounds 103–5, 111
Bailey, F. Lee 81
Bakers, Henry 246–7
Barnard, Ursula 247
Baton Rouge Killer 126–9
bed-wetting 42–3
Beethe, Carol 191–3, 195
behavior changes 105
Bernardo, Paul 173–5
Bisoli, Gianni 206
Bissett, Samantha & Jazmine 110–11

Blair, Judy 236
Blake, Jack 48–9
Blanchard, Roger Collin 176–8
Bockova, Blanka 152
body language, suicide bombers 274–7
bombers
  Atlanta Olympic Games bomber 258
  Mormon bomber 249–51
  signatures 190
  suicide bombers 272–7
Bond, Dr. Thomas 18
Booth, Charles, *Master Map of Poverty* 19
Bowyer, Thomas 13
Britton, Paul 109, 145, 211
Brussel, Dr. James 25–8, 31
Buckland, Richard 144–6
Bukhanovsky, Alexander 215
Bundy, Ted 33, 34, 148–51
Burakov, Viktor 216
Byleveld, Piet 180

C

Calabro, Carmine 170
Cameron, Alice 97
Canter, David 34–5, 36–9, 132
Caratachea, Rolando 96–7
Carpenter, David 40–3
Center City rapist 160–1
Chandler, Oba 234–6
Chapman, Eliza (Annie) 12
Chase, Richard Trenton 118–21
Cheney, Vivian 135
Chikatilo, Andrei 213–17
child kidnapping 209–10
child molesters 205–21
child murder concealment 87–9, 90–3
Cho, Diane 164
Christensen, Steve 249
Cicero, June 48
Claremont murders 138–43
Clarkson, Pamela & Amber 141–2

closed-circuit television (CCTV) 8
Co-ed Killer 68–73
Code, Nathaniel 134–7
Code, William 136
Coles, Frances 15, 17
Colomb, Treneisha Dene 127–8, 129
Comfort, John 194
communication,
    extortion/kidnapping 223–39
commuter criminals 35, 131, 147
    Bundy, Ted 33, 34, 148–51
    Sutcliffe, Peter 147
    Unterweger, Jack 152–5
Consolidated Edison 24, 27, 28
crime scenes 75–80
    staging 76–99
Cronin, Captain James 25
Culbert, Jerry 136

D

Dahmer, Jeffrey 34, 35, 196–9
DaRonch, Carol 150
Davis, Debbie Dudley 163
Day, Alison 37, 38, 39
DeBardeleben,
    James Mitchell II 176–8
Devier, Darrell Gene 252–5
disorganized killers 41, 53, 101, 104–5
    Chase 118–21
    Lawson & Odom 106–7
    Napper 108–17
DNA matching 9
    Harman 270–1
    Lee 127, 128, 129
    Masters 261, 262
    Napper 108, 111, 114
    Pitchfork 144–7
    Prince 142–3
    Russell 195
    Troy 161
dog food extortion case 226

Doody, Jonathan 94, 97
Douglas, John 33, 41–2, 85–7, 124–5, 157,
    178, 189–90, 230, 253–5
Driscoll, Gerald 269
Druitt, Montague John 19, 20, 21
Duffy, John 36–9

E

Eddowes, Kate 13, 17
Edwards, Tracy 198
Ellis, Shirley 172
Elveson, Francine 170
extortion 223–30
extortioners, making contact 223–4, 225,
    230
Exxon kidnapping 231–3

F

FBI Behavioral Science Unit 31–3, 250
fingerprint matching 135, 137
Finney, Inspector Howard 25–6
fixated child molesters 207–8
Ford, Deborah 134–5, 136
forensic odontologists 150
Franklin, Linda 266–7
Frazier, John Linley 68
Freemasons 19
French, Kristen 174

G

Garcia, Alessandro 94, 97
Geiger, Ernst 154
Gentilcore, Pasquale 169
geography, marauders 132–3
Gilbert, Leigh 212

Giuttari, Michele 169
Golding, Paula 122
Grant, Ed 44–9
Graves, Troy 160–1
Green, Gina Wilson 127
Green Chain Rapist 108–11
Green River Killer 33

intermediaries, police contact 78, 80–1, 84
interpersonal coherence 35
investigative psychology courses 34–5

J

Jack the Ripper 10–21
Jaeger, Susan 32

H

Haertle, Steve 42–3
Hallett, Sally 73
Hammerer, Heidemarie 152–3, 154
Hammond, Richard 261–2
handwriting, matching 235, 237–9
Hansen, Ellen 42–3
Hansen, Robert 122–5
Harman, Craig 270–1
Harris, Billy Joe 135–6
Harris family 58–60
Hasib Hussain 272
Hazelwood, Roy 33, 41–2, 208, 261
Heaton, Joan 55
Hellems, Dr. Susan Elizabeth 163–4
Hercules, Fouzia 65
Hettrick, Peggy 260–2
Hicks, Steven Mark 196
Hill, Karen Ann 48
Hofmann, Mark 249–51
Homicide Information Tracking System
   (HITS) 33
Homolka, Karla 173–5
Hoover, Michelle 94, 97
Hughes, Tony 197
Humphries, Abbie 211–12

K

Kane, Edda 40–1
Keller, Elissa 140
Kelley, Julie 211–12
Kelly, Ian 146
Kelly, Mary Jane 13, 17
Kemper, Ed 68–73
Keppel, Robert 33
kidnappers, making contact 223–4, 231–3
kidnapping
   attempts, staged 87–9, 90–3, 98–9
   child 209–10
   see also abductions
Kinamore, Pam 126–7
Kinge, Michael 58–62
Kinge, Shirley 61
Koli, Surender 218–21
Koo, Aiko 71, 72
Kosminski, Aaron (Isaac) 19–20

L

Lano, Renee C. 172
Lawson, James Clayton Jr 106–7
Leach, Kimberley Diane 150–1
Lee, Derrick Todd 126–9
Levine, Andrea 193
Lewis, James William 229–30

I

I-40 killer 171–2
inadequate child molesters 207

literacy, profiling 27
Little, Michael 270
Liu, Alice 72
Locke, Anne 37, 38, 39
Lotti, Giancarlo 166, 168
Luchessa, Anita 71

M

Maake, Cedric 179–80
Mad Bomber 22–9
Mahaffy, Leslie 174–5
Mainardi, Paolo 167
Malvo, Lee Boyd 264–9
Mann, Lynda 144
Manson, Charles 69
marauder criminals 35, 131, 132–3
    Code 134–7
    Pitchfork 144–7
    Prince 138–43
Masser, Brunhilde 152, 153
Masters, Timothy 260–3
May, Shauna 41
Maybrick, James 20
McCrary, Gregg 44–9, 55–7, 60,
    79–80, 94–7, 155, 232, 250
McKenzie, Alice 14, 15, 17
McPhaul, Jean 178
means, non-serial killers 102
Meirhofer, David 32
Meredith, Dan 120
Messina, Joanne 122
Metesky, George 22–9, 34, 39
Metropolitan Police
    and Whitechapel killings
    17–21
    scenes of crime investigation 51
Milat, Ivan 181–5
Milton, Rod 182
Miroth, Evelyn 120

modus operandi (MO) 188–90
Monster of Florence 166–9, 179
morally indiscriminate child molesters 207
Moreland, Cynthia 41
Mormon bomber 249–51
Morrow, Sherry 122
mothers, child murder concealment 87–9,
    90–3
motives, non-serial killers 102
Mottram, Barbara 236
Muhammad, John Allen 264–9
Mulcahy, David 36, 39
Mullany, Patrick 31, 32
Mullin, Herbert 69
Myburgh, Elmarie 179
Mylett, Rose 14, 17
mysoped child molesters 207–8, 208–9
    Koli 218–21

N

Napper, Robert 108–17
National Center for the
    Analysis of Violent Crime (NCAVC)
    33, 34
Neal, Clara 49
New York bomber 22–9
New York Journal American 23
Nichol, Mary Ann 11, 17
Nickell, Rachel 112–17
Nickell, Stella & Bruce 228
non-serial murders 102–3
Norsworthy, Derrick 247–8

O

O'Connell, Diana 41
Odom, James Russell 106–7
Ohta, Dr. Victor 68

Onions, Paul 183–5
opportunity, non-serial killers 102–3
organized killers 41, 53, 71–3, 101, 104
   Hansen 122–5
Ostrog, Michael 19, 20

P

Pacciani, Pietro 168
Pace, Charlotte Murray 127, 129
Pandher, Moninder Singh
   218–21
Paramount Theater, Brooklyn 24
paranoia, profiling
   paranoid psychoses 27, 68–73, 111,
      119–21
pedophiles 205–21
Pennell, Steven Brian 171–2
personality, profiling 27
Pesche, Mary Ann 71
Peterson, George 97
Pettini, Steffani 169
Pistorius, Micki 65, 180,
   200–1, 202–3, 247
Pitchfork, Colin 144–7
Pohlreich, Mary Ann 191
power-assertive rapists 33, 157, 162, 188
   Graves 160–1
Prasad, Arti 220–1
preferential child molesters 207–9
Price, Craig 55–7
priests 206
Prince, Cleophus Jr 138–43
product tampering cases 226–30
profiling
   effective 31–49
   errors, 126–9
   misreading 115

Q

Qasem Odeh, Abedal Basit Mohammed 274
questioning suspects 241–4
   Devier 252–5
   Hofmann 249–51
   Wests 244–5
   Wilkin 246–8

R

Railway Rapist 34, 36–9
ransom kidnappers 210
rapists
   anger-excitation/ sadism 157, 168–9,
      189
   anger-retaliatory 157, 162–5
   power-assertive 157, 162
   power-reassurance 157, 158–61, 188
   serial, profiling 157
Rapodile, Amelia 203
reconstructing crime 54–5
regressed child molesters 206–7
Reso, Sidney 231–3
Ressler, Robert 32, 33, 118, 157, 202
Robinson, Joe 136
Rocky Mountain Child Killer 32
Rogers family 234–6
Rontini, Pia 169
Russell, George Waterfield 191–5

S

Sacramento Vampire 118–21
sadistic kidnappers 210
Salp, Tom 94–5
San Quentin Prison 43
Savvas, George 185

Scaggs, Heather Roxanne 43
scene of crime investigation 51–5
Schaefer, Margaret 153
Schall, Cindy 71–2
Schenner, August 153
Schrempf, Elfriede 153
Schrieber, Shannon 160–1
Schultz, Tiffany 139
Schwartz, Barbara 40
Seale, Arthur & Jackie 231–3
Selepe, David 200–2, 203
Shawcross, Arthur 44–9, 52
Sheets, Kathleen 249
Sheppard, Dr. Sam 77–80
Sheppard, Marilyn 77–80
Shreveport marauder 134–7
Sickert, Walter 19, 21
signatures 187–90
    bombers 190
    Dahmer 196–9
    Russell 191–5
    Selepe & Sithole 200–3
Simons, Avzal Norman 63–7
Sithole, Moses 200, 202–3
situational child molesters 206–7
Smith, Emma Elizabeth 11, 17
Smith, Susan 90–3
Smith, Theresa 199
Snow, Susan 228
Spencer, Timothy 163–5
Stagg, Colin 112–14
staging, crime scenes 76–99
stalking, power-reassurance rapists 159
Station Strangler 63–6
Stefanacci, Claudio 169
Stoner, Mary Frances 252–5
Stott, June 45, 47, 49
Stowers, Richard 41
stress reactions 104, 105
Stride, Elizabeth 12, 13
suicide bombers 272–7
Surrey University, investigative psychology
    courses 34–5

suspects, questioning 241–4, 244–8
Sutcliffe, Peter 147
Swart, Jan 246

T

Tabram, Martha 11, 17
Tamboezer, Maartje 37, 38, 39
Tarr, Holly 140
Teten, Howard 31, 32
Thai Buddhist temple murders 94–7
Thethe, Amanda 203
Thorpe, Rosalind 72
Trailside Killer 39, 40–3, 53
trigger events
    Code 137
    non-serial murders 102
Tucker, Susan 164
Tumblety, Dr. Francis John 19, 20
Turner, Anthony 58–62
Tylenol blackmail case 229–30

U

Unterweger, Jack 152–5

V

van Rooy, Elroy 65
Vanni, Mario 166, 168
Vasquez, David 163, 165
Violent Criminal Apprehension Program
    (VICAP) 33–4, 143, 155
victim profiling 52–3
Vorpagel, Russ 118

W

Walter, Richard 33, 157

Wardell, Carol & Gordon 98–9

Washington snipers 258, 264–9

Wat Promkunaram, Phoenix, Arizona 94

weaknesses, and questioning 243–4

Weinhold, Janene 139, 142

West, Fred & Rosemary 244–5

West, Raymond 230

Whitchelo, Rodney 227–8

White, Joanna 61–2

Whitechapel killings 10–21

Wilken, Stewart 246–8

Williams, Eric 136

Williams, Vernon 230

Wollin, Teresa 118–19

Wolsieffer, Betty Jayne 82–7

Wolsieffer, Dr. Edward Glen 82–7

Wolsieffer, Neil 84

Y

Yoder, Carrie Lynn 128–9

Z

Zanasovsky, Major 214–15